TO ANDRÉ TCHELISTCHEFF

FOR HIS ENDURING INSPIRATION OVER THE YEARS
AS HE HAS LED US, THROUGH SCIENCE AND IMAGINATION,
TO THE REVELATION OF THE POETRY IN WINE

WINES OF CALIFORNIA

BY ROBERT LAWRENCE BALZER

EDITED BY DARLENE GEIS

HARRY N. ABRAMS, INC.

PUBLISHERS · NEW YORK

OTHER BOOKS BY ROBERT LAWRENCE BALZER
CALIFORNIA'S BEST WINES
BEYOND CONFLICT
THE PLEASURES OF WINE
ADVENTURES IN WINE
ROBERT LAWRENCE BALZER'S BOOK OF WINES & SPIRITS
THIS UNCOMMON HERITAGE
DISCOVERING ITALIAN WINES

ULRICH RUCHTI, DESIGNER
RUTH EISENSTEIN, ASSOCIATE EDITOR

Library of Congress Cataloging in Publication Data

Balzer, Robert Lawrence.
    Wines of California.

    Bibliography: p. 256
    Includes index.
    1. Wine and wine making—California. I. Title.
II. Title: Wines of California.
TP557.B26   1978   641.2'2'09794   77-26955
ISBN 0-8109-0750-X

Library of Congress Catalogue Card Number: 77-26955

CONTENTS

VINEYARDS AND WINERIES: BAY AREA AND CENTRAL COAST COUNTIES 165

FOREWORD

This is Robert Balzer's very personal testimony to wine, or, as he writes, "a prolonged personal essay on the pleasures of wine." From his long experience with California wines, he certainly has a right to his opinions. Furthermore, he personally enjoys wines, and these opinions on the quality of specific wines are worth our careful consideration.

The chapter on grape varieties introduces a much-needed perspective as to the basis of California wine quality. The influence of climate on wine quality is clearly outlined. The influence of soil is repeatedly emphasized.

On individual wineries, we find a historical discussion of the genesis of the winery and in some cases something about the ideals of the winemakers. In other cases, there are discussions of specific wines. Since Balzer is a wine connoisseur, we should listen to his recommendations. Of course, one has to remember that wines disappear from the market and what was available in late 1977 may be off the market in 1978.

Thank you, Robert Balzer, for telling us again about the important wines of the world, particularly those of California.

MAYNARD A. AMERINE

WHAT IS WINE?

"Wine itself is but Water sublim'd, being nothing else but that Moysture and Sap, which is caus'd either by Rain or other kind of Irrigations about the Roots of the Vine, and drawn up to the Branches and Berries by the virtual attractive Heat of the Sun; the Bowels of the Earth serving as limbec to that end."   —James Howell

When Galileo wrote "Wine is light held together by water," his meaning was clear to those who had worked the vineyards in the sun, gathered the grapes, and attended the transformation of the fresh juice into living wine. Realism is served by André Simon: "Wine is the naturally fermented juice of fresh, ripe grapes." But the late grand seigneur of all true wine-lovers was not content to leave it there. He continued: "Wine is, indeed, a living thing, brash in its youth, full-blossoming in its maturity, but subject, if not used in time, to senility, decay and death. It is gregarious, appearing at its best in the company of food, and as a constituent of food; and in the society of moderate men and women, priming their wit, assisting at their worship, and serving as a medicine for some of their ills."

Almost two thousand years earlier, the Roman naturalist and author Pliny the Elder had documented the people's regard for wine in the imperial city: "It has become quite a common proverb that in wine there is truth" (*in vino veritas*). Petronius Arbiter, his contemporary and a consummate bon vivant, concentrated his definition into three words: "Wine is life."

Holding up a glass of wine so that its jeweled brilliance can be seen, its fragrance noted, and then allowing its warmth to flow over the taste buds, today's connoisseur might declare cryptically: "Wine *is!*" This would recall the silent sermon of Siddhartha Gautama, the Buddha, to his disciples when, in a deliberately calm gesture, he held up a single lotus flower. Truth was apparent, needing no description, analysis, or discussion.

Throughout recorded history, in every age, appreciation of wine has been verbalized by the articulate taster. Aeschylus commented on the liquid's reach toward man's affections: "Bronze is the mirror of form; wine, of the heart." While there is poetry in such phrases extolling wine, they neither describe it nor reply to the universal question, "Which wine is best?" My answer for years has been the one offered by Pliny the Elder: "The best kind of wine is that which is most pleasant to him who drinks it." Those who find this an irritating cop-out must go further into the catechism involving the spectrum of taste, and ask whether mind or body dictates the preferences of a prejudiced palate.

In one swallow of wine some three hundred known chemical compounds may exist simultaneously in "a chemical symphony," to quote Professor Emeritus Maynard A. Amerine of the University of California's Department of Viticulture and Enology at Davis. But to appreciate this balance, this harmony, with every conceivable shade and variation, requires experience as well as sensory alertness. A learning curve is involved. It follows a natural progression from the early preference for sweetness, which is the springboard of the Pepsi generation, to those pop wines of obvious fruit taste, to more subtle flavors. The innocent charms of a simple Liebfraumilch, a light and lovely white

Antonio Perelli-Minetti, founder of the family-owned winery, tasting the dark red wine from one of his experimental grapes. Photograph taken in 1975

14

German Rhine wine with its edge of sweetness, or of a California Chenin Blanc, have obvious appeal for the neophyte, whereas red wines, with their astringency and lack of sweetness, are often a quick turn-off. The unfamiliar needs repetition to become welcome.

The recognition of quality arises through comparison, in which the index of memory serves the winelover as his most reliable ally. It is the winetaster's greatest asset. Immediately upon tasting an older red wine with age-enhanced bouquet, you may find it better than another red wine of a similar kind. How better? Is the difference in the grape? The soil? The method of vinification? Most probably it is in all three. Memory of other wines will hold the clues and give the answers.

In its complexity, wine is the most thought-provoking beverage known to man. Sometimes the sight of a great painting, an architectural monument, a sunset sky, the sound of a great voice, or the concentrated wonder of poetry expressing the common experience in an uncommon insight, seems almost to open your eyes to a deeper vision, with a glimpse of Truth. It happens with wine, great wine, when in moments of experiencing its complex perfection with all your senses you attain a flash of understanding. Great wines and ordinary wines differ in their component structure only by micro-minimal degrees. The source of these differences —be it the soil, the vine, or the winemaker's skills—is the fascinating enigma of what we may call "winespell," challenging us to a discriminating appreciation.

During the international congress of wine producers held in 1976 in San Francisco, I had the good fortune of being the luncheon companion of a well-known German vintner who had come there as a delegate. He had visited the wineries of the North Coast counties and tasted many of the wines of current challenge to the world market, and we fell into a discussion of the relative merits of California wines and those of Germany.

"I've enjoyed California red wines very much," he told me, "but the white wines have a much too aggressive bouquet, a pronounced nose and definite taste of the grape variety. For us, as an example, the Gewürztraminer of Alsace is too strong, too assertive; it jumps out of the glass. It is completely lacking in subtlety. I found that to be the case with many of the California white wines."

Had he, I asked, tasted the Wente Bros. 1975 Johannisberg Riesling from Monterey County, an opulent young wine of the most extraordinary fruitiness, its bouquet and flowery freshness almost room-filling? Alas, he had not tasted this outstanding California wine produced from the grape so preeminent in his homeland. But it is safe to assume that since it would "jump out of the glass" he would not have found it to his liking. As the revered California winemaker Louis M. Martini observed many, many years ago, "We like that best to which we are accustomed."

The freshness and opulence—the fruitiness—of the Wente Johan-

Fourth-generation Wentes standing in front of the stainless-steel tanks where the harvest is stored

nisberg Riesling, as of many of the young California white wines, is due to the new methods of vinification, perhaps dreamed of ten years ago but realized only with today's technological developments. Long, slow, cool, temperature-controlled fermentation, in stainless steel, of clean, morning-fresh grape juice cleared of extraneous matter by a variable-speed centrifuge enables the winemaker to achieve better results than ever before. Such technological changes and advances are not peculiar to California; they are also the pride of leading wineries in Germany, France, Spain, Australia—in fact, wherever established winemaking can afford the capital investment required. These impeccable and ultramodern systems of vinification are enhancing the richness of current vintages at Château Latour and Château Haut-Brion in Bordeaux. Where vintners cannot afford the millions of dollars required to effect such changes, they have perforce to hold fast to yesterday's methods, rationalizing their adherence as "traditionalism."

We are in a period not only of changing, improving systems of vinification but of taste transition as well. While this is a book primarily about California wines—their history and their growing significance to the winelover—its scope will include other winelands. Only a few weeks have intervened between my visits to vineyards in Bordeaux pridefully growing Cabernet Sauvignon and Merlot grapes and hillside slopes in California where wines are being made from these same species of *Vitis vinifera*. New vineyards at home and abroad seek the finest budding stock, to upgrade the quality of fruit that is to come to the press.

Things were different when Robert Louis Stevenson wrote the chapter "Napa Wine" in his *Silverado Squatters*. Most California wine buffs are familiar with his vignettes of the California wine scene of 1880. "From those paragraphs," Brother Timothy, winemaker of The Christian Brothers of Napa, told me one winetasting afternoon, "we know Stevenson's stance, and the winelover's views of his day. He raved about Golden Chasselas. We know all about the Golden Chasselas in the Napa Valley today. There's none growing at Schramsberg, where Stevenson discovered it, nor in any of the best vineyards today, because it just doesn't make a wine we think is good any more! Johannisberg Riesling can beat it all hollow."

In the post-Repeal renaissance of California wines, the route to finer wines led directly to the grape, to a new emphasis on varietal individuality. While there was some emphasis placed on the importance of region, the consumer was led to believe that the varietal name was synonymous with

A fruity, rich, vintage Chardonnay is the Golden State's pride and treasure

The post-Repeal renaissance of California wines has resulted in many more thousands of acres planted in vineyards

superior wine quality. It dominated winelovers' approach to California wines to such a degree that by the early 1970s ambitious French vintners were exporting Bordeaux and Burgundy wines to the United States with varietal titles! We had come full circle in the roundelay of imitative labeling. It was no longer Burgundy that arrived in America from La Bourgogne but "Pinot Noir," and good claret from Bordeaux came here as "Cabernet Sauvignon." The trend even went so far that Spanish wineries which had never seen a Zinfandel grape on the vine were sending us "Zinfandel" in addition to "Pinot Noir" and "Cabernet Sauvignon," named after grapes that were equally rare, if not nonexistent, in the vinelands of Old Castile.

We are now, happily, beyond this varietal madness. We are moving toward the next plateau: each regional winery in California is beginning to develop its own style within each single varietal category. Style derives from the third element in our triptych of soil, vine, and the winemaker's skill. As Brother Timothy points out, "We, as artists, are stamping our wines with our own style. The wines of one winemaker will always have the style of that winemaker, like an artist's signature. Even in wineries of adjacent acreage, each wine from the same varieties of grapes will be different in style."

It has been my good fortune to spend the major part of a lifetime among the wines and vines and winemakers of California. I came under the winespell only months after I was out of Stanford. Over these forty-odd years I have come to know the dreams and goals of hundreds of winemakers, not only in the states of California, Washington, and Oregon, but in Mexico, France, Germany, Spain, Italy, Sicily, Portugal, and Australia. They are everywhere men of intense dedication. Their wines, like the leaves and snowflakes of nature's divine and inexhaustible variety, are never the same, and it is a blessing. Why and how they are so different, one from another, though from similar vines, is partially answered between the covers of this book. What is wine? Which is the best wine? Curiosity may lead you to many answers, culled from the wisdom of the ages, all affirming that wine is one of man's more noble concepts, as eternal as the seasons, beginning anew with every vintage. For primary answers, we move on to the vineyards and their fruit, enjoying along the way the words of James Howell, seventeenth-century winelover and court historian to Charles II of England, who, from his many days in the vineyards of France, formulated the definition that stands as epigraph to this chapter.

THE VINES AND WINES OF CALIFORNIA

"... the wine
Must taste of its own grapes."
—Elizabeth Barrett Browning

One of the first plants to flourish in the rich mud left by the subsiding waters of the Deluge quickly became the blessing of Noah and his family and myriads of his descendants. The vine, throughout the Scriptures, rivals the olive and the fig tree for dominance. Wherever it was found among the peoples of antiquity, its origins were assigned to a divinity in appreciation of its fruit and the miraculous beverage derived therefrom— everywhere a signal of health, joy, and celebration. The Dionysus of the Greeks became the chubby Bacchus of the Romans, still today a familiar fellow with his endearing image.

Most of the world's wines evolve from one of the oldest species of the grape, *Vitis vinifera,* which followed the spread of civilization from its cradle in the rich, warm Mediterranean basin of Asia Minor. Of the genus *Vitis*—from which the Latin word evolved in Spain to *vid,* in France to *vigne,* to bring us the English *vine*—there are literally hundreds of species, vinifera being almost alone the noble parent of noble wines. America has its own indigenous *Vitis labrusca, Vitis riparia,* and *Vitis rupestris* of Eastern and Middle Western origins, from whose berries are made significant amounts of wine, enthusiasm for which is seldom shared far afield. But to these native American vines, the whole world of winelovers owes a debt of gratitude. In the last century, when the treasured vineyards of Europe were in withered ruin from the devastating scourge of the root louse *Phylloxera vastatrix* (2 1/2 million acres of vines in France alone had been destroyed), in an eleventh-hour experiment it was found that native American species such as *Vitis riparia* and *Vitis rupestris* were phylloxera-resistant. American vinestocks were imported and planted, and the noble species Cabernet Sauvignon, Pinot Noir, and Chardonnay were grafted onto them. The foreign vinestocks flourished and bore these vinifera grapes, thought to have been lost forever. Today the vines of almost every vineyard in Europe grow on American rootstocks.

A less well-known part of the story subtracts somewhat from the flag-waving glory of our to-the-rescue act: the pest was brought to Europe from America, quite innocently, on cuttings imported to England about 1860 by a botanist curious to experiment with these native American grapevines, who shared his cuttings with a fellow botanist in France. The blight spread through Europe's vinelands like fire in a dry wheatfield. French wine income dropped from over 545 million francs to 8 million francs by 1889. Mass emigrations of vineyard and winery workers began. Bordelais victims of the phylloxera disaster crossed the Pyrenees into Spain (reestablishing themselves in the Rioja district, and bringing with them winemaking techniques which continue there to this day, and which account for much of the claret style of that fine Spanish red wine). Other émigrés from France found their way to California. But so did the phylloxera, just as those new lands, in Robert Louis Stevenson's words, "already weary of producing gold, began to green with vineyards."

The bounty of California's orchards and vineyards: a still life of fruits and wines

22

In a remarkable instance of retribution, cuttings of *Vitis vinifera*, imported to California in the hope of making the Golden State the new wine capital of the world, brought the root louse back to America. Its toll was substantial but not as ruinous as it had been in Europe, for now the cure—resistant rootstocks—was known. Soon many California vineyards were growing the fine vinifera varieties on American rootstocks. While many regions today, with advanced systems of soil fumigation in preparation for planting, are growing the noble viniferas Chardonnay, Cabernet Sauvignon, Pinot Noir, Johannisberg Riesling, and others, on their own roots the prudent vinegrower puts down resistant American rootstock, waits the extra year, and then field-buds his choice of vinifera stock. I would defy anyone to detect a difference between the wine from grafted vines and wine from vines growing on vinifera roots.

Each grape has its own intrinsic taste, its own flower, its own scent; indeed it must move us to a state of wonder as we realize these countless subtleties of nature that differentiate the varieties. The mere mention of Concord, Muscat, or Tokay brings instantly to mind a unique and individually different taste. These are but three well-known table grapes. There are thousands of different wine grapes: every wineland has its own champion stock and esteemed varieties.

In the Zind-Humbrecht cellars of Winzenheim in Alsace, I recently tasted a 1975 vintage Tokay d'Alsace, sometimes known as Pinot Gris, which "jumped out of the glass" with its own perfume almost as positively as that Alsatian wonder wine called the spicy Traminer, or Gewürztraminer. The latter is the only accepted wine in Alsace today; old Traminer vineyards are being replaced with improved vinestock, which assures the vintner that the wine will be *gewürz*. Under the *Appellation d'Origine Contrôlée d'Alsace* only Gewürztraminer vines may now be planted. In California vineyards both Traminer and Gewürztraminer vines are growing, but one can rest assured that the better native examples of this exotic table wine are coming from Gewürztraminer vines.

But, it will be asked, why is there so much difference between Alsatian and Californian Gewürztraminer? The obvious difference is in the degree of sweetness elected by many of California's winemakers (Louis M. Martini is one exception), supporting their belief that this edge of residual grape sugar, aside from making the wine more widely popular, balances its natural acidity.

Taste analysis of a straightforward wine like Gewürztraminer is relatively simple. But we move into a profound complexity when we investigate the true taste of the Burgundian Pinot Noir. Here, we are inquiring not into the taste of the noble grape alone but, by extension, into the taste of rich red Burgundy.

The world's concept of generic Burgundy has been formed by centuries of advocates. Arguments concerning the true taste of Burgundy are

Part of Moët-Hennessy's $12-million-dollar investment in Napa Valley—the gleaming steel tanks that hold the Domaine Chandon *cuvée*

not new. The first came in 1395 with an edict by Philip the Bold, ruler of the Duchy of Burgundy, banishing the heavier-yielding Gamay grape forever from the already hallowed regions of Chambertin, Musigny, La Romanée, Clos de Vougeot, and Beaune. Resident monks in the area, noting the more generous harvest from the Gamay, were inclined to expand its planting, since revenues exceeded those from the shy-bearing Pinot Noir. The fate of Gamay was sealed forever by Philip's pronouncement against not only the greedy monks but the grape itself, which he declared to be "très mauvais et très desloyaux." It found a new home in Beaujolais, to the subsequent joy of Parisians and the worldwide fans of this jolly refresher. Pinot Noir continued its history of noble production in the Côte d'Or as the exclusive vine of the great growths of red Burgundy.

With this preamble, it is possible to understand the gravity of any question that dares to challenge such exalted traditions. Yet Robert Mondavi, one of California's preeminent winemakers, passionately devoted to the task of extracting the fullest potential from every wine-grape species, believes his experiments yield revealing answers to our question about Pinot Noir.

With every vintage, he and his staff make countless small batches of wines, harvested from specific areas, sampling various methods of crush, fermentation, cooperage (French oak versus Yugoslavian or American, new wood versus old), yeasts, temperatures, blendings with free-run juice and press wine . . . all toward a better, finished wine of greater finesse and flavor. Every morning, at the winery, during the bedlam of harvest and winemaking, of incoming grapes and bubbling casks, Robert and his sons, with their crew of technicians, set up for tasting a circle of glasses filled with embryonic wines when they are but hours out of the vineyard. To the layman, these are an unappetizing assembly of opaque liquids in varying dull shades suggesting anything but the jewel-bright vintages they will become. But to the knowing, the potentials are revealed in clues from scent, body, and even taste, as raw and unfinished as the wines are.

Through such dedicated experiment, Robert Mondavi's belief about the proper fermentation of Pinot Noir, progressed from 1970 (the year that produced his 1970 Pinot Noir, which took first place in the *Los Angeles Times Home Magazine* tasting) to the still greater enlightenment with his 1972 Pinot Noir as a breakthrough. Break through what? Mondavi does not believe that the accepted *typical* taste of top-ranking Burgundies either realizes the fullest potential of Pinot Noir or is even its healthiest manifestation. Connoisseurs are generally united in admiring the bouquet, the penetrating scent, of fine Burgundies, which have a pungency not present in the softer fragrance of fine clarets. Some call it smoky, some call it medicinal, and someone I know who adores great Bordeaux wines, and

Veteran winemaker Myron Nightingale of Beringer/Los Hermanos plays host to a visiting wine class

dislikes Burgundy, declares it "mousy." Heresy, of course, to thousands upon thousands of Burgundy lovers all over the world who are accustomed to that pungency as a hallmark of the finest Burgundies.

Robert Mondavi believes this scent is a result of the autolysis (breakdown of cell tissues) involved in prolonged malo-lactic fermentation. The odorous materials which are the products of this autolysis, in his opinion, are responsible for the characteristic Burgundy bouquet, present in his prize-winning 1970 wine, which triumphed in the Los Angeles tasting over '70 Chambertin-Clos de Bèze, '70 Clos Vougeot, and '70 Nuits-Saint-Georges, Clos de la Maréchale. In his 1972 wine from the same grapes Mondavi deliberately curtailed the fermentation and thus the odor. He regards this Pinot Noir as a step toward better Burgundy-style wine. It is rich, with an unobstructed bouquet from the grape, touched with the incense of oak, but lacking the overriding (autolysis) scent that connoisseurs have long sought and accepted as an attribute of Burgundian wine character.

There are confirming results from Burgundian wines produced from Pinot Noir in the Côte de Beaune at the villages of Monthélie and Savigny-les-Beaune—lovely, endearing, and straightforward wines of pure Pinot Noir, but atypical in their lack of that penetrating wood-smoke adjunct of more famed, more expensive Burgundies. The celebrated Beaulieu Vineyard 1968 Beaumont Pinot Noir and generic 1968 Burgundy were equally atypical in this respect, as was the outstanding Louis M. Martini 1968 Pinot Noir Special Selection.

After two thousand years of winemaking, and despite the intensive technological advances of recent decades, areas of uncertainty still abound. Only within recent years have we understood the function of malo-lactic fermentation in reducing total acidity and realized its importance. Once prayed for as an unpredictable development that would or would not come in its own time, it can now be induced, and at the appropriate time. In this fermentation, a wine's total acidity (the combined acids that give wines the tart sprightliness without which they are dull and insipid), when it is too high in malic acid, can be reduced by half, and the malic acid converted to lactic acid by bacterial action. Lowering of the total acidity in Pinot Noir assures a more palatable taste. Robert Mondavi's method involves a malo-lactic fermentation that is simultaneous with the yeast fermentation and of relatively shorter duration than is traditional in France. The wine is thus not in contact with the odorous cells resulting from post-fermentation activity. Experiments in the whole area of yeasts, including all their multiple strains, are part of the enological development in California, possibly accounting for some of the mysterious differences in the emergent wines of the Golden State.

In the field of viticulture there are few persons more honored than

Robert Mondavi holding a cluster of Pinot Noir grapes; in the background, his distinctive Mission-style winery

Professor Harold P. Olmo of the University of California at Davis, a lifelong and talented plant geneticist. In his monograph on Chardonnay he veers away from science to describe the indescribable: "In matured wines of the highest quality there is often an exquisite aroma of ripe apples or of ripe peaches, but who can document it?" Others have suggested that fine examples of this splendid white wine of Burgundy and California often evoke nostalgic memories of warm dry grasses, or ripe pears. None of these are the same... *nor are the wines*. Is that any more curious than the familiar description of Château Mouton-Rothschild as being reminiscent of black currants? Or the fragrance of wood violets that haunts superb vintages of Haut-Brion?

Academicians tend to put down such verbal flights that go beyond laboratory analysis, but after years and years of pursuing the elusive tastes and bouquets of wines, and attempting to capture them in terms that make for easy communication, I believe this is the best route to follow—free, not reining in the imagination and not losing in the toils of science the poetic mystery that fascinates the true winelover.

We can leave speculation there. It does provide some answers in the tug-of-war of taste preferences when the riddle of differences between California and European wines is posed. But even in the comparison of French wines, district with district, vineyard with adjacent vineyard, we see differences revealed. Is it soil alone that makes La Tâche differ from Richebourg, from Echézeaux... all produced from Pinot Noir? Why Mouton's black currant against Haut-Brion's violet?

It is not necessary to have the answers to all the questions in order to enjoy wine, but with the knowledge that some of the answers bring comes awareness that deepens appreciation. Enology, viticulture, botany, and plant physiology are only partial routes to knowing wine and understanding its nature. It is not as a botanist, or a viticulturist, or an enologist, or a chemist—for I am none of these—but as a devoted winelover of forty years' standing that I write. And this is not a textbook but a prolonged personal essay on the pleasures of wine, and of California wines in particular.

"It is a myth," enologist Richard Peterson of The Monterey Vineyard told me, "that wine is made in wineries. It is really made in vineyards!" This is a tribute to the vineyardist who raises the grape, as opposed to the winemaker who develops the wine. Since the vineyard contributes so importantly to the quality of wine, let us take a look in the next chapter at the terrain and climate where the vine is most likely to thrive in California.

CALIFORNIA'S FIVE WINE REGIONS

"But before we plough an unfamiliar patch,
It is well to be informed about the winds,
About the variations in the sky,
The native traits and habits of the place,
What each locale permits, and what denies.
One place is good for crops, one happier
With grapes. . . ."

—Virgil

On the return of Augustus from Asia, in 29 B.C., Virgil read him the four books of the *Georgics*. In this work, which the emperor had commissioned, the poet's intention was to describe in verse the close relation of man and nature, with full appreciation of the seasons' round of labor, the importance of soil and weather, and the particular joys of cultivating the vine and the olive. Two thousand harvests later, with the riddles of sun and soil only partially solved, for all our theories and experiments, we still stand in awe and wonder before the vagaries of nature.

The vine thrives in most well-drained soils, even producing some of its most illustrious wines from relatively infertile, rocky terrain where nothing else will grow. Above and below the equator, two loosely defined isothermal belts demark the vine-growing potentials of the Northern and Southern hemispheres. The northern belt includes the broad east–west reach from Washington, Oregon, California, Arkansas, Iowa, Ohio, Michigan, and New York across the ocean to the Mediterranean Basin and extending eastward into China and Japan, with wide variations north to south, from Germany to North Africa, from Russia to Iran. Below the equator, in the Southern Hemisphere, are the enormously productive vineyard regions of Chile and Argentina, the tip of South Africa, and the burgeoning vineyards of Australia.

In our time, we have seen deserts transformed to veritable paradise gardens through the miracle of modern irrigation, drawing upon faraway sources of water. Where natural rainfall is inadequate, as in Monterey County, California's new wonderland for the grape, overhead sprinklers not only provide controlled moisture but, by means of efficient new drip systems, deliver the amount of water essential to each vine with conservation-oriented economy.

The old adage "Bacchus loves the hillsides" implies, among other advantages of site, the blessings of natural rainfall. Irrigation of the flatlands can be abused, of course, when the grower's objectives place quantity above quality. But with today's enlightened understanding of viticulture, man-made "rain" from overhead sprinklers is generally used judiciously not only to provide the necessary moisture for vine roots but to serve as a frost-protection system. When the temperature falls below freezing, clouds of spray over a vineyard can raise the temperature of the area, the water being warmer than the air. In more extreme cold, water from the overhead sprinklers will freeze, coating the vines with ice. The freezing action of the water gives off heat, and the ice-coated vines, looking like crystal sculptures, are saved.

Old hands say that the weather in June (in the Northern Hemisphere) determines the quantity of a vintage and that the subsequent weather of the summer, until harvest, determines the quality. Rainfall during blooming can cause a poor "berry set." When it is time for the berries to set, in late spring, other unfavorable conditions as well are cause for anixety.

Michael Stone, one of the directors of Sterling Vineyards, demonstrates the duplex pruning that makes possible mechanical harvesting

A system of drip lines radiating from a tank of water irrigates the vines in the high, dry Chalone Vineyards

32

Strong winds, temperatures that are excessively high (over 95° F.) or too low create "shatter": some of the tiny jade-green flowers with their delicate pistils fail to develop into berries, and fall off. Following the berry-set days, the vineyardist can test for shatter by cupping the cluster loosely in his hand and gently drawing his open fingers over the baby berries; shatter is present if more than a few fall off. Rainfall in the ripening period, when followed by extended high humidity, brings on leaf mildew and bunch-rot.

But weather is only one of the factors to be considered in determining the natural endowments of a wine region. Virgil was aware of the importance of soil composition, making specific recommendations about the location of plantings. The *Georgics* were serious in their intent, touching upon the vine, the olive orchard, herds and flocks, and even bees, as they related to the basic wealth and industry of ancient Rome. It was a similar concern that prompted the California State Legislature, in an act signed by Governor Perkins on April 15, 1880, to direct the Regents of the University of California to "provide for special instruction to be given in the Agricultural Department of the University in the Arts and Sciences pertaining to Viticulture and the theory and practice of fermentation, distillation and rectification . . . also, to direct the professor . . . or his assistants, to make examinations and reports upon the different sections of the state adapted to viticulture. . . ."

Count Agoston Haraszthy, an energetic, dynamic immigrant from Hungary, with prophetic visions of viticulture and winemaking in California, introduced a program of state-sponsored studies, beginning with his own authorized tour of European vineyard and winemaking regions in 1861. In Europe he purchased 100,000 vines of about 1,300 varieties. "It may take us a hundred years to find out where these vines should be planted," he wrote, adding, "To the people of this State they will in time be worth many millions." Haraszthy's seemingly extravagant prophecy was to prove to be an understatement. Agriculture is California's number one industry today, with revenues of eight billion dollars. And winegrowing, a uniquely aesthetic branch of farming, is the third-largest segment of the industry.

Recent comparative tastings of European and California wines by acknowledged experts support Haraszthy's boast, made in his 1862 report: "California can produce as noble and generous a wine as any in Europe; more in quantity to the acre, and without repeated failures through frosts, summer rains, hailstorms, or other causes." While it is generally true that "every year in California is a vintage year," in the sense that the relatively uniform climate allows grapes to ripen to acceptable sugar levels, variations in California vintages do exist. However, chaptalization—the addition of sugar to the must (fermenting grape juice) to ensure adequate

alcoholic content of the wine—which is common practice in France and other European countries, is both unnecessary and illegal in California.

The importance of climate for winemaking is not limited to its effect on grape-sugar content; acid levels as well as grape-sugar content depend upon benign weather conditions. The right vine in the wrong location produces wines irrevocably out of balance. Where red-wine grapes are concerned, the wrong climate can even cause problems with coloring.

Why do wines vary so enormously in taste? Why is the Pinot Noir grape of Alsace suitable for making only an indifferent rosé, when the same vine in Burgundy, under equally optimum weather conditions, produces the liquid ruby that has elicited encomiums from popes, emperors, and poets? California's ubiquitous Zinfandel thrives as a money-crop vine in every region of the state but produces great and exciting wines of rare longevity and finesse only when it has the temperate warmth of Napa and Sonoma hillsides, the Sierra foothills of Amador County, or the blessings of similar exposure in comparable microclimates.

The concept of the microclimate (a word that crept into the wine buff's vocabulary only about a decade ago) becomes a handy explanation to account for some very fine wines now coming out of hitherto unsung southern California vineyards. By weather-station measure, the microclimate of Temecula, on a high plateau 23 miles inland from the Pacific Ocean, less than an hour's drive north of San Diego, is comparable to some northern California winegrowing regions more famed for quality.

The temperature-summation scale used to classify California's winegrowing regions is arrived at by totaling the number of degree-days above 50° F. during the days of the growing season. On the basis of this scale, the state is divisible into five regions:

REGION I   Very cool: 2,500 degree-days or fewer—Napa, Santa Cruz (Rhine in Germany, Champagne in France)

REGION II   Cool: 2,501 to 3,000 degree-days—Middle Napa, Sonoma, Monterey (Bordeaux in France)

REGION III   Moderately cool: 3,001 to 3,500 degree-days—North Napa, Livermore (Tuscany in Italy)

REGION IV   Warm: 3,501 to 4,000 degree-days—Ukiah, Lodi (Sicily, Central Spain)

REGION V   Very warm: 4,001 degree-days or more—San Joaquin Valley (Jerez de la Frontera in Spain)

It may be noted that the famous Napa Valley, considered by many to have one climate, is listed under three regions. Near the northern tip of San Francisco Bay, from the Carneros region below Napa all the way up to Yountville, it is very cool. In the central region around St. Helena, Oakville, and Rutherford is the heartland similar to Bordeaux and Burgundy. Where the valley narrows at its northern tip, below Mount St. Helena near Calistoga, it can get quite warm, but just move up the hillsides and you have the microclimates of Stony Hill and Schramsberg, with their blessings of southeastern exposure and the coolness of the Champagne French region.

Present and succeeding generations of California winelovers owe an eternal debt of gratitude to the University of California and its staff, including Professor Amerine, for their prodigious studies of vine, soil, and climate undertaken at UC–Davis over forty years ago. From the comfortable vantage point of the present, all seems right with the world as today's wine pilgrim surveys the healthy green rows of vines ribbing the hills and valleys of each California wine district. But forty years ago, some of those areas were cattle-grazing land with no recognized potential for grapes, and even in yesterday's prime areas, like the Napa Valley, many vulgar, heavy-bearing varieties were grown. They made poor wines, debasing the post-Repeal California vintages to such a degree that their reputation suffered a serious setback when compared with European wines. The prejudices formed then against California wines are only now being slowly overcome in the mind of the European-oriented winelover.

"Golden Chasselas makes the greatest white wine ever produced in the Napa Valley," one winegrower in that area boasted in the mid-thirties. "Alicante Bouschet is *absolutely* a *great* variety!" To the men who owned and praised vineyards of those grapes, young Amerine's findings to the contrary were revolutionary. Rip them out? Ridiculous! Plant low-yielding Cabernet Sauvignon, Pinot Noir, or that difficult Pinot Chardonnay instead? Ridiculous!

Amerine's fieldwork continued during the years from 1935 to 1938 with Chairman A. J. Winkler of the UC–Davis Department of Viticulture and Enology. I first met Maynard Amerine in 1937 in the courtyard of the Davis experimental winery laboratories as he was unloading lugs of grapes from a pickup truck, grapes gathered from a remote vineyard at the proper harvesting moment a few hours earlier. He had little time to talk. I moved along with him and the grapes, back and forth from the truck to the labs as darkness came on. When I left, he drove off into the night to another vineyard, and another, and another, all over the state, spending sleepless weeks to harvest varieties that would provide the field knowledge resulting in today's golden age of wines in California . . . with the right vines in the right places.

CALIFORNIA WINE GRAPES: AN AMPELOGRAPHY

The beginning of vine-planting is like the beginning of mining for the precious metals: the wine-grower also "prospects." One corner of land after another is tried with one grape after another. This is a failure; that is better; a third best. So, bit by bit, they grope about for their Clos Vougeot and Lafite. Those lodes and pockets of earth, more precious than the precious ores, that yield inimitable fragrance and soft fire; those virtuous Bonanzas, where the soil has sublimated under sun and stars to something finer, and the wine is bottled poetry. . . .

—Robert Louis Stevenson

The following ampelography includes all the *Vitis vinifera* species flourishing in California's 328,352 acres of wine grapes (as of 1975). It lists, in alphabetical order, the great and the small, the famous and the little-known varieties, first the grapes destined for the production of white wine. then those destined for red.

CALIFORNIA WHITE-WINE GRAPES

Burger

Early vineyardists set out moderate-sized plots of this heavy-bearing variety to fulfill their ambitions for quantity. Known in Germany and Alsace as the Elbling, this is not the grape a vineyardist shows to visiting nabobs. Alone, it produces a commonplace wine, usually low in acidity. Its principal virtue is as an extender for the cheaper versions of generic California wines such as Chablis and Sauterne. Total planting: 2,018 acres.

Chardonnay

Professor Olmo solved the perplexing problem of the proper name for the elegant grape of the elegant white Burgundy wines Meursault and Montrachet and of Pouilly-Fuissé, Chablis, and Champagne. In his monograph "Chardonnay," published by the Wine Advisory Board in 1971, he states: "The Chardonnay should be recognized as a distinct and well-marked variety and not a white-fruited form of the Pinot Noir. It appears desirable to end the confusion by omitting any reference to Pinot in the name." Commercially launched in California as Pinot Chardonnay, the wine remains incorrectly designated on many labels and wine lists. Many wineries perpetuate the error for commercial reasons. Others, of a more purist bent, have switched to "Chardonnay," with little loss of trade acceptance.

By premium vinification in California in recent years, wines made from the Chardonnay have challenged and surpassed some of the French wines of legendary fame produced from the same grape. It was not until 1962 that a sudden flurry of widespread cultivation of Pinot Chardonnay (as it was then known in California) took place. Land devoted to that vine, according to statistical reports, increased from fewer than 150 acres in 1962 to 11,500 in 1975. This agricultural focus upon Chardonnay was probably triggered by the representative of the *Guide Michelin*, who, in a *Life* magazine article in 1962, declared that the Wente Bros. Livermore Pinot Chardonnay was the finest wine produced in America, on a par with some of the finest white Burgundies of France.

The Wente wine was in sudden demand all across the nation. Winemakers from San Diego to Mendocino wanted to buy, sell, plant, and make Pinot Chardonnay. By the boom year of 1973, choice harvests of

Young Chardonnay berries from Beaulieu's vineyards in the cool Carneros region pioneered by André Tchelistcheff

Chardonnay in Napa and Sonoma counties were bringing $1,000 per ton. By 1977, over 2 1/2 million cases of 100 percent Chardonnay wine were produced, a staggering amount. It is a sobering truth, however, that all the vines of this elegant species do not produce equally elegant wines. The wines vary not only with the region in which the vines grow but with subtleties of both harvesting and vinification.

In very cool regions such as Chablis and Champagne in France and California's North Coast counties, Chardonnay produces a high-acid, crisp wine, ideal with oysters and shellfish. In slightly warmer areas, as in the Burgundian Côte d'Or and the warmer but well-drained and sun-favored hillside vineyards of northern California counties, the microclimate difference and soil variations enable the completely ripe grapes to achieve that full-bodied richness of which Le Montrachet is the classic ideal.

It was just such a California wine, Château Montelena 1973 Chardonnay, that made history in a Paris tasting in May 1976 in a first-place triumph over a lovely Meursault-Charmes 1973 and Puligny-Montrachet Les Pucelles. Many members of the judging panel of French experts believed the California wines to which they were giving high scores were French wines!

Chardonnay vines planted in regions of California's interior valleys, in relatively less extensive acreage than in the favored coastal counties, may, if the necessary irrigation is provided, produce a heavier yield per ton, giving table wines of unremarkable character, though they are drinkable and even pleasing. But these wines lack the famed finesse of the grape variety at its best.

Chardonnay is not an easy vine to grow. An early bloomer, it is vulnerable to spring frosts. The translucent, easily ruptured skin makes it easy prey to flocks of migratory birds, and for such delicate grapes hand harvesting is mandatory. Short cluster stems make even hand harvesting a demanding task.

While sun is vital for ripening, Chardonnay berries are particularly subject to sun-scald damage when exposed, even in the cooler coastal regions. The consequent browning impairs wine quality. Innovative trellising and pruning methods are now being used to provide ample foliage for shading the delicate fruit. The moment of harvest is of the utmost importance, for, according to Professor Olmo, "There is very little in the way of distinct flavor, in either the grape or the new wine, until the fruit is almost overripe. Even experienced tasters cannot detect any mark of varietal distinctiveness in the usual wines of high acidity. However, it is exactly this delicacy and cleanness of taste that makes the variety an excellent base for champagne and a delight to the connoisseur." It is the moment of picking—whether the grapes are just ripe or very ripe—that marks the difference between the Chardonnays of Chablis and Champagne

Winemaker Walter Schug of Joseph Phelps Vineyards keeps careful watch over his temperature-controlled fermenters, in which white wines develop slowly

and the mellow Montrachet. Happily for American consumers, Chardonnay vines in the California sun are currently producing vintages of distinction costing half or even less than half as much as their European counterparts.

Chenin Blanc

This popular grape (also known as Pineau de la Loire, though it does not belong to the Pinot family) is the predominant variety in nearly all the wines of the Loire Valley—Vouvray, Saumur, Anjou, and the Côteaux du Layon—to which the ancient province has given its name.

The Chenin Blanc story in California really began in 1955, when the Charles Krug Winery won a gold medal at the Sacramento State Fair for a pale golden wine which Peter and Robert Mondavi had rechristened "Chenin Blanc." Before this, the good wine had limped along under the designation "White Pinot," one of the misleading names for the French grape. The gold medal, the new name, and, more important than anything else, prolonged cool-fermentation techniques, allowing residual sugar in the finished wine, combined to make a wine that appealed to public taste. Demand quickly outran supply. An abundant-yielding vine, producing an average of 9 to 12 tons per acre in California, Chenin Blanc repeated the Chardonnay story. When spotlighted by public favor, the limited plantings were expanded throughout the state, and today Chenin Blanc is the second most extensively planted white-wine variety in California. From the 19,826 acres in bearing in 1977, a whole sea of 100 percent varietal Chenin Blanc—8,913,000 cases—would be possible with but a 4-tons-per-acre yield! However, much of the wine goes into generic blending, and it is favored by many sparkling-wine producers as a gentle addition to their basic *cuvées*, or blends.

Walter Schug examining young vines

There are many additional reasons, beyond its high productivity, for the popularity of the vine with growers. The sturdy grapes ripen mid-season, in compact clusters that are easily harvested and are capable of being transported from the vineyard to the crushers with minimum damage.

Cool fermentation in stainless steel preserves the wine's most distinctive asset—its clean, ingratiating, thirst-quenching fruitiness. This good balance of natural grape sugar and fruit acidity allows the wine-maker a challenging latitude in style. Since the grape thrives in nearly every one of the state's viticultural regions—in both cool coastal counties and warm interior valleys—subtle differences beyond sweet or dry finish can inspire the winemaker and afford varied taste experiences to the winelover.

The grapevine is essentially a pump, drawing moisture from the soil for the ultimate development of the fruit. Grapes are roughly 80 percent water. Obviously the "pump" is not drawing distilled water from the ground. A good proportion of the grape's composition, beyond wetness,

Brooks Firestone of the new Firestone
Vineyard supervising the Willmes press

is probably a concentrate of the mineral elements of the earth that supports
the vine-root system. It is my belief that this is what we notice when there
is too much earthiness in a wine's taste—what the French term *goût de
terroir,* usually in derogation. But in this native complex of primordial
elements there are the distinguishing differences that make some minute
portions of the planet's surface more precious than others—worth, in
centuries past, a veritable king's ransom. All because the grapevine found
them good.

Some California vintners elect to produce a Chenin Blanc that is
wholly dry. Beyond the sweet-edged market leaders, broad differences in
taste exist. One vintner may prefer to age his wine entirely in stainless
steel, preserving its freshness and fruitiness, never letting the wine touch
wood. Another may keep his wine in wood for a few months. Still others
may combine the two techniques. Differences in oak and in the many
other sizes and kinds of aging containers also contribute nuances of taste,
bringing individuality—its own intrinsic finesse of flavor—like a signature, to each vintaging of this grape.

Emerald Riesling

One of the most popular of the vinifera hybrids developed by Professor Olmo at UC–Davis, the Emerald Riesling, is a cross of the White Riesling of Germany's Rhineland with Muscadelle, one of the many variants of Muscat, a white-wine grape of Bordeaux, where it contributes to the richness of Sauternes. The resulting vine, introduced in 1946, is suitable for planting in California's warmer regions. Invariably the Emerald Riesling produces a wine of freshness and high acidity. With its floral fragrance (happily subdued) from the Muscadelle, it suggests to many the well-balanced charm of Moselle wines of good vintage. Of the present plantings totaling 2,869 acres, more than half grow in Kern and Fresno counties in the San Joaquin Valley, with commercial quantities in Monterey County.

Flora

Only 427 acres of this vinifera hybrid, developed in the course of the grape-breeding studies conducted by Professor Olmo at UC–Davis, currently exist. Produced by crossing Gewürztraminer, the highly aromatic Alsatian grape, with Sémillon, the dominant vine of French Sauternes, the sturdy moderate-yielding vine was introduced in 1958. Intended for the cooler regions of the coastal counties, Flora has appeared in a varietal wine in Napa and Sonoma counties. Its most distinguished and prominent use, taking full advantage of its distinctive bouquet, came in its contribution to the *cuvée* for the Schramsberg Crémant Demi Sec dessert champagne.

Folle Blanche

Formerly the leading grape of the Cognac regions of Charente, the Folle Blanche is easily the best variety for brandy, which is distilled from its pale, light wine of high acidity. A scant 261 acres are being propagated in the moderately cool coastal regions of California. The tightly packed grape clusters are susceptible to bunch-rot and mold in wet seasons, and this limits its popularity among growers; it is sometimes produced as a varietal wine, appealing for its tart, fresh, clean taste. When chilled it is as crisp and refreshing as iceberg lettuce, whose taste it suggests. Because of this almost neutral taste and its high acidity, it is recommended frequently for blending in *cuvées* of champagne and other sparkling wines; it adds the zest and zing necessary in effervescent wines.

Franken Riesling (See Sylvaner)

French Colombard

In France this vigorously productive white-wine grape is sometimes called the Colombar. It arrived in the 1870s in California from France, where it

Giumarra grows a French Colombard in the San Joaquin Valley that makes a fresh, fruity white wine

was valued in the Cognac regions for the high acidity which is desirable in wines for brandy distillation. For a long time grape growers called it "West's White Prolific," but following Repeal, Professor Winkler correctly identified it as the white-wine grape of Charente, and ever since, in California, it has been known as French Colombard. It flourishes in both coastal and interior regions, with present plantings in excess of 26,185 acres. It is a good ripener and will yield 8 to 12 tons per acre.

The amazing versatility of this very popular varietal, which produces a wine of tart, crisp acidity and floral bouquet, has made it a mainstay in California Chablis. But as a distinctive varietal, often made with more than a trace of residual sugar, French Colombard gains fans for its apple taste, unique, ingratiating, and appetizing.

Gewürztraminer

One of the oldest identifiable vinifera varieties in the wine world, the Traminer supposedly enchanted Roman soldiers marching across the Alps two thousand years ago when they encountered it in the village of Tramin (since 1919 known as Termeno) in the Italian Tyrol. Cuttings of the vine traveled north with the Roman legions, were planted along the Danube, and ultimately arrived in Alsace and Germany under the name of Traminer, which it still bears.

Throughout the vine's planting evolution, Alsatian growers propagated those clones of the pinkish grape which had the most outstanding spicy character. From the mother vine, the Traminer, came the dominant vine we know today as the Gewürztraminer, *gewürz* being the German word for "spicy." Under Alsatian *Appellation Controlée* it is now the only strain designated for planting in that wine country. Both Traminer and Gewürztraminer vines exist in California vineyards, but a similar trend

Traminer grapes at Sebastiani Vineyards in Sonoma make their slightly sweet, spicy Gewürztraminer

46

toward the more distinctive variety has trebled the planting in the cooler regions to the present 2,616 acres. Shy-bearing, an early ripener, yielding 4 to 6 tons per acre in irrigated plantings, the Gewürztraminer produces tough-skinned grapes which can be delivered intact to the fermenters.

With cool-fermentation techniques, the grape's very assertive characteristics are preserved. In Alsace the wine is almost always fermented totally dry, but in California some winemakers have found that vinification with an edge of sweetness from residual grape sugar wins favor. The wine requires little or no aging upon release from the winery. It is at its best when its fruitiness and spicy grape taste are fresh and young.

Golden Chasselas

This is one of the most beautiful grapes to behold on the vine, with luxuriantly long, conical clusters of yellow-gold berries to inspire an artist's eye. It is prized in California's San Joaquin Valley vineyards as a sherry grape, but for table wine it is inconsequential, producing wines that are dull, flat, readily oxidized, and almost wholly lacking in acidity. In Switzerland, where the Chasselas is known as the Fendant, it is the leading variety for the pleasant white wines of Vaud, Vallais, and Neuchâtel.

Green Hungarian

The appeal of Green Hungarian, like that of Golden Chasselas, is not inherent in the character of the grape itself, which is neutral to the point of being almost flavorless. But there is no denying the attraction of the name. Like Zsa Zsa Gabor, it has dollar-earning romantic appeal. Lee Stewart, who launched Souverain Vineyards in the Napa Valley in the early forties, was the first to introduce Green Hungarian as a varietal wine. With the renaissance of the Buena Vista Winery in Sonoma, it was only natural that its new owner, Frank Bartholomew, taking full advantage of the Hungarian background of dashing Count Agoston Haraszthy, the founder, would offer Buena Vista Green Hungarian. Poured well-chilled from its tall, slender green bottle, it attracted an immediate following. Other winemakers, seeking to improve upon the wine's rather colorless character, gave it generous additions of Chenin Blanc and/or French Colombard. The M. Lamont Vineyard at the foot of Bear Mountain on the Tehachapi slopes near Bakersfield is producing a Green Hungarian with a very distinctive taste, obviously resulting from the special qualities of that region's soil.

Grey Riesling

This grape, called Chauché Gris in its native France, came to California in the last century. By 1884 it was already known in the Napa Valley as

(overleaf) Almadén owns nearly 4,000 acres of vineyard at Paicines in San Benito County, where much of its Johannisberg Riesling is grown

Modern glass-lined tanks for storing wines at Weibel's historic Mission San Jose winery, founded in 1869 by Senator Leland Stanford

Grey Riesling, even though it had been brought from the Poitiers district, northeast of Bordeaux. Propagated in San Jose nurseries along with the Chauché Noir, it came into favor in the Livermore Valley because it thrived in that warmer climate. Dubbed "grey" because the reddish-tan berries are covered with a dusty bloom as they ripen, the grape acquired the "Riesling" moniker, one can only assume, because the wine was thought to resemble the crisp, clean, popular Rhine wine.

As Grey Riesling the wine has had a success that is nothing short of phenomenal. That it is not even a kissing cousin of any Rhenish grape matters not a whit to those who enjoy its charms. The wine looks like a Riesling in its tall, slender bottle.

An early ripener, harvested in the hot weather of the vintage season, the fruit must be brought in when it is at the peak of its most desirable sugar–acid ratio. With cool-fermentation techniques, often with no wood at all in its aging, it comes to market flowery and generous in mouth-filling refreshment. Although the wine has been criticized for its lack of character, its many adherents find its mildness pleasing.

Malvasia Bianca

This grape with its heady fragrance, luxurious body, and rich history has only 934 acres in bearing in California. Of Greek origin, cuttings established on the island of Madeira in the fifteenth century produced the famed Malmsey wine in which, as reported in Shakespeare's chronicle of King Richard III, the Duke of Clarence was drowned. Malmsey Madeira, laced with brandy, and syrup-sweet, has its own traditions connected with George Washington and Thomas Jefferson. But today in California the muscat-flavored varietal is used to produce a white table wine, sweet-finished and appropriate to serve with dessert, though it cannot rival a great French Sauternes.

Muscat

Cheap California Muscatel, the skid-row tipple, all but annihilated any acceptance for Muscat wines among connoisseurs. It remained for the late Louis M. Martini to make Muscat appealing with his still scarce Moscato Amabile, delicately sparkling and carrying an ineffable freshness of the lovely grape into light, light wine.

The present vogue for other Californian versions of *moscato*, and even the growing popularity of Asti Spumante, attest to the potential of Muscat varietals when used by talented winemakers. Bone-dry Muscat can be exciting and fully satisfying. Muscadelle de Bordelais is classically, but sparingly, blended into French Sauternes. But no matter whether it be the revered Moscato di Canelli of Asti, the Muscat of Alexandria, or Muscat de Frontignan, the perfume is inescapable. How the grape is used is the secret of making captivating wines. If it is harvested too late, the acidity is gone and a flat, dull wine results.

Souverain of Alexander Valley makes a new dessert wine, Moscato Bianco, from the muscat grape

Palomino

In California the Chasselas has sometimes been mistakenly thought to be the same as the Palomino, the leading grape variety in Spain for fine sherry.

Pinot Blanc

In the family of *Vitis vinifera* there is magic to the name Pinot, associated as it is with Romanée-Conti, Le Musigny, Corton, Beaune, and Pommard, made from Pinot Noir. Cross-breeding and selective vine propagation through the centuries have produced different strains with distinctions that often confound and mystify even professional viticulturists who attempt to identify the vine varieties. Pinot Blanc is a proper member of the Pinot family, of which the illustrious Chardonnay is but a cousin. Both are most frequently used in champagne *cuvées*. In California, Pinot Blanc is an often overlooked and underrated varietal white wine. It should not be confused with "White Pinot," which is most often produced from Chenin Blanc.

A shy-bearing vine whose grapes grow in very small, compact clusters, Pinot Blanc thrives in the cooler regions of Monterey, San Benito, Alameda, and Napa counties. Its wine is invariably completely dry; sometimes aged with a slight touch of oak, it is ready to be enjoyed in its first year after the vintage. As produced by premium wineries, it is usually a 100 percent varietal wine. Though its presence is difficult to detect, some Pinot Blanc is employed in the better generic versions of California Chablis.

Pinot Chardonnay (A misnomer. See Chardonnay)

Riesling (See White Riesling)

Sauvignon Blanc

In the hierarchy of wine grapes, Sauvignon Blanc is outranked only by Chardonnay and the White Riesling of the Rhineland. Its ability to last long on the palate gives distinction to the white wine of Graves and contributes body to Sauternes. It is prized in the upper Loire Valley as the dominant variety in Pouilly-Fumé. There it is called Blanc-Fumé because the ripe grapes are a smoky grayish color (*fumé* being the French word for "smoked"), and the name has been adopted by California winemakers in recent years for their varietal interpretation of this grape of many styles.

The earthy, almost wet-sand taste of Sauvignon Blanc serves the winemakers of California as well as of France in producing wines of individual style and taste. A Livermore Valley Sauvignon Blanc is apt to be paper-dry, while one celebrated Napa Valley "château" edition is frankly sweet, styled after Sauternes. Other North Coast county wine-

The fog blanket that sometimes rolls in from the Pacific over the North Coast vineyards keeps the grapes cool and allows them to ripen slowly

makers have found preference in the market by calling their Sauvignon Blanc wine Fumé Blanc or Blanc Fumé. Alas, the labels do not indicate the degree of dryness, which can range from zero residual sweetness to the detectable level of more than 1 percent. Proprietary designations such as Sauvignon Fleur or Blanc de Sauvignon tell you only that the breed is there, but you may be sure that wine from this grape has more than ordinary distinction.

Sauvignon Vert

A low-acid grape, of very pronounced flavor, Sauvignon Vert is used mainly in blending generic white wines; however, California wineries produce a varietal Sauvignon Vert. Used in a varietal, the grape has modest virtues of crisp dryness, the result of early harvesting, and a slightly Muscat flavor brought out by cool fermentation. Sauvignon Vert is usually low in acid.

Sémillon

The late Frank Schoonmaker, who sponsored varietal labeling for California's premium wines, is responsible for the nationwide fame that this excellent grape attained after Prohibition. It is dominant in the blend that constitutes French Sauternes: Sémillon, Sauvignon Blanc, and Muscadelle de Bordelais. "Dry Semillon" from the Livermore Valley was one of the country's most popular wines. There are, of course, those who prefer Sweet Semillon, and still others who enjoy the very sweet Chateau Semillon golden wines.

As *the* Sauternes grape, Sémillon's illustrious destiny may lie in Monterey County plantings, where *Botrytis cinerea,* the "noble rot" of French Sauternes, is a relatively common phenomenon. The benign mold not only draws out moisture, concentrating the grape sugar, but by its presence on the shriveled, fuzzy clusters adds a complexity of taste that enriches the wine. When he was employed as the winemaster of Cresta Blanca in the early sixties, enologist Myron Nightingale produced California's first French-styled sauterne (California sauterne is spelled without the final *s*) by induced humidity and hand-implanted spores of botrytis mold. Several vintages of this "Premier Semillon" were produced, noble experiments that were far ahead of their time. Despite its excellence, the wine offered no serious competition to Château d'Yquem. Today, when we look more and more to California for all kinds of wines, including sweet sauterne, Monterey County may provide an exceptional product for this popular demand.

St.-Émilion (See Ugni Blanc)

Sylvaner

For reasons no one understands, Sylvaner as a wine name has little public appeal. The grape has wider planting than the White Riesling in Germany, where it produces a soft, earthy wine, which when young is fruity and charming. Because it is cultivated widely in Franconia, the Sylvaner is sometimes called the Franken there. In California the Sylvaner appears under other names, too: wines labeled Riesling or Monterey Riesling or Grüner Sylvaner are all made from this grape. Each is likely to have more than 51 percent of Sylvaner, and some may have 100 percent of the varietal. The wines are fairly dry, soft, round, and modestly priced.

Traminer (See Gewürztraminer)

Ugni Blanc

For many years, Wente Bros. in the Livermore Valley produced a varietal Ugni Blanc wine that enjoyed acceptance by a small, enthusiastic group of customers—the only ones who could pronounce the name. But even those who asked for "Ugly Blank" could sometimes be understood, and then the wine would come, chilled, delectable, crisp, tart, and fragrant. Ugni Blanc was not a real winner until the Wentes blended it with Chenin Blanc and renamed it Blanc de Blancs. What's in a name? Nearly everything, where a wine's popularity is concerned. Brookside winery, of Guasti, California, produces a varietal wine from this grape and calls it by the name it enjoys in the French Cognac region—St.-Émilion. Sold in Burgundy bottles, it is a puzzler to the traditionalist who orders from a wine card expecting a red Bordeaux-type wine, only to be presented with a white wine in a Burgundy bottle.

In Italy, this high-yielding vine is called Trebbiano and is one of the grapes used in Soave, which many consider the best white wine of that country. You can stop looking for Ugni Blanc, but don't be surprised someday to find a California Trebbiano that is competing for the Soave market. There are more than 1,500 acres growing in the Golden State, most of it in Central Valley vineyards. It is used for ordinary California Chablis, Sauterne, or Dry Sauterne. Ugni Blanc's lack of acidity is perhaps its greatest defect.

White Riesling (Johannisberg Riesling)

The correct name of this noble grape is Weiss Riesling but it is more commonly known in California as Johannisberg Riesling, in honor of the famous Schloss Johannisberg—and for obvious commercial reasons. It is the outstanding vinifera not only of the Rhineland but also of the Mosel, where it makes the great Bernkasteler Doktor and Wehlener Sonnenuhr. The Riesling of Alsace, Austria, Chile, and Australia is the same

Almadén Vineyards, one of the oldest and largest, must irrigate some of its 15,000 far-flung acres

At the Firestone Vineyard, late-harvested Johannisberg Riesling grapes show evidence of the prized *Botrytis cinerea*, or "noble rot"

species, but the famous Schloss Johannisberg of the Rheingau is the name that holds public favor, even when the wine is made thousands of miles away.

Native to the coldest wineland of Europe, the White Riesling's adaptation to the warmer plots of California has been productive of wines with character and finesse. But they are seldom even close in taste or nature to the fine wines of the Rhine or the Mosel. The grapes develop differently in the warmer environment, often having a higher sugar content, which means greater alcoholic strength and less delicacy.

White Riesling in California is produced in varying styles by different winemakers within one growing area. A flowery bouquet may be the aim of one winemaster, while another balances the grape freshness with the modifying fragrance and flavor that comes from aging in new oak. Vintage becomes important with some producers, whose wines may vary from year to year. Late-harvested versions will benefit from cellar aging, the higher sugar and alcoholic content acting as a preservative, but the wholly dry or even ever so slightly sweet versions are never better than within months of their release from the winery.

In recent years—with the recognition of botrytis in vineyards along the Russian River in Sonoma County, in isolated locations in the Napa Valley, in Monterey County, and in the region of Temecula in southern California—it was realized that, if late-harvested, Johannisberg Riesling can make wines that approach the *Auslese* and even the *Beerenauslese* richness of German wines. These botrytised wines have the splendor of yellow-gold liqueurs whose color and body promise extraordinary taste. Such great wines are uncommon in Germany, and equally rare in California, but all are treasures the true winelover may enjoy. Comparison is incidental, of minor significance.

CALIFORNIA RED-WINE GRAPES

Aleatico

An exotic member of the Muscat family, this grape, which thrives in the warm vineyard regions, is used to produce a very aromatic, soft and spicy table wine of pleasing pink color, and also a deeper-colored red dessert wine. Of Italian origin, Aleatico is the source of the Tuscan *vino santo*, but its greatest claim to fame is its reputation as the finest wine produced on the island of Elba. In California Aleatico table wine is produced by fewer than half a dozen wineries; a scant 144 acres are in bearing.

Alicante Bouschet

One of the very few wine grapes in the world with blood-red juice, Alicante Bouschet zoomed into popularity during Prohibition as a juice grape for home winemakers. Heavy-skinned, with high sugar content,

Angelo Papagni gives Alicante Bouschet oak aging worthy of Pinot Noir and Cabernet

Alicante's blood-red juice gives it some value as a color agent

John Moramarco, viticulturalist at Callaway Vineyard, exhibits their Cabernet Sauvignon grapes, which he cluster-thins to a two-ton-per-acre yield of richly concentrated berries

generous-bearing, and easy to harvest, it afforded California vineyardists an appealing money crop during the dry era. Later, when, following Repeal, fine winemaking transformed the standards of the California wine industry, the vulgar virtues of Alicante ceased to be advantages. But Alicante Bouschet remains the leading grape for thousands of home winemakers, and during the harvest season 175,000 tons are shipped from the San Joaquin Valley to Eastern states and Canada. Not only do the grapes ship well, but the home winemaker is assured of a wine of good (though not long-lasting) color, quick maturing, and soon ready to drink. The grape, though misprized by other winemakers (except as a color agent for California port wine), is a variety no longer touted among the ranks of the state's growers of fine wines, whose attention is focused upon the more noble varieties.

Barbera

The Barbera grape produces a big, full-bodied wine in its home region of Piedmont. Though some 20,576 acres are in bearing in California vineyards at present, much of the wine is used in Burgundy and Chianti blends. Some California vintners of Italian background give premium status to the vine, and their wines are favored by consumers seeking deep-flavored, deep-colored wines to accompany highly seasoned Italian foods. Barbera is cultivated in all the state's wine regions, and in each region the wine reflects the particular climate and soil and the style of the individual winemaker. Some wines will be wood-aged to a rich softness, while others, with accent on the berry-like bouquet, will be young wines best consumed early.

Cabernet Sauvignon

Cabernet Sauvignon ranks easily as the world's most highly prized red-wine grape. It is responsible for the great clarets of Bordeaux and the best red wines of California. The velvet-soft and deeply fragrant ruby-red wine from this vigorous *Vitis vinifera* species offers every winemaker the challenge that will test his creative skill and enhance his name. Synonymous with superior red wine, the name Cabernet Sauvignon and its appeal to the world of wine consumers accounted for much of the wine boom in California, extending the planting from 1,966 acres in 1965 to the present 24,539 bearing acres—an increase that can only be called phenomenal.

In the famed French château vineyards of Bordeaux, the vine is trained low, the rows often punctuated with red roses which flower simultaneously with the vine. It is perhaps only viticultural superstition that the rosebushes are there to warn of an onset of mildew, they and the grapevines being subject to similar diseases, or to attract bees to pollinate the berries. In California the vines are often trellised, the branching canes providing a luxuriantly shady arbor frequently more than seven feet tall.

At Freemark Abbey, Cabernet Sauvignon grapes are crushed in a cylindrical press

58

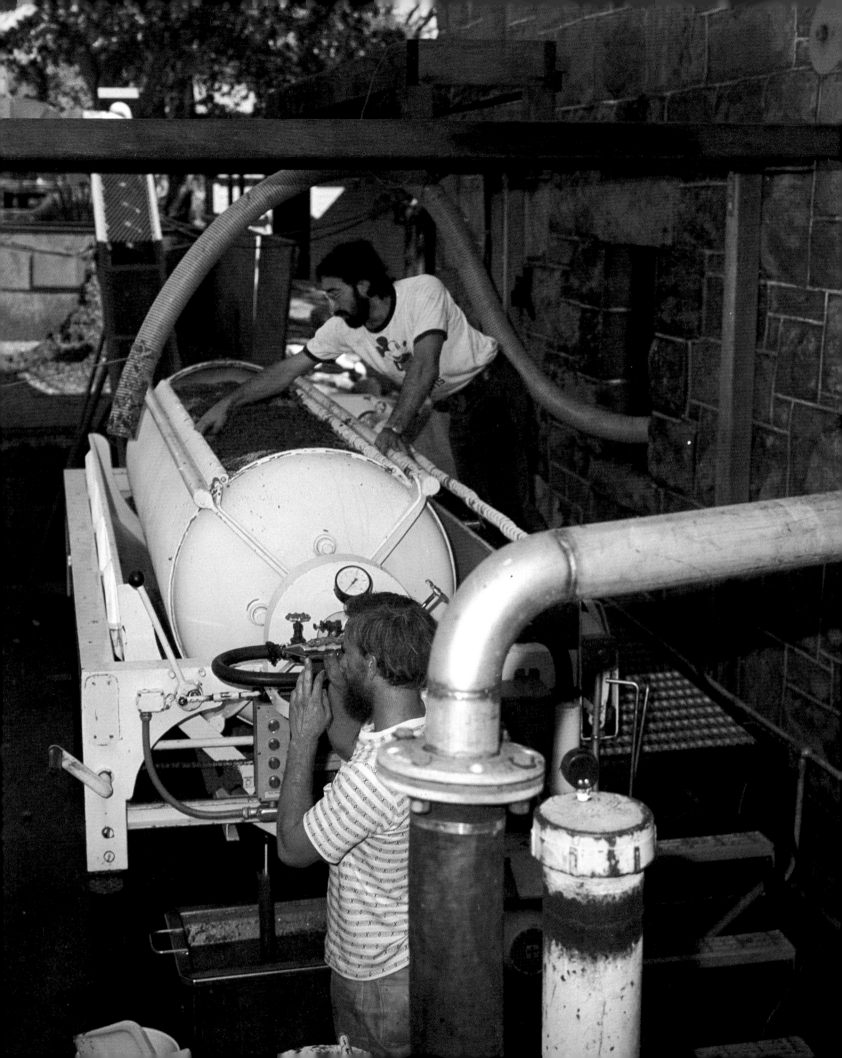

Under normal conditions a fairly good set of the blue-black small clusters can be expected, with a yield of 4 to 6 tons per acre. Monterey, Napa, Sonoma, and Santa Barbara counties are preeminent in Cabernet planting, but there is scarcely a winegrowing region in the state that has not been tempted to plant this aristocratic variety.

The grape has a tough and durable skin, which not only makes for easier harvesting but is an advantage in case of rain late in the season, since the heavy-skinned clusters can dry without danger of bunch-rot. The heavy skins are also responsible for the high percentage of tannin in the wine, a factor that increases the winemaker's options as to method of vinification.

Professor H. W. Berg of UC–Davis demonstrated that nearly all the color is extracted from the skins of the grapes in the early period when the juice is in contact with the pomace (the skins and seeds) and suggested that further contact extracts excessive amounts of tannins that only age can soften. An accelerated maturity is thus possible if the emerging wine is taken off the skins even before the full sugar/alcohol fermentation is completed. Winemakers can argue for hours this theory versus the Bordeaux tradition of leaving the wine in contact with the pomace for two weeks or longer. From such points of difference in winemaking emerge the different styles of clarets, not only in California but in France as well.

The astringency of young Cabernet wines is decreased through aging in wood. The classic French method is to age new wine in new wood, an expensive process requiring new 50-gallon oak barrels for each vintage. The choice of Limousin, Nevers, Yugoslavian, German, or American oak will affect the taste of the wine almost as much as climate, soil, and blending with other claret grapes. But the distinctive bouquet of Cabernet Sauvignon, which is enhanced with bottle age, is the attribute that gives the breed its universal appeal.

The complexity of the Cabernet Sauvignon bouquet tests the descriptive powers of its passionate adherents. There are 100 percent Cabernet Sauvignon wines that smell like roses, others that are richly herbal, and the woodsy, cedar scents from oak aging can often marry with the fruit to give a wine an indescribable complexity.

Cabernet Franc

This leading member of the Cabernet family in Saint-Émilion also produces the popular rosé wines of the Loire, but it is not cultivated in any appreciable quantity in California. Cabernet Franc has been produced as a single varietal by Spring Mountain Vineyards in the Napa Valley and Veedercrest of Emeryville. Growing in small, compact clusters, it is valued as a grape to blend with Cabernet Sauvignon.

Cabernet pomace—the skins, seeds, and stems left after the juice has been drawn off—being poured into a basket-press at Jordan Winery for added essence

The winemaker at Jordan draws from the wood a sample of '76 Cabernet Sauvignon, the first wine from the third-leaf harvest

Carignane

The most widely planted wine grape in California, Carignane was once second to Zinfandel, but today, with 30,710 acres in bearing, it is the most important commercial red-wine grape in the state. Produced as a single varietal wine by several wineries, it belies its reputation for being ordinary through vinification methods that achieve outstanding results for the grape. For example, the normally high-yielding vine is cultivated without irrigation. Hillside grapes from North Coast counties can produce a powerful varietal wine, its robust flavor intensified by lower yield. But for the most part heavy yield remains Carignane's chief virtue, and it becomes a payload variety for almost all generic red wines of California.

Carnelian, Carmine, Centurion

The University of California has experimental vineyards at Davis where continuing research to improve the quality of California wine production is carried on. Distinguished hybrids like Emerald Riesling and Ruby Cabernet are the results of Professor Olmo's patient work, based on the belief that the outstanding virtues of two, and sometimes even more, crossed plants may combine to produce a superior vine, with the best characteristics of each, adaptable to climate and soil environments in which no one vine had before excelled. Such a vine is Carnelian, a Cabernet × Carignane × Grenache hybrid developed for the warm San Joaquin Valley, with more than 2,000 acres now in commercial planting. Newer is Carmine, another Cabernet type, which yields a distinctly more flavorful wine than one of its august parents, Cabernet Sauvignon; the progeny of Cabernet Sauvignon × Carignane were crossed with early-ripening Merlot, a first cousin to Cabernet Sauvignon. Professor A. Dinsmoor Webb, the present chairman of the UC–Davis Department of Viticulture and Enology, believes Carmine's 20-year history of development will make it a bell-ringer for California Cabernet-type production. Centurion is another hybrid just beginning to move into the spotlight after the long wait of growing cycles designed to determine its standing in the family of Cabernet hybrids. Begun, like all the cross-variety samples, as a number, it has achieved the dignity of a name.

Charbono

This currently rare varietal, imported from Italy in the last century, probably declined in popularity because of its coarse, deep-colored, rough wines, which when blended with other wines tended to overpower them. Viticulturist Charles Wetmore condemned it in 1884 in no uncertain terms: "Those who desire to produce only high-grade wines should not plant this variety."

The present story of Charbono is a full turn-around to glory. In the late 1930s, Professor Winkler studied the vines from which Inglenook

VARIETAL WINE LABELS

was producing a medal-winning Barbera and identified them not as the popular vinifera of Piedmont for which the wine was named, but positively as Charbono. Today, Inglenook draws upon fewer than 20 acres of Charbono, but winemaker Tom Ferrell tells me there are present plans to extend the planting, with added vines almost within the shade of the winery buildings at Rutherford. Keep Charbono on your list of California specialties. Taste it young. It will upholster your mouth with brash tannin. Age is really needed to bring it around to the greatness found in it by its admirers.

Gamay

Quite simply, Gamay is the grape which produces that darling of Parisian bistros called Beaujolais. Light and gay, always to be consumed young, with the delicate appeal of vine-fresh raspberries, it is the ideal candidate for generous pouring and carefree occasions when a more illustrious wine would be out of place. The grape is known in France as *Gamay noir à jus blanc* ("black Gamay with white juice"). It thrives in California, where only recently it has begun to emerge under the proper name, Gamay Noir, as a varietal wine. There are currently 4,760 acres in bearing.

The grape has extensive use for rosé wines. To make a rosé, the juice is fermented on the skins for only a few hours, until just the desired hint of color is obtained. Both red and rosé Gamay wines require little aging and are at their best the moment they reach the wineshop.

Gamay Beaujolais

Recently discovered to be a member of the Pinot Noir family, the Gamay Beaujolais is an early ripener, with small, oval, black berries growing in compact clusters. With a yield of 4 to 6 tons per acre, it adapts well to varying types of soil, thriving almost entirely in Monterey, Napa, Mendocino, San Benito, Sonoma, and Santa Barbara counties in 4,490 bearing acres.

Though Gamay Beaujolais is not the grape of carafe wine in French bistros, several California vintners vinify the grape in the style of Beaujolais *nouveau*, bottling it young for consumption while the wine is fresh and fruity. Other winemakers give the wine added aging in wood, releasing it a year, instead of weeks or months, after harvest. Essentially a light wine, its ideal service comes with barbecue dinners and picnics.

Grenache

Charles Wetmore, executive officer of California's first State Board of Viticultural Commissioners, writing in 1884, found the Grenache "so vigorous and fertile, and so well adapted to dry, warm regions, that there is danger that it may be planted too numerously." More than half of the

Gamay Beaujolais and Sauvignon Blanc from Monterey Vineyards

20,244 acres now thriving in the state are planted in the warm central San Joaquin Valley and give varietal distinction not only to Grenache rosé wines but to blended generic vin rosé. Many examples of generic vin rosé are slightly sweet, while others are quite dry, depending upon the winemaker's marketing aims. All should be consumed young, while still fresh and fruity.

The Grenache's pronounced, almost spicy, aroma contributes to the complexity of Châteauneuf-du-Pape of the Rhône, and in Spain, where it is known as the Garnacha, its reddish-purple grapes enhance the appeal of Rioja wines. The vogue for pink wines was born of the Grenache rosé produced in the Tavel district of the Rhône. When the late Frank Schoonmaker discovered Grenache flourishing in the California vineyards of Almadén in Los Gatos, it was only a matter of months before Almadén Grenache Rosé was on its way to becoming an American favorite.

Grignolino

The reputation for individuality possessed by this unique Italian grape of the Piedmont region arises from its unusual strawberry-like fragrance and the hints of orange in its light crimson color. While the most famous editions of Grignolino have been produced in the widely separated areas of Cucamonga and the Napa Valley, as a red-wine varietal or rosé table wine, blended with Pinot Noir, it gave distinction to Beringer Brothers' original proprietary blending called Barenblut. Grignolino remains one of the favorite grapes of Joe Heitz of the Napa Valley, and customers line up for their share of each release. A total of 241 acres are currently in bearing in California, principally in Santa Clara and Napa counties.

Mataró

Plantings of Mataró, which makes a rather coarse red wine, are largely confined to southern California. The grape's utilitarian role in bulk wine production in France and Spain is responsible for whatever popularity it had. It is to the credit of California winegrowers that Mataró is rapidly being replaced as a wine grape by finer varieties. Not even its very limited use in Châteauneuf-du-Pape could rescue it from its California decline.

Merlot

While the role of Merlot is subsidiary to that of Cabernet Sauvignon and Cabernet Franc in the Médoc, the grape rises to great distinction in the wines of Saint-Émilion and Pomerol—and especially the noble Château Pétrus—to which it imparts softness and roundness. With bigger berries than Cabernet, growing in loose clusters, the grape gives suppleness and flower delicacy to wines with which it is blended.

An early ripener as a grape, Merlot is an early bloomer as a wine. In years when frosts or hail wipes it out, the wines of the Haut-Médoc that

66

The modern winery's ranks of stainless-steel fermenting and storage tanks represent an enormous investment

usually incorporate it into their blends will have heavier, slow-maturing Cabernets. When the weather has been kind to the grape, Merlot joins the other Médoc varieties to make winsome, graceful wines of lighter mien.

First cousin to the Cabernet family, Merlot is just beginning an independent varietal career in California. It thrives in the Napa Valley, where 100 percent Merlots from Sterling Vineyards have shown that the wine can have the same soft grace and charm as endear it to the winegrowers of Saint-Émilion and Pomerol. Quicker-maturing than Cabernet wines, Merlot, as an ingredient along with Cabernet in claret blending, is coming into vogue among California winemakers. Their customers are beginning to understand that 100 percent Cabernet Sauvignon is not essential for deluxe editions of that famous varietal. Acreage of Merlot in California had a hundredfold increase from its scant 35 acres in 1966 to 3,988 in bearing ten years later.

Mission

Few grape varieties have as romantic a history as the Mission grape or have played a more important role in the development of a region. Long thought to be a Criolla seedling first brought to the western world by Cortez and the conquistadors, it is believed today by UC–Davis viticulturists to be a variant of the Spanish Monica. Named after the Spanish missions established by Franciscan fathers throughout California, the grape was first planted by Padre Junípero Serra in San Diego de Alcalá in 1769. From San Diego north to Sonoma, twenty-one Franciscan missions grew up along El Camino Real, each with its vineyards proving the land was receptive to *Vitis vinifera*.

Reminders of earlier times at Mission San Jose along El Camino Real, where the Mission grape was first planted by Franciscan friars

The blue-black grapes, "round as a musket-ball," from abundant-yielding vines taller than a man, produced a wine reminiscent of Málaga. The Mission grapevine continued to be the only species in California until the 1830s, when Jean Louis Vignes arrived in Los Angeles from Bordeaux bringing French vine cuttings and winemaking traditions that would improve upon the product of the padres. There are still 6,356 acres of Mission vines yielding abundant crops from San Diego to Sonoma.

The Mission grape is used in California today for both port and sherry, but its finest role is in the production of a rich, sweet, golden dessert wine called Angelica, named after the city of Los Angeles.

In the Livingston vineyards of Ernest and Julio Gallo, Mission vines, with gnarled and sturdy trunks indicating an age of several decades, are planted along the bank of the Merced River, where they are prized for their contribution to Gallo's Livingston Cream Sherry.

Montonico

Only 8.4 acres of this rare vinifera, brought from Calabrian vineyards by members of the Filice family of San Martin Vineyards, are known to exist in California. Originally thought of as a sherry grape, it went almost unnoticed until, in 1973, 11,000 gallons of the 1967 vintage were found by winemaster Ed Friedrich, quietly resting in oak. Unbaked, slowly aged in wood, the wine was a facsimile of the *vino santo* made in small amounts by farmers all over Italy. The ancient grape species has a heritage that dates back at least to 720 B.C., when the Calabrian city of Sybaris was founded.

Nebbiolo

Only 383 acres of this splendid Italian red-wine grape are in bearing in California—in Fresno, Stanislaus, Tulare, and Amador counties. But it is not unlikely that its distinctive and compelling varietal flavors, which give recognizable character to the great Italian wines, Barolo, Barbaresco, and Gattinara of Piedmont, will inspire extended planting in California; at present only the Monteviña winery of Plymouth produces a varietal Nebbiolo. The vine is named for the *nebbia,* the cool morning fog that

rides softly across the rolling vineyard landscape of Piedmont during the hot pre-harvest months, allowing the grapes to mature gradually. The sturdy red wines of Nebbiolo grapes require considerable aging, but when mature they have outstanding attributes of bouquet, assertiveness, and class.

Petite Sirah

André L. Simon wrote: "The true origin of the Syrah grape is unknown." Clonal descendants of the ancient Shiraz vine from Persia allegedly thrive today in the vineyards of France, Switzerland, California, Australia, and South Africa. Whether or not the California Petite Sirah, currently enjoying tremendous popularity among winelovers with an appreciation for bold red wines, originated in Persia, its charms are not to be denied.

When the French crusader Gaspard de Sterimberg quit the Holy Land in 1225 and built himself a hermitage near Lyons, legend tells us that he not only took home to the valley of the Rhône his taste for the wines of Persia; he brought back vine cuttings as well. And here the legend accommodates the fact that the oldest vineyards in France, those that resisted Domitian's edict against the vine, A.D. 92, were in this region of Roman Gaul. The vineyard of the crusader-turned-hermit produces wine that has been called "the manliest of all French wines"—Hermitage.

The Syrah vine came to dominate the Rhône. It is the grape that gives longevity, color, and flavor to Châteauneuf-du-Pape. In color, wines of the Syrah or Petite Syrah vine will vary from dark garnet to almost transparent ruby. The bouquet is a complex that may suggest almond, cedar, or raspberry. In the mouth-filling taste there is strong tannin that may be puckery in young wines, giving way to softness as the wine ages. Intensity of color, acid, and tannin increases as the temperature of the region in which the vine is grown decreases.

California Petite Sirah thrives in 13,074 acres with plantings in the foothills of the Sierra, in the northern reaches of Mendocino County, in Napa and Sonoma, in the great San Joaquin Valley, and as far south as San Diego. Frank Schoonmaker suggested that the California Petite Sirah, while presumed to be the Syrah of the Rhône, was probably a more vulgar vinifera called Duriff, a heavy-bearing variety that also grows in the Rhône Valley and that resembles the Petit Syrah of Hermitage. This is probably a partial truth, but I believe that some true Syrah clones, descendants of the ancient Shiraz, give greatness to some California vinifications of Petite Sirah wines. André Simon, after his visit to Australia, declared the Shiraz, widely propagated there, to be "the same variety that is planted extensively in the Rhône Valley of France, where it is the basis of Hermitage wines." In Australia I tasted the wine against memories of Rhône wines, and agree.

Pinot Noir

Pinot Noir, both the grape and the wine, remains an enigma to California viticulturists and winemakers alike. More than 200 clones, or variants of the species, have been identified, but it is also known that numerous differences in the species exist in the celebrated vineyards of the French Côte d'Or. We can only speculate on how many of the differences found in the true Pinot Noir wines of California and France result from soil or vine variations.

The shy-bearing vine can be as temperamental as a spoiled child. The early-ripening grapes come to maturity during the warmest period of the harvest season and can quickly become overripe, losing their proper sugar/acid ratio. Thin-skinned, the clusters require careful handling. Although it is primarily used for red wines, the white juice of the black grapes has an elegant fruitiness that recommends it for *cuvées*, or basic blends, in champagne. In Blanc de Noirs editions, consummate skill is required to keep the pigment of the skins from "bleeding" into the wine, giving it an unwanted blush of color.

Pinot Noir in California seems to elude even the most intelligent application of enological science in the production of wines comparable in stature to those of the French Côte d'Or. In the words of wine writer Norman S. Rody, "Pinot Noir is the thorn in the side of the California wine industry."

I can cite isolated examples of superlative California Pinot Noir, but they are few and far between. California Pinot Noir, like fine French Burgundy, is affected by the soil in which the grapes grow and by the vinification methods and aging procedures. Few wineries can afford more than a year or so of bottle age before general release. That aging is the beginning of the refinement necessary to achieve a wine's full potential. It is up to you, the wine buyer, to allow your wines the time they need to reach their peak.

Pinot St. George (Red Pinot)

Though a true vinifera, it is doubtful that Pinot St. George is a member of the regal Pinot family. Grown in hillside vineyards of the Napa Valley, it produces a wine of distinctive character, which, with added age, deepens in complexity. The obvious advantages of the Pinot name have been responsible for increased planting of the variety, though at present only 654 acres are in bearing, mostly in Monterey and Napa counties.

Refosco

Transplanted to France in the last century, the Refosco grape of Italy fooled even the famed ampelographer Count Oudart, who listed it as Petit Pinot, which obviously made it a more attractive candidate for importation. Some believed that the Refosco which arrived in California

was in reality a Pinot Noir, but to settle the question for a while, one planter gave it his own name; Crabb's Black Burgundy enjoyed a lively fame as a red-wine grape in turn-of-the-century California vineyards. Today Refosco is often used in small amounts in Cabernet blends. The number of acres planted in the Napa Valley, currently 231, will probably decrease.

Royalty

This California-developed hybrid, like the Rubired, Salvador, and Alicante Bouschet, has red juice. It has long been used to give color to California port. Beyond the pigment of the skins and juice, Royalty has little interesting potential as a red-table-wine grape. It does not, despite its name, belong in the company of truly noble varieties. At best, it is a rather commonplace wine, sweet-edged and as obvious as a Valentine.

Ruby Cabernet

The distinctive flavor and bouquet of Cabernet Sauvignon and the high yield of Carignane inspired the marriage of these two viniferas at the Agricultural Experiment Station of UC–Davis in 1936. Their offspring was released for commercial planting as Ruby Cabernet in 1948, and it did indeed seem to inherit the hoped-for parental characteristics. Even when planted in warm Central Valley regions the grape produced wines of a quality to gain immediate acceptance. Public recognition of the wine's attractive bouquet, good fruit, acidity, and excellent color accounts for the steady growth of the plantings to the 17,583 acres currently in bearing. As a varietal, it has even earned some gold medals at the Los Angeles County Fair.

Souzão

In the production of fine port wine, beyond the aesthetic importance of the mellow ruby color derived from the skins of the grapes, sufficient acidity to balance sweetness is critical. Without acidity, the most beautiful, velvet-soft port would be cloying. The virtue of the Souzão grape resides in its peculiar ability to retain, in the process of ripening, a good balance of natural acidity, even as it develops a high sugar content.

Valdepeñas

The vine takes its name from the large wine-producing area of the ancient province of Spain whose rocky soil earned it the name "Valley of Stones." The wine from this vinifera is undistinguished even in its homeland, but the generous yield is the reason it is propagated for *vino corriente*, the inexpensive wine for daily or "current" consumption. More than 2,000 acres in California vineyards are planted in Valdepeñas, important for the same reason: the vine thrives and gives a bountiful yield per acre for generic blendings of inexpensive and undistinguished red table wines.

The noble Pinot Noir, autumn-ripe, is used primarily for red wines, but the white juice can also add a touch of elegance to champagne blends

Zinfandel

Zinfandel is California's own wine, unique, complex, and as varied in its character as the climate in which it grows. While it enjoys the distinction of being produced from one of the most widely planted vines in the state, no one has yet been able to establish the land of its birth with certainty.

History and legend tell us the vine was brought back from Hungary in 1862 by Count Agoston Haraszthy, but today it is totally unknown in that country. Zinfandel thrived in America long before Haraszthy made his famous grape-gathering trip to Europe. In his authoritative volume *The Wines of America*, Leon D. Adams reveals the existence of a European grape named Zinfandel "grown under glass by William Robert Prince on Long Island, N.Y., as early as 1830, 10 years before Haraszthy immigrated to the United States." In his own *Treatise on Grapes,* Prince declared that Zinfandel came from Hungary.

The most recent clue to the possible origin of Zinfandel emerged in 1967, when Dr. Austin Goheen, plant pathologist with the U.S. Department of Agriculture, visited vineyards in Puglia, in southeastern Italy, where he saw rows of vines that looked to him like California Zinfandel. Called *Primitivo di Gioia* in reference to their early ripening, the big, heavily winged bunches of compactly clustered black grapes were first gathered in August. A second crop, well-shaded by foliage, ripened much later and produced a fine, full-flavored red wine capable of great age.

Almadén makes nearly every variety and kind of wine produced in California, and many of its thousands of vineyard acres thrive with the help of sprinkler systems

The deep red Zinfandels from cooler North Coast regions of California resemble the wines of the Médoc. A lighter, fruitier version from the warmer districts suggests Beaujolais

Like other vinifera species, California Zinfandel also will set a second crop of fruit, and it matures both in the middle of the growing period and late. Dr. Goheen reported his observations to Professor Olmo, casting new light on the mystery of Zinfandel's origins.

Three different Primitivo vines that flourish in the Taranto area of Puglia are now growing in the UC–Davis experimental vineyards under the watchful eye of Professor Olmo. As a result of his study of leaf conformation, fruiting and ripening characteristics, and ultimately by wine analysis, it may eventually be determined that Zinfandel had an Italian rather than a Hungarian origin, but we will have to wait perhaps five or ten years for confirmation.

Today, of the 328,352 acres of wine grapes growing in California, Zinfandel with 29,889 acres in bearing is second only to Carignane. There are heavy plantings in the warm central and southern counties and also in the cooler North Coast counties. Since in the warmer districts grapes mature much earlier, and with the same degree of sugar have less total acid and less color, it is immediately apparent that two different types of Zinfandel, one lighter and one heavier, will emerge by reason of vineyard location. California's highly skilled winemakers today produce not merely two types of Zinfandel but five:

1. A light, young, and fresh Zinfandel, its berry-like flavor suggesting the French Beaujolais.

2. A heavier-bodied, deeper-colored wine, capable of long cellar aging, comparable to the finest French clarets of the Médoc. Such wines are most likely to emerge from the cooler regions.

3. Late-harvest Zinfandels, with alcohol content as high as 17 percent by volume and with minimal residual sugar. These have rare aging potential and suggest the results that will be possible when viticulture and enology marry in the science of winemaking.

4. The rare Blanc de Noirs Zinfandel, white wine from black grapes. Cool, controlled crushing and fermentation preserve the grape's characteristic aroma and bouquet and give satin richness of body. Only a few examples of this wine exist.

5. Zinfandel Rosé, incomparably fresh, fragrant, usually dry, to be enjoyed young. This is a stunning surprise to winebibbers accustomed to pink wines that are innocuous and lacking in character.

TWO HUNDRED YEARS OF WINE HISTORY

"And all these tidal gatherings, growth, and decay,
Shining and darkening, are forever
Renewed; and the whole cycle impenitently
Revolves, and all the past is future. . . ."
                    —Robinson Jeffers

Long before the Pilgrims landed on Plymouth Rock, three small ships sailed into the harbor near what would later be the town of San Diego. They belonged to the expedition of Juan Rodríguez Cabrillo, a Portuguese navigator in the service of Spain. The year was 1542, less than a quarter of a century after the conquest of Mexico for Spain by Hernando Cortez, which brought about the capture of Montezuma in chains, followed by the plundering of one civilization by another and the cruel imposition of Spanish rule. Out of this high drama came the transposition of cultures that still marks the land. Spanish colonists were commanded to plant, every year for five years, one thousand vines for every one hundred Indians living on the land. Mexico, it was hoped, might become one enormous vineyard.

It was not fertile California in which Cabrillo planted the first flag to fly over that land, on October 10, 1542. With the ensign of Carlos V of Spain, he took possession of California near Mugu Lagoon in Ventura County, a cactus-studded, rocky, sun-drenched peninsula, hot as a furnace, according to some of the explorers.

In England, Queen Elizabeth's interest in the New World inspired a rather piratical voyage by Sir Francis Drake. On his freebooting expedition around the world in the *Golden Hind* he managed to raid every Spanish ship he encountered, but beyond raising the English flag with the Cross of St. George, and nailing a sixpence to a post on the shore of Drake's Bay, just north of San Francisco, Sir Francis failed to make "New Albion" a real threat to Spanish empire.

However, reverberations of Drake's exploits troubled the Spanish court and ultimately set in motion the expedition of Gaspar de Portolá and Padre Junípero Serra. The simultaneous planting of the Cross, the sword, and the vine at San Diego in 1769 truly begins the romantic wine history of California, with the ultimate establishment of the chain of the twenty-one missions, the presidios, and the pueblos that have become today's cities, ranches, and farming communities.

The gentle face of Padre Junípero Serra in the portrait by a contemporary artist belies the enduring strength and dynamic force that marked his leadership of the missionary expedition until his death at the Mission San Carlos Borromeo del Rio Carmelo, in January 1784.

His is a life story of overcoming the most incredible hardships, pushing against the impossible toward accomplishment, and achieving the miraculous. It was this superhuman drive in Serra that converted the dry, thorny thickets and desert land of California into gardens, orchards, vineyards, and thriving communities. At every mission vine roots went into the ground as certainly as the foundations were begun.

The wines of San Gabriel and San Fernando, San Juan Capistrano and Santa Barbara gathered such fame, life in Alta California became so like paradise, that reports to the viceroy in Mexico brought orders from

The Serra Chapel in Mission San Juan Capistrano honors the memory of Padre Junípero Serra, who brought wines and vines to California in 1769

jealous administrators to curtail even small luxuries. All the wooden *carretas* were burned to keep the good friars from riding. Shoes and stockings were forbidden. Rooms that were large and comfortable were taken from the friars and assigned to travelers.

San Juan Capistrano, the seventh of the missions founded, and permanently established in the year of our nation's birth, 1776, played a tiny but significant part in our beginnings—the mission padres donated $229 to help the cause of the American Revolution, and among their early records is a notation that a priest said a prayer "for the success at arms of Mr. George Washington, whose cause seems to be just."

At this same mission in 1818, raiding French pirates flying the revolutionary flag of Buenos Aires and allegedly seeking to achieve Argentine independence from Spain, so enjoyed the wines of San Juan Capistrano that some of them had to be dragged back to the ship and lashed to the cannons. Who could blame the poor sailors, after months at sea, for wanting to stay at this virtual palace garden? Like the swallows who return to Capistrano every March 19, those tipsy pirates must have had wishful urgings to return to this bit of Paradise on earth!

Over the years, revolution, secularization, earthquakes, plunder, and desertion reduced most of the missions to adobe ruins. Because their chapels could serve as granaries, a few were spared, among them San Juan Capistrano, sold to a private buyer for $710. With the admission of California to the Union in 1850, the Catholic Church began petitioning for a return of its properties. President Lincoln deeded Capistrano and other missions back to the Church in 1865. But restoration of the whole chain along El Camino Real had to wait for future generations to realize the profound meaning resting in the ghostly walls of those once happy oases for pilgrims and travelers in California.

It is significant that the California wine industry makes its own divisions of the two centuries from 1769 to the present, as here summarized.

The Mission Period (1769–1834) saw the establishment of the first vineyards at most of the twenty-one missions along El Camino Real from San Diego to Sonoma, the present Coast Highway 101. Established at sites one day's walking journey apart, with orchards, grain fields, and livestock (including riding horses), they became way-stops for California's first tourists. The arrival of the Russians at Fort Ross in 1812 determined the location of the last of the mission/forts at Sonoma under the command of General Mariano Vallejo as a barrier to any further inroads by the intruders. The garrison still stands, as does Vallejo's house, whose vineyards were admired by Count Haraszthy. John Chapman, the first American vineyardist in California, planted a vineyard of 4,000 Mission grapevines in Los Angeles in 1824. But the breakthrough to imported

Padre Junípero Serra in a contemporaneous portrait

Vitis vinifera came with Jean Louis Vignes, whose El Aliso Vineyard, on the site of Los Angeles's Union Station, was established in 1834, the year in which the secularization of the missions took place.

The Pioneer Period (1835–1861) fulfilled the rich promise of the Los Angeles area for vinifera wines which would exceed in quality the wines already being produced in large quantities by Mission San Gabriel and Mission San Fernando. The discovery of gold at Sutter's Mill in 1848 and the ensuing gold rush brought the forty-niners; many of them came from France, Italy, and Germany and found more enduring riches in vineyards and winemaking than in the goldfields. In 1858, bearing vineyards in Los Angeles were selling for $1,000 an acre. Poor harvests in 1859 and 1860 brought on the inevitable bust after the boom. It was at this time that Count Agoston Haraszthy, sensing the potential for California to become the leading wine region of the world, applied to the governor for sponsorship of his voyage to European wine countries. Étienne Thée arrived in the San Jose area in 1852, beginning the Almadén/Paul Masson saga, and Pierre Pellier arrived in the same area in 1854 and started the Mirassou Vineyards.

The Founders' Period (1861–1919) saw the establishment of Buena Vista in Sonoma by Count Haraszthy. A succession of winemakers—including Gustav Niebaum of Inglenook, Jacob Schram, Charles Krug,

In the house of General Mariano Vallejo, commander of the garrison at Sonoma around 1812, is California's first piano

Carl Wente, James Concannon, Joseph Korbel, and Georges de Latour of Beaulieu—put down their first vines. Each of these men established a dynasty as well as a fine *Vitis vinifera* vineyard, and enjoyed growing acceptance for their wines not only in America but in the wine markets of the world. The disaster of Prohibition allowed only a small handful of wineries making wine for medicinal and sacramental purposes to continue to function. Thousands of acres of low-yield noble vinifera were uprooted or regrafted to heavy-yielding juice grapes for shipping to Eastern communities where home winemaking was being carried on. And many vineyards were turned into pastureland. For thirteen years the California wine industry was virtually nonexistent.

The Post-Repeal Period (1932–1945) found an eager and enthusiastic, if inexperienced, generation of Americans ready to buy California wines. Stocks of aged, well-made wines were tragically small; the fine vineyards had been destroyed during Prohibition. Through the assistance of the well-organized viticulture and enology classes at UC–Davis, the evolution of quality wines began its long progression from the vineyard to the cellar. Newly planted vines require three years before a commercial crop can be obtained. From this "third leaf" onward, tonnage increases. But experienced European vintners have always held that the measure of a vine's true quality cannot be determined until the tenth year, and, to its sorrow, California found this to be true. Its immature wines were at first rejected by many emerging "experts," who could, with safety, evaluate the established clarets and Burgundies of France to build their reputations.

The Prestige Period (1946–1965) brought a new generation of graduate viticulturists and enologists onto the scene in the California dynasties, and more understanding of winemaking skills into the industry itself; the technological advances that resulted from scientific breakthroughs during World War II were applied to the fields and laboratories of California wineries.

After World War II, microbiology was applied to winemaking, and the millipore filter, capable of screening out a single yeast cell, seemed an indispensable answer to wine stability. It was not until 1962 that the best California wines were recognized as the equals of their fine French counterparts. Brilliant wines were everywhere. Consumer enthusiasm grew. There was talk about the "golden age of wines" in California. Another boom was beginning.

The Corporate Investment Period (1965–1974) saw the expansion of wineries as they moved from the traditions of yesterday into the technology of today, subjecting the juice of the grape to impeccable scientific methods —a development that ran into millions of dollars of capital investment. With every journal in the land reporting the consumer boom in wine buying, and diversification being touted as the key to success for large

Charles LeFranc, partner and son-in-law of Etienne Thée, was one of the founders of Almadén

The original cellars of Agoston Haraszthy at Buena Vista, tunneled out of the rock by Chinese laborers in 1857 and still in use

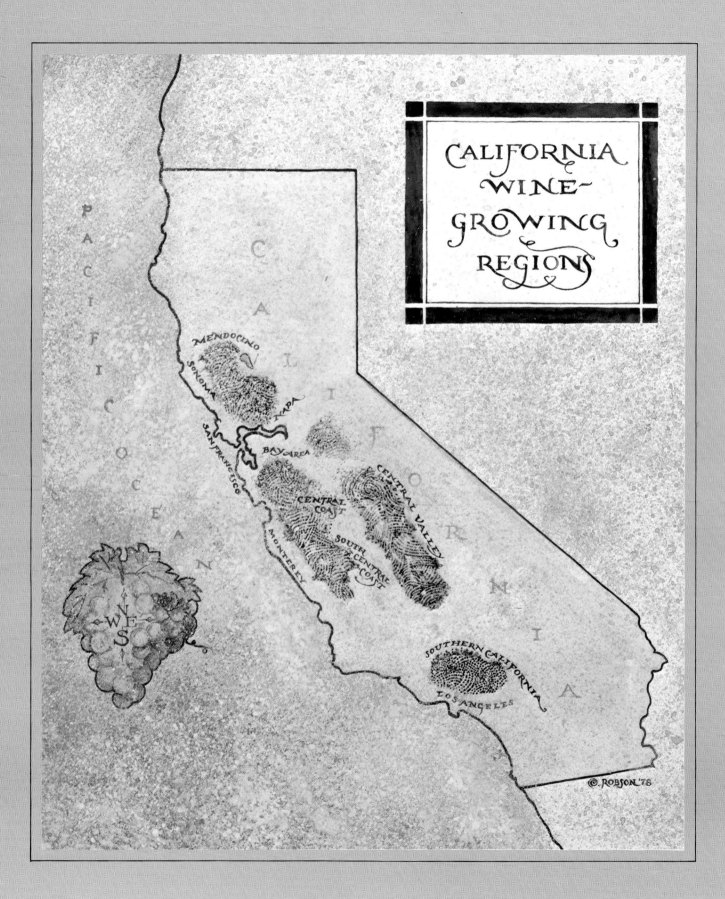

corporations, wineries one after another were acquired by giant companies, many of which had had no experience in the wine business.

Both tax shelters and get-rich-quick schemes lured land investors to new vineyard areas such as Monterey County, and farther south to Santa Maria and Santa Barbara. The golden wand of Nestlé of Switzerland transformed Beringer in the Napa Valley with a $6-million-dollar investment, dwarfing the earlier purchase of Inglenook by Petri. In turn, Petri was swallowed up by United Vintners, which bought 82 percent of its stock, as well as all of Beaulieu Vineyard. Coca-Cola Bottling of New York bought Franzia; Pepsi-Cola moved into wines with Monsieur Henri imports. Southdown of Texas acquired heavily in San Martin; Pillsbury invested in both Napa and Sonoma with its acquisition of Souverain, which was sold to North Coast Cellars in 1976. Rainier Brewery of the Pacific Northwest invested in Robert Mondavi when he split off from the family enterprise of Charles Krug Winery. In 1943 Seagram had acquired Paul Masson, and in 1967 National Distillers acquired Almadén. Schlitz embarked upon a multi-million-dollar enterprise in Sonoma County called Geyser Peak. Beatrice Foods of Chicago, a two-billion-dollar corporation, acquired the Brookside Vineyard Company. And even the illustrious Moët-Hennessey of France bought 600 acres in Napa and Sonoma to produce sparkling wine in large commercial quantities. This is but a partial listing of acquisitions and investments made during the hectic nine-year period that altered the character of the California wine industry. Telephones rang in every winery with offers to purchase at inflated prices that few could resist. But nothing lasts forever. With inflated values, a crisis was in the air.

Financial Adjustment and the Post-Boom Crisis (1974–1976) followed as the recession of the seventies loomed. A wine scandal in Bordeaux, which should have created immediate and large benefits for the California wine trade, helped a little, but two years of abundant harvests and tightened spending by the American consumer slowed the industry's growth. Speculators lured by the high prices paid for grapes—as high as $1,000 per ton for Chardonnay in 1973—faced a declining market, and by 1975 some grapes were left unpicked, with no offers. An anticipated glut of wine from large '73 and '74 harvests, and the depressed grape market of '75 threatened the outlook for 1976. Nevertheless, consumer purchases of wines increased 10 percent beyond previous record highs. The 1976 drought, which affected the vineyards of Europe and California, substantially reduced the quantity, and in some instances the quality, of the vintage. Many speculators were wiped out in marginal vineyard operations. Some untended vineyards were overgrown with weeds, others were uprooted and converted to orchards or row crops. But the market was stabilized, and the price for premium grapes returned to comfortable levels. A rapid increase in consumer consumption of white wines affected everyone in the industry, and once more the happy signal of demand brought smiles to the faces of growers and vintners.

The wine industry is subject to moments of inspiration, visionary goals and ideals, impractical aspirations like those of the artist, but it is also subject to the demands made on the farmer for endurance, strength, and the psychological stamina to face the tests imposed by the often cruel caprice of nature. There are heroes in this history, like Padre Junípero Serra, Count Agoston Haraszthy, and, in modern times, dynamic innovators like Frank Schoonmaker, Louis M. Martini, Ambassador J. D. Zellerbach, Ernest and Julio Gallo, Georges de Latour, and Herman Wente. To these moving forces must be added the scientific leaders on whose breadth of knowledge the industry depends, the teachers Maynard Amerine and André Tchelistcheff. The shadows of all these men are long upon the California wine country. To them the wineries we shall visit in later chapters make deep obeisance.

VINEYARDS AND WINERIES: NORTH COAST COUNTIES

"Let the great world spin for ever
down the ringing grooves of change."
—Alfred, Lord Tennyson

The Golden Gate Bridge crosses San Francisco Bay to the North Coast wine country

As we move into the wine country, we find yesterday, today, and tomorrow coexisting. Our inventory of wineries includes stable, entrenched establishments along with almost unknown fledgling enterprises. There can be no permanence to such a listing, nor claims to completeness. As Rodney Strong of Sonoma Vineyards said to me, "Wineries are springing up, and dying off."

Logic, as well as geography, dictates our division into these unofficial groups of counties: North Coast, Bay Area and Central Coast, South Central Coast, Central Valley and Southern California. Our odyssey begins in Sonoma County, where, by general historical agreement, the roots of the modern California wine industry were first established in 1857.

As we go from winery to winery in the California wine regions, what are the criteria of judgment? My answer always remains the same, and it bears repeating,

like a theme song. The focus must be upon the three basic elements: the soil, the vine, and the winemaker's skill.

In each wine-growing region there are different pockets of soil, and within one block of the same vines the berries will differ. Add to this that each winemaker picks at a different time, makes his wine in changing ways, for changing goals. The explanation of why and how wines differ cannot be further simplified. Change is the only constant.

SONOMA AND MENDOCINO COUNTIES

Once across the Golden Gate Bridge and heading north to the wine country, we encounter the coastal mountain barriers that hold back the cool—even cold—ocean cloud banks, and they seem almost inhospitable; the native shrubs and trees are wind-pruned, and angled landward from the constant onslaught of the Pacific wind currents. This is Marin County, a cold area, which in pre-Prohibition days had extensive vineyard acreage. On one steep, protected slope there are 11 acres of Cabernet Sauvignon—the pride of the Cuvaison winery of the Napa Valley—but otherwise,

Wines aging in European-oak barrels at Cuvaison

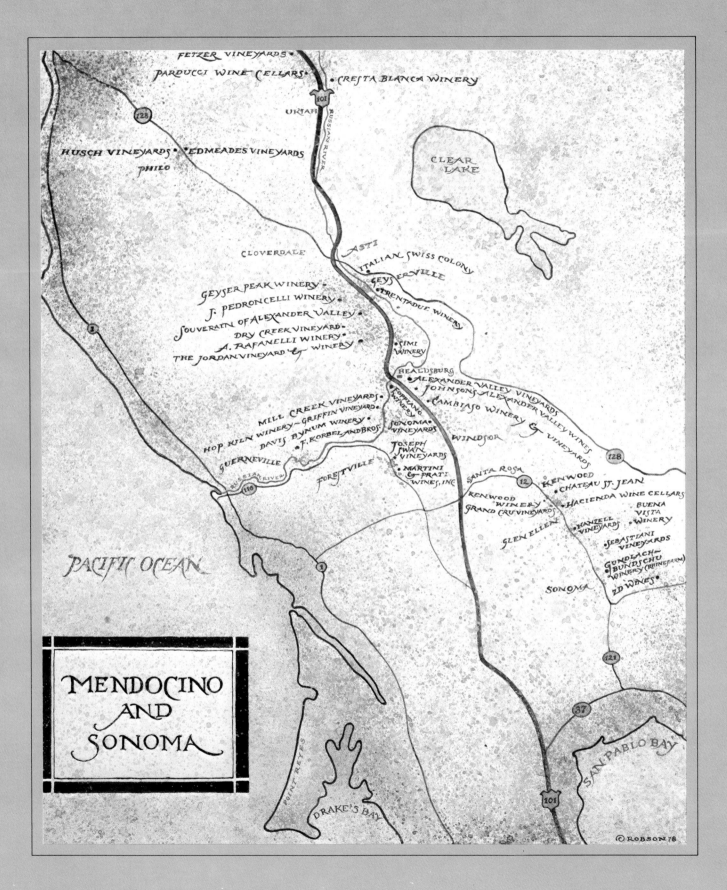

FETZER VINEYARDS •
PARDUCCI WINE CELLARS • • CRESTA BLANCA WINERY
101
128 UKIAH RUSSIAN RIVER
CLEAR LAKE
HUSCH VINEYARDS • • EDMEADES VINEYARDS
PHILO
CLOVERDALE ASTI
ITALIAN SWISS COLONY
GEYSERVILLE
GEYSER PEAK WINERY • TRENTADUE WINERY
J. PEDRONCELLI WINERY •
SOUVERAIN OF ALEXANDER VALLEY •
DRY CREEK VINEYARD •
A. RAFANELLI WINERY • • SIMI WINERY
THE JORDAN VINEYARD & WINERY
HEALDSBURG
ALEXANDER VALLEY VINEYARDS
JOHNSON'S ALEXANDER VALLEY WINES
FOPPIANO WINERY
MILL CREEK VINEYARDS • CAMBIASO WINERY & VINEYARDS
HOP KILN WINERY ~ GRIFFIN VINEYARD • WINDSOR
DAVIS BYNUM WINERY SONOMA VINEYARDS
F. KORBEL AND BROS.
GUERNEVILLE JOSEPH SWAN VINEYARDS
128
1
RUSSIAN RIVER FORESTVILLE • MARTINI & PRATI WINES, INC
SANTA ROSA KENWOOD
116 12 • CHATEAU ST. JEAN
KENWOOD WINERY • HACIENDA WINE CELLARS
GRAND CRU VINEYARDS BUENA
GLEN ELLEN • HANZELL VISTA
VINEYARDS WINERY
SEBASTIANI VINEYARDS
PACIFIC OCEAN GUNDLACH–
BUNDSCHU
WINERY (RHINEFARM)
SONOMA ZD WINES
1
121
37
101
POINT REYES SAN PABLO BAY

DRAKE'S BAY © ROBSON 78

MENDOCINO AND SONOMA

as a result of today's realization of the importance of the microclimate environment, few vines remain. Hence "Marin County" as an appellation has no real significance, and the area functions (at least insofar as wine interest goes) chiefly as a border to the broad region of Sonoma and the westward approach to Napa.

As a wine district, Sonoma County includes both the Sonoma Valley—called Valley of the Moon by the Indians and made famous by Jack London—and the winding course of the Russian River Valley. Two-thirds of California's red wines were once produced in this region, where there are areas (the Sonoma Valley) that have a climate comparable to Burgundy's and (along the Russian River) as cool as the Rhineland's. But there are also inland valleys with the same temperate climate as Bordeaux. These include the new appellation of the Alexander Valley, once pastureland and prune trees, today boasting some of the state's finest varietal vineyards. In the foothills of the Mayacamas Range, the tree-clad mountains that separate Sonoma and Napa, new vineyards with limestone, shale, and granitic rock beneath them are indicative of the renaissance of this once first-ranking wine region.

Mendocino, to the north, is having its merits appreciated with the establishment of wineries proud to place this appellation on their labels. The land is rolling and warm, favorable for fine red wines, but there is also a considerable richness to the white wines of this incomparably Californian redwood country.

ALEXANDER VALLEY VINEYARDS

8644 Highway 128, Healdsburg, California 95448

The first finished wines of the Alexander Valley Vineyards from the vintage of 1975 are newly on the market: Johannisberg Riesling, Chardonnay, and, after further aging, Cabernet Sauvignon. The winemaker, Harry H. Wetzel III, is one of the youngest in California, with his degree in viticulture and enology from UC–Davis, class of '74. His father, Harry H. Wetzel, Jr., bought vineyard property in Alexander Valley, having caught the fever from Russ Green, his associate in the Signal Oil Company, who initiated the

conversion of the Alexander Valley from prunes and pastureland to varietal grapes. When Green acquired the Simi Winery in 1970, part of the Wetzel vineyards' harvest was pledged to Simi until 1974. Young Hank Wetzel helped out at Stony Hill and Freemark Abbey while his own winery was being readied. He made his first wine from his own grapes when the winery was completed in the fall of 1975. Father and son have reason to rejoice. The Alexander Valley Vineyards 1975 Johannisberg Riesling, especially, signals a proud beginning.

SAMPLER SELECTION

Johannisberg Riesling (Alexander Valley). Estate-bottled vintage wine. Rich in fruit, sweet-edged, delicate, silky.

Pinot Chardonnay (Alexander Valley). Hint of ripe pears lends subtle complexity to this French-style, oak-aged fine wine.

Cabernet Sauvignon (Alexander Valley). A splendid varietal, touched with Merlot; an aristocratic wine.

BUENA VISTA WINERY

1800 Old Winery Road, Sonoma, California 95476

References to Count Agoston Haraszthy must abound in any account of the wineries and winemakers of California because this remarkable man played an important part in the formative years of the California wine industry. Some may question the authenticity of his title, but his right to the sobriquet "the father of California viticulture" is indisputable. Haraszthy planted grapevines wherever he lived in America—in Wisconsin, in San Diego, in San Francisco near Mission Dolores. But it was not until 1857, when he bought 560 acres northeast of the old Spanish garrison town of Sonoma, called it Buena Vista, and planted vinifera vines there that his influence on California wines began.

As early as 1859, anticipating a shortage of oak casks, which had to be brought from Europe on long sea voyages, he had some small casks constructed of redwood, filled them with wine, at the same time filling similar oak casks with the same wine, and set both

Built by Cyrus Alexander when he owned the valley that bears his name, the one-room schoolhouse now stands among young vineyards

redwood and oak casks aside to watch developments. It was the beginning of redwood cooperage for aging a large volume of young red wines—which still endures significantly in California.

At the Sonoma County Fair of 1860, Haraszthy anticipated the establishment of the state viticultural college of the University of California by twenty years: "How differently we should be situated," he declared, regretting the paucity of general winemaking knowledge, "if we had an Agricultural School, where a vineyard would be planted and cultivated, and wine made by competent professors. Our youths would there be taught the business in all its branches, and the older farmers, during their seasons of leisure, would learn all the various manipulations at a trifling cost."

The following year Haraszthy went on his historic mission to Europe, from which he brought back the priceless collection of vine cuttings that were to have so great an effect on California winemaking.

The lavish years at Buena Vista, with its Pompeian villa, its formal gardens, its wine cellars tunneled into the sandstone hill by Chinese coolies, were not many. By 1868 heavy taxes—and a costly fire—had led to financial troubles. Haraszthy went to Nicaragua, where, after only a year, he perished. In his fifty-seven

Antonia and Frank Bartholomew take their ease at Buena Vista

years his accomplishments were noteworthy and of lasting significance.

Buena Vista continued its long decline—the vineyards were decimated by phylloxera, the winery cellar collapsed in the 1906 earthquake, the estate was sold and allowed to fall into decay. But the legend of Haraszthy's Buena Vista was to have an exciting revival after World War II. Frank Bartholomew, executive vice-president of the United Press, had bought the property in 1941. By 1949 he and his wife, Antonia, were happily settled in a comfortable country house on the property. In the fields, gnarled survivors of Haraszthy's Zinfandel vines still bore grapes. The collapsed cellars had been reopened and crushing equipment installed. Ambitions and hopes were directed at goals of which Haraszthy himself might have dreamed.

In 1951, Al Brett was hired as winemaker and André Tchelistcheff was engaged as consultant. Two fascinating wines that are still popular emerged—Rosebrook, a vin rosé produced from Cabernet Sauvignon, one of the first in California from this varietal, and Green Hungarian, its name a reminder of the colorful founder.

In 1968 the Bartholomews sold the winery to Young's Market Company of Los Angeles, retaining the vineyards and their house. Philip Gaspar was appointed managing director and Jan Haraszthy, great-grandson of the founder, was appointed to become the goodwill ambassador and public relations director, a job for which he is eminently suited. His own son, a fifth-generation winemaker, works in the winery, sharing in the exciting challenge as each gondola of grapes arrives at the crusher.

In 1971, with the planting of Chardonnay and Pinot Noir in mind, Buena Vista acquired 600 acres of untried pastureland in the cool region of Carneros. In 1974, an additional 150 acres were purchased as the project flourished, and today row upon row of Cabernet Sauvignon, Pinot Noir, Chardonnay, and Gewürztraminer are growing on the lower slopes of the Mayacamas.

Al Brett has earned his retirement, and René Lacasia, an intense, superbly trained enologist with

Wine and roses—Buena Vista's Gewürztraminer and Zinfandel

experience in South American winelands, is supervising the new technological installations. The first part of a new winery, at Huichica, nine miles south of Buena Vista, was ready for the 1975 crush. Here in addition to the ultramodern press—a leviathan that can handle 5 tons of grapes—are the first in the series of stainless-steel tanks, standing like a file of armored giants on their sloped concrete platforms (sloped for ease in removing pomace after fermentation). Additional construction, scheduled for 1979, will give the new winery an ultimate storage capacity of 500,000 gallons.

SAMPLER SELECTION

Gewürztraminer (Cabinet). The winemaker's pride. Intensely fragrant, edged with sweetness. Seductive grace.

Green Hungarian. Undeniably popular, with more going for it in the name than in the rather neutral taste. Dry and light.

Zinfandel. Not to be missed; from the vineyard and winery where its fame began. Deep red, tannic, rather sharp.

Rosebrook. A Cabernet rosé from Sonoma County vines. A Tchelistcheff creation from the beginning.

DAVIS BYNUM WINERY

8075 Westside Road, Healdsburg, California 95448

Journalist Davis Bynum unquestionably got into winemaking through family influence: his father, Lindley Bynum, UCLA historian for the famed Bancroft Library, was among the pioneer wine judges of the Los Angeles County Fair. Davis started making wine in the East Bay suburb of Albany. He bought grapes, sold home winemaking equipment, and made such good Cabernet in his converted store that connoisseurs pushed him into serious winemaking. A facetious label—"Barefoot Bynum's Burgundy"—for his more ordinary, yet good-value, table wine spread his fame, but today, with the Albany tasting room serving merely as a salesroom, with a full-scale winery in the Russian River area eight miles downriver from Healds-

burg, "we're out of the Barefoot business," he told me. The 14,000-square-foot winery of 85,000-gallon capacity, acquired in 1973, on the way to 25,000-case annual sale goals, is concentrating on Pinot Noir and Chardonnay. Son Hampton Bynum, with some UC–Davis training, is winemaker, and under the new Davis Bynum label a limited number of choice varietals are giving new stature to the name.

SAMPLER SELECTION

Pinot Chardonnay (Sonoma). From adjacent vineyards of Joseph Rochioli, Jr., and Howard Allen on the Russian River. Vintage.

Fumé Blanc (Sonoma). Russian River Sauvignon Blanc grapes give this very dry, brilliant, pale gold wine its luster and taste.

Davis Bynum, journalist-turned-winemaker

Chateau St. Jean's elegant mansion at the foot of The Sugar Loaf Rid

Pinot Noir (Sonoma). A translucent ruby wine of aristocratic and noble bouquet, which, with added age, will have true finesse.

Camelot Mead. A Bynum honey-wine specialty, deservedly popular, with a gentle sweetness of 3 percent.

CAMBIASO WINERY & VINEYARDS

1141 Grant Avenue, Healdsburg, California 95448

Shortly after the repeal of Prohibition, in 1934, Giovanni Cambiaso, who had learned winemaking in his native Italy, established this small winery with his wife, their son, and two daughters. Though the winery, which produced generic and varietal wines for bulk sale for many years, has now been sold to non-resident conglomerate financiers, The Four Seas Investment Company, Cambiaso remains a family affair. Son Joseph makes the wine, and his sister Rita is general manager. These are sturdy regional wines, patiently attended in stainless steel until they are ready for bottling from the veteran redwood aging tanks.

SAMPLER SELECTION

Cabernet Sauvignon (Sonoma County). A pleasant claret-style wine of nonirrigated hillside grapes of modest value.

Petite Sirah (Sonoma County). A full-bodied wine from long-established vines.

CHATEAU ST. JEAN

8555 Sonoma Highway, Kenwood, California 95452

It was Lord Byron who said, "Glory, the grape, love, gold . . . in these are sunk the hopes of all men of every nation." In winemaking today, when one stainless-steel fermenter costs more than a tract home, a centrifuge more than a Rolls-Royce, the gold must come before the grape, with wisdom a close third. For Robert and Edward Merzoian and their brother-in-law, Ken Sheffield, their hopes have come together in the Valley of the Moon. They bought an elegant mansion surrounded by 255 acres of virgin land for vines. Named for Edward's wife, Chateau St. Jean is pro-

nounced in the American way. Of the 255 acres, 105 are given over to Chardonnay, Johannisberg Riesling, Sauvignon Blanc, Pinot Blanc, and Pinot Noir. On the remaining 150 acres a complex of separate buildings is being built. For fermentation, aging, bottling, and storage, rows of Limousin, Nevers, Yugoslavian, and American oak barrels and casks are already filled and in place. The first wines released were of the 1974 vintage. The Chateau St. Jean 1974 Sonoma County Johannisberg Riesling, Selected Late Harvest, earned a gold medal from the Sonoma County Fair in 1975. The 1974 Sauvignon Blanc brought Chateau St. Jean a bronze medal. As for the Chateau St. Jean Chardonnays, no description fits them as well as "custom-made." There are seven of them at this writing, each separately produced from the individual vineyards designated on the labels. They differ as much as children of one family; each has its own distinctive personality.

Glory, the first in Byron's inventory of man's ambitions, has come early for Chateau St. Jean, winemaker Richard Arrowood, and the Merzoians. If their goal of about 30,000 cases per year of premium varietal wines, plus a judicious amount of *méthode champenoise* Blanc de Noir and Blanc de Blanc champagnes is reached, fame will follow as a result of distribution in leading metropolitan restaurants and wine shops.

SAMPLER SELECTION

Chardonnay (Wildwood Vineyards). Rich in varietal character, oak-scented. Deep and languid.

Sauvignon Blanc (Mendocino County). From grapes grown along the Russian River. Flowery, sweet-edged.

Johannisberg Riesling (Late Harvest). Botrytis, or "noble rot," emerging on the ripe grapes gives a rich sweet wine of some complexity.

Blanc de Noir Champagne (Vintage). A golden *tour de force* of balanced yeasty nose and varietal depths.

CRESTA BLANCA WINERY

Ukiah, Mendocino County, California 95482

If it is confusing to find San Francisco as the

address of the winery on the label, a quick spin through the history of this well-known winery will answer the question of where the wine is made and why the label also reads "Since 1889."

The original winery was established by Charles Wetmore at Livermore in Alameda County in 1882. The vineyard was set out with cuttings from Château d'Yquem and Château Margaux, and wines from those grapes were the first California wines to be honored with a Grand Prix at the Paris Exposition of 1889. The name Cresta Blanca was derived from the sheared-off chalky cliff into which the aging tunnels of the Livermore winery were dug.

In 1940, Cresta Blanca was bought by Schenley, Inc., and in 1971 Guild Wineries acquired it with Roma Wine Co. There are generations who can remember the radio jingle that hammered out the spelling "C-R-E-S-T-A B-L-A-N-C-A. . . . *Cresta Blanca!*" almost ad nauseam. And there are wine merchants who can remember how the brand later faded almost into oblivion. It had one moment of glory, however, before the winery was closed and the operation moved to the gigantic Roma winery in Fresno. That was in 1961, when enologist Myron Nightingale produced the first French-style sauterne ever made in America.

Guild, which is the nation's largest grower-owned cooperative, with over a thousand members in every winegrowing area of the state, had an increasing inventory of remarkably fine wines produced at their Mendocino winery in Ukiah. The decision was made to set up a separate marketing and production division for Cresta Blanca with executive offices in San Francisco, and that is the address on the label.

SAMPLER SELECTION

Gewürztraminer (North Coast). A happy discovery as an aperitif wine; fragrant, light, thirst-quenching.

French Colombard (North Coast). Delightful luncheon wine. Crisp and clean, but not bitingly dry. Flowery nose.

Triple Cream Sherry. Honored with gold-medal acclaim for its rich depth and luxurious satin-smoothness.

Zinfandel (North Coast). Beyond the grape, there is a souvenir of pine and cedar forests in its fascinating bouquet.

DRY CREEK VINEYARD

3700 Lambert Bridge Road, Healdsburg, California 95448

David Stare and his burgeoning winery are further evidence that with youth, intelligence, and single-focus drive you *can* make it from scratch as a grape grower and winemaker. It's not easy, nor in any sense a get-rich-quick process. But all is in order today for this Harvard graduate, who got fed up with a civil-engineering career in West Germany, chucked it, and headed California way to become a winemaker.

With missionary zeal, young Stare obtained and promoted an appellation of origin for his vineyard area—Dry Creek Valley. If it's on the freeway signs, why not on a wine label? His first wine to come to market was a 1973 Dry Chenin Blanc which showed immediately that there was nothing imitative or compromising in his approach. It was bone-dry, crisp, clean, and fragrant, but very different from everyone else's Chenin Blanc, tending toward gentleness and grace. There is the same rugged individuality about Stare's Zinfandel of 1973, the first heavy red wine released.

SAMPLER SELECTION

Fumé Blanc (Sonoma County). Vintage wine of Sauvignon Blanc bouquet; deep, richly complex dry wine of high style.

Dry Chenin Blanc (Sonoma County). An unusual and refreshing wine eminently suited to service with shellfish, poultry.

Zinfandel (Sonoma County). A big wine that collectors can age with assurance; it will round out in balanced mellowness.

EDMEADES VINEYARDS

5500 California State Highway 128, Philo, California 95466

Winding over the rugged, tree-clad flanks of the Coast Ranges between Boonville and Mendocino's Pacific Coast, Highway 128 follows the Navarro River to the sea. Philo is here in this remote mountain-valley region, and nearby is the 40-acre vineyard of Cabernet Sauvignon, Chardonnay, and French Colombard which are bringing recognition to Anderson Valley. The wines offer a sound argument in favor of Anderson Valley's having its own appellation of origin as a cool Region I.

Dr. Donald Edmeades planted the vineyard in 1963, when winemaking was his hobby. In 1972, Paula and Daron Edmeades took up their father's quest for good wines and bonded an old farm building to be used as a winery. The erstwhile hobby is now a small and pleasant business.

SAMPLER SELECTION

Apple Wine (Anderson Valley). Produced with great pride from Baldwin, Spitzenberg, Golden Delicious apples; aged, like Chardonnay, in French-oak casks. Intriguing and refreshing.

Gewürztraminer (Anderson Valley). The unmistakable fragrance of the varietal grape is achieved with notable success.

Cabernet Sauvignon (Anderson Valley). Vintage; small lots of this popular varietal concentrate the grape's richness.

FETZER VINEYARDS

1150 Bel Arbres Road, Redwood Valley, California 95470

"Fine winemaking is ideally a family enterprise." That was Bernard Fetzer's thought when, with his wife and eleven children, he moved to California from Oregon in 1954 to accommodate the needs of his lumber business. While Mendocino County is basically lumber country—redwoods, pine, cedar—it is also making dramatic inroads into the premium-wine business.

To house his family, Bernard Fetzer bought a ranch in Redwood Valley, two hours north of the Golden Gate Bridge and two minutes north of Ukiah.

After some careful research, Fetzer decided to plant his 150 acres of vineyard land with Bordeaux varieties— Cabernet Sauvignon, Sémillon, and Sauvignon Blanc. But as the third-leaf commercial crop came on in the early sixties, even though famed major wineries bought Mendocino County grapes, "they kept it a secret, beggaring the price below Napa levels" according to Bernard Fetzer. So he sold his grapes to amateur wine-makers all across the country, most of them doctors. Many won local prizes for their wines made from the Fetzer grapes and began singing his praises. It was enough to inspire him to think about building his own winery.

And so a small cluster of buildings grew, housing winemaking equipment of stainless steel geared to the vineyard's less than heroically proportioned needs. Tiers of French, Yugoslavian, and American oak in casks and barrels neatly accommodate 100,000 gallons of aging wines. John Fetzer, in his twenties, moved into the role of winemaster, with James to help and with Richard and Robert assisting as and where needed.

Long vatting on the skins of Fetzer's red wines makes further aging in bottles necessary, but just taste a Fetzer Zinfandel or Cabernet Sauvignon, Petite Sirah or Carignane, and you will understand why he is a firm

Bernard Fetzer measuring the sugar level of his wine with a saccharometer

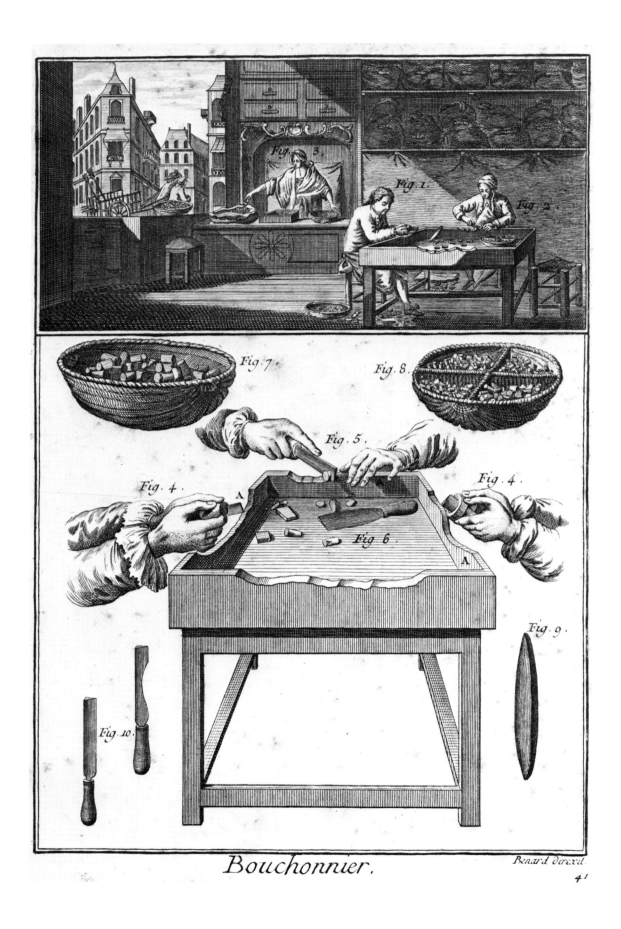

Bouchonnier.

41

believer in the procedure. These are big wines, possibly requiring decanting at least an hour before serving.

SAMPLER SELECTION

Zinfandel (Ricetti Vineyard). A big, big wine that is soft and round, with the bouquet and spice of the Mendocino region.

Cabernet Sauvignon (Estate Bottled). Pure, 100 percent Cabernet Sauvignon, always vintage, deep, complex.

Carmine Carignane. From grapes high in the benchlands of the area, an uncommonly big wine from a rather common grape.

FOPPIANO WINERY

12707 Old Redwood Highway, Healdsburg, California 95448

John Foppiano arrived in the Russian River Valley from Italy in 1864. The original lure had been the goldfields, but the most lasting reward, for him, came from grapes and wine. In 1910 his eldest son, Louis, took over the winery. In those days the Foppianos sent wagonloads of cask wine to San Francisco wine merchants for customers who had their own jugs refilled. The third and fourth generations of the family are now operating this 200-acre winery. In addition to selling bulk wines to other wineries, they present a wide range of varietal wines from the Cabernet Sauvignon, Pinot Noir, Petite Sirah, Chardonnay, Sauvignon Blanc, Gamay Beaujolais, and Zinfandel vines now in bearing, an advance beyond the generic Burgundy and sauterne of yesterday.

GEYSER PEAK WINERY

Old Redwood Highway North, Geyserville, California 95441

Geyserville was one of the early California boom-towns developed by the gold seekers, many of whom were also attracted to this area because of the hot mineral baths fed by geysers, famed for their health-giving properties from the time of the Indians. August

Quitzow established the first winery in this area in 1880, in the belief that the volcanic soil was ideally suited for growing wine grapes. Today's Geyser Peak Winery is located on the site of the original Quitzow Winery, a 600-acre tract of land acquired in 1972 by the Jos. Schlitz Brewing Company of Milwaukee. George Vare, a dynamic merchandiser, is president of Geyser Peak and Al Huntsinger is the winemaster.

The new Geyser Peak Winery is prepared to accommodate the increasing demands of the American wine market for the next three generations, both qualitatively and quantitatively. Vare recently stated: "I think the tastes of the country are going up, and California has the wines to meet those tastes at very attractive prices as lower grape prices are passed on to the consumer."

Under the Geyser Peak label, the unusual brand names given to the two lines are "Voltaire" for the better varietals, and "Summit" for the mountain jug wines. There have been some good values already in Cabernet and Zinfandel under the Summit label. Aside from its own 600 acres of fine varietals, the winery draws upon 200 acres of the Kiser Ranch, some 40 miles farther south, in a cooler region more suited to Pinot Noir, Chardonnay, and Johannisberg Riesling. Vintage estate bottling of varietal wines is adding new status to the winery.

Geyser Peak's present emphasis is upon the broad distribution of popularly priced wines of outstanding value. It is among the first American wineries to successfully launch boxed wines, that is, wines equipped with self-sealing pouring spouts in one-, three-, and five-gallon cartons. An interior vacuum liner of plastic prevents oxidation as the wine is used. You can keep a three-gallon carton of Summit Chablis in your refrigerator for a month. Every glass you pour will cost a modest 15 cents, but will be worth at least twice that for taste and convenience. The boxed wine is ideal for picnics, sports events, or to serve around the swimming pool, where its unbreakable container is a distinct asset.

These are mighty modest beginnings, considering

Le Bouchonnier (The Corkmaker). Engraving by Robert Benard from Denis Diderot's *Great Encyclopedia*, Paris, 1762. (The Christian Brothers Collection)

the magnificence of the installation, but with technology, skill, and experience combined with the right grapes, Geyser Peak is on the road to success.

SAMPLER SELECTION

Pinot Chardonnay. Vintage wine of Sonoma and Lake County grapes, given subtle oak aging under Al Huntsinger's hand.

Johannisberg Riesling. Very fresh and fruity wine; no wood, so the grape comes through, sweet-edged and refreshing.

Cabernet Sauvignon (Santa Maria). Flood ranch grapes make a limited bottling; fine wine aged in French oak.

GRAND CRU VINEYARDS

No. 1 Vintage Lane, Glen Ellen, California 95442

Here in the Valley of the Moon six enthusiastic young men have joined forces to produce a limited number of wines, each to be the finest that grapes and men can achieve. The original winery was established on these 36 acres in 1896. Closed down during Prohibition, the winery was reactivated during the 1950s, the cellars being converted to accommodate numerous open concrete fermenting vats for bulk wine production. When it was acquired by the young vintners of Grand Cru in 1970, the vats were remodeled into neat aging vaults, with a grandly arched entrance from the ground level, where, as the label shows, a row of shining stainless-steel fermenters now stand like sentinels guarding the new wines.

Administrative chief of the winery is viticulturist Allen B. Ferrara, who shares an electronic-engineering background with Robert Magnani, the winemaker, now a full-time enologist. Parker Taft, a Vallejo attorney, is secretary of the corporation, Bob Balassi, a CPA, its treasurer. Joe Nichelini, a director, brings a lifetime of experience in vineyard management from his family's long-established winegrowing activities in the Napa Valley. Completing the team is James Miller, who supplies Pinot Noir, Gewürztraminer, and Cabernet Sauvignon grapes exclusively to Grand Cru from his 200-acre ranch in the Alexander Valley.

Ferrara and Magnani produced an extraordinary Gewürztraminer wine by using an induced botrytis culture on Gewürztraminer grapes—a first for this berry in the United States. This quite sensationally fragrant and sweet dessert wine, the Grand Cru 1975 Alexander Valley "induced botrytis" Gewürztraminer, has moved into history, and a 200-case lot was produced in 1977. Acclaim also came for Grand Cru's 1971 White Zinfandel, served to the International Federation of Wine Brotherhoods in Paris in 1974, where it was declared "excellent" and compared favorably with the finest wines in the Loire Valley.

A pair of gold medals for the Late Harvest Zinfandel assures its continuation, but now with Jim Miller's fine Alexander Valley grapes, the main thrust —beyond the "induced botrytis" Gewürztraminer— will be upon Blanc de Noir Champagne and still wines, Muscat Canelli, and Cabernet.

SAMPLER SELECTION

Gewürztraminer (Alexander Valley). Award-winning wine of extraordinary varietal charm; sweet-edged, full-bodied.

Zinfandel (Sonoma County). Vintage and estate-bottled; from ancient vines that provide a fine, fruity, intriguing wine.

Pinot Noir Blanc (Sonoma County). A slight blush of color in a special-occasion wine with a popular fruity sweetness.

GUNDLACH-BUNDSCHU WINERY (RHINEFARM)

2000 Denmark Street, Vineberg, California 95487

Gundlach, Bundschu, and Dresel are among the pioneer names of winemaking and wine selling in nineteenth-century California. Karl Bundschu was general manager of Inglenook forty years ago. Emil Dresel, a great friend of Agoston Haraszthy, is said to have helped the Count plant the greater portion of the famed Zinfandel and other vines at Buena Vista. He was also one of the original partners in the Gundlach-Bundschu Rhinefarm, a recently replanted 300-acre ranch in Sonoma, now owned by Towle Bundschu, Karl's great-nephew. Today, Towle is consultant to his son, Jim, and son-in-law, John Merritt, respectively vineyardist and winemaker at Rhinefarm. The revered old trade name returns to the marketplace, offering wines made from grapes grown on the original land.

The Rhinefarm is unique in having two acres of a rather celebrated and rare clone of Johannisberg Riesling called Kleinberger. Another exclusive proprietary wine, in addition to the Kleinberger Riesling, is a slightly sweet Sylvaner christened Dresel Sonoma Riesling, honoring the pioneer vintner Emil Dresel. Vintage Zinfandel and Cabernet Sauvignon complete the roster of one of the newer Sonoma wineries.

SAMPLER SELECTION

Kleinberger (Sonoma County). The Rhinefarm's own clonal berry of Riesling makes an always pleasing, fruity wine.

Johannisberg Riesling (Sonoma County). "Late Harvest" editions carry a golden-rich sweetness, intense bouquet.

HACIENDA WINE CELLARS

1000 Vineyard Lane, Sonoma, California 95476

After Frank Bartholomew had sold the Buena Vista Winery in 1968, some grapes from the Alexander Valley Buena Vista Vineyards were made available to him. The temptation to make wine again was strengthened by the fact that an area of the ranch had been devoted to nursery plots for new strains of resistant rootstock and fine *Vitis vinifera* varietals, under the supervision of Don Van Staaveren, a graduate of Cal State's Viticultural College. Why not transform one of the old buildings on the property into a winery and salesroom and make wine from the new grapes?

Steven MacRostie, with UC–Davis training, became winemaker.

The first wine marketed by Hacienda Cellars, the 1973 Clair de Lune Chardonnay, came home from the First Annual Sonoma County Fair with a gold medal, accompanied by another gold medal for the huge, dark, spicy, and fragrant 1973 Zinfandel. Hacienda took two of the three gold medals given by a panel of

Steve MacRostie of Hacienda sampling the contents of a 2,387-gallon tank

judges among whom were Frank J. Prial of the *New York Times*, Ruth Ellen Church of the *Chicago Tribune*, Burgess Meredith, and myself. The 1973 Chardonnay is now a collector's item, but subsequent editions are certain to be as lingeringly haunting to the taste.

SAMPLER SELECTION

Clair de Lune Chardonnay (Sonoma). Distribution is limited, but visitors to Hacienda Wine Cellars shouldn't miss it.

Gewürztraminer (Sonoma). Slightly sweet, unlike most Alsatian versions, but with the same spicy fragrance.

Zinfandel General Meszaros. Conceived without compromise as a big, powerful wine, almost pungent, to last forever. Named for the Hungarian who shipped Haraszthy the first vines.

Cocktail Sherry (Sunshine of Sonoma). Take it away as a souvenir of the Buena Vista vineyard of Count Agoston Haraszthy.

HANZELL VINEYARDS

18596 Lomita Avenue, Sonoma, California 95476

The late Ambassador James D. Zellerbach, founder of the paper company bearing his name, had a connoisseur's appreciation of fine Burgundies, nourished no doubt during the years between 1948 and 1950 when he served as chief administrator for the Marshall Plan in Europe. In 1947 he acquired a rolling 200-acre expanse of foothill land in the Valley of the Moon. The first Pinot Noir and Chardonnay vines were planted in 1948, but spill-water erosion indicated that they were improperly located. In 1953 the vineyard—11 acres of Pinot Noir, 5 of Chardonnay—was completely replanted in semicircular terraces, banked below the site for the winery building. If California counterparts of the ruby Romanée-Conti and golden Montrachet, the Ambassador's favorite wines, were to be produced here from the ground up, nothing short of perfection would do.

The winery project was undertaken with equally high goals, and no expense was spared. Bradford Webb, a California-trained biochemist, was employed to design the functional facilities. These were fitted into a building that externally resembled the Château Clos de Vougeot, but any similarity to a Burgundian installation ended there. Stainless-steel fermenters were designed and built to accommodate the imported crusher's capacity. In the 1950s, stainless steel was priced for custom use, and it cost nearly as much as platinum. Temperature-controlled fermenters on calibrated levels were unknown outside the UC–Davis laboratories for winemaking. The new wine, like its Burgundian models, would age in wood from the oak forests of Limousin coopered in Nuits-Saint-Georges. Preparations for the revolutionary concept were made with little awareness of their eventual effect upon the industry.

Samples of the first 1956 Chardonnay were forwarded to Zellerbach in Rome, where he was then serving as our ambassador to Italy. You can imagine his delight when local experts thought it was a white Burgundy from the Côte d'Or! The Ambassador's million-dollar project had succeeded. It was the first

ripple of a wave that was to roll over the California wine industry during the next decade, causing more changes than the shift from wood or concrete to stainless steel as the material of fermenters. It also increased the necessary capitalization for winery equipment, including French-barrel cooperage, to six- and seven-figure sums, an amount well beyond the limits of most private fortunes.

When Zellerbach died, in 1963, orders were given to dispose of all the wine in bottle and barrel. (It was bought by Joe Heitz of the Napa Valley, who cared for it meticulously.) All winemaking ceased during '63 and '64. In 1965 the estate was bought by Mary and Douglas Day, who followed Ambassador Zellerbach's lead and planted 4 more acres of Chardonnay, making a

A stainless-steel, temperature-controlled fermenter, one of the sophisticated pieces of winemaking equipment pioneered in California

total of 20 planted acres. Mr. Day died in 1969, and Mrs. Day in 1973. The early 1970s were the height of the wine boom, and in 1975 a buyer of vast means looking for a very small winery on a large country estate was found in Barbara de Brye, the major stockholder in Easton United Securities, Ltd., of Calgary, Canada.

In assessing the contribution made by Ambassador Zellerbach, we find that two factors were responsible for his revolutionary impact on the winemaking industry: the stainless-steel tanks, which made possible the maximum preservation of bouquet through cool, slow fermentation in a vessel that did not impart any taste to the wine, and the touch of French Limousin oak on a white wine. These two factors wrought the subtle difference that delights American connoisseurs of California Chardonnay and makes it competitive with Burgundian white wines for the first time.

The role of wood in the aging of both red and white wines is important. With the American rush to buy European-oak cooperage, the prices for 50-gallon barrels has more than trebled in the last five years. When you see tiers of French-oak barrels in a California winery, often more than 5,000 in one room, you are looking at an investment of half a million dollars or more, excluding the contents or inventory aging costs. The arithmetic is even more staggering when you try to estimate the costs of great batteries of stainless-steel tanks. Such multi-million-dollar installations explain why large corporations and conglomerates were needed when the Zellerbach-launched revolution overtook the small family business of winemaking.

For Hanzell Chardonnay, and all those other California Chardonnay wines which have enjoyed preeminence through the touch of French wood, it would seem that success was achieved. But, alas, wood has not wrought the victory with Hanzell Pinot Noir. It is good but not great, though, like the Chardonnay, it now costs $8 per bottle.

SAMPLER SELECTION

Chardonnay (Sonoma Valley). Vintage wine, grown and bottled at the estate. On allocation at the winery.

Pinot Noir (Sonoma Valley). A marked peppery, earthy taste gives this deep ruby wine a less than ideal personality.

HOP KILN WINERY–GRIFFIN VINEYARD

6050 Westside Road, Healdsburg, California 95448

The artistic dedication of the owners of this 65-acre vineyard and winery located beside the state-landmark hop kiln, one of the most handsome of the chimneyed buildings indigenous to the region, promises fine, interesting wines. The first crush, in 1975, carried the subsidiary label "Sweetwater Springs," commemorating one of the oldest vineyard ranches of the Russian River Valley.

These oddly shaped buildings for drying hops (a form indigenous to Sonoma County) adjacent to Hop Kiln Winery are a state landmark

Winemaker at Hop Kiln Winery is Marty Griffin, who also serves as chairman of the Health and Social Welfare Committee of the Wine Institute of San Francisco. All wines are produced in small lots, are racked by gravity or siphon to avoid any bruising by pumping, and are unfiltered, with a view to achieving full body, complexity, and long life.

SAMPLER SELECTION

Zinfandel Primitivo. A big, dark, heavy-bodied wine with a familiar "briar" nose. Sold only at the winery.

Petite Sirah (Russian River Valley). A big, mouth-filling wine from Marty Griffin's "1880" vineyard of established vines.

HUSCH VINEYARDS

4900 Star Route, Philo, California 95466

You don't have to be a millionaire to achieve the goal of winemaking in California. Inflation was not yet as devastating as it was to become later when, in 1968, Tony and Gretchen Husch decided to abandon city life in San Francisco. They found a hillside ranch in the cool Anderson Valley, 13 miles southwest of Ukiah. There on a southerly slope they planted their first 8 acres of Chardonnay vines. As a result of loving care, the vines prospered despite the cool Region I climate. The Husches bonded a tiny winery in Philo in 1971, the first for the area. Their Chardonnay had such character that they expanded the vineyard to 25 acres and included some Pinot Noir and Gewürztraminer plantings. In 1974 they enlarged the winery to a capacity of 5,000 gallons. From their timid beginnings, with only textbooks to guide them, they have now flowered into first-rate winemakers.

Husch Vineyard wines—all from grapes grown in their own vineyards—are 100 percent varietals, dry, assertive in character, and crisp with the natural acidity of the cool growing conditions.

Pinot Chardonnay (Mendocino). Vintage and estate-bottled. Expensive. Just enough French oak. Needs development time.

Pinot Noir (Mendocino). Also vintage wine, confirming the wisdom of planting this grape in this area.

Gewürztraminer (Mendocino). Vinted with a hint of sweetness, in the California style, which seems to balance the grape well.

ITALIAN SWISS COLONY

Highway 101, Asti, California 95413

The history of this commercial giant of the California wine industry began with organizational turmoil in 1881, and today the courts are wrestling with problems emanating from the company's size.

Andrea Sbarboro, a boy of thirteen, arrived in San Francisco from Italy in the middle of the last century. For twenty years he worked in his brother's grocery store, nurturing ambitious dreams in which the ownership of land would put him on the road to security and wealth. He founded five mutual loan groups, which handled receipts of $6.5 million dollars. This led to the purchase, with a group of local businessmen, of a 1,500-acre tract of pastureland. Italian and Swiss immigrants working this land contributed as little as $5 per month from their wages toward ultimate ownership. The pastureland became the vineyard still known as Asti, but the immigrants decided they would rather keep all of their wages instead of having shares in the land.

Sbarboro raised more money and by 1900 had a thriving winery operation. A 300,000-gallon stone winery built in 1887 made wines that won gold medals in competitions as far away as Genoa, Dublin, Bordeaux, and Paris. The winemaster was Pietro Rossi.

With Repeal, Rossi's twin sons, Robert and Edmund, revived Italian Swiss Colony. The present organizational troubles began after World War II, with a series of changes in ownership following the Rossis' sale of the Asti winery to National Distillers. In 1953, National sold Italian Swiss Colony to Louis Petri, who had merged his family winery with United Vintners. In 1969, Heublein acquired 82 percent of United Vintners, and also acquired prestigious Beaulieu Vineyard. The tangled skeins of Heublein's corporate holdings are made more complex by their marketing ties to Allied Growers, one of the larger cooperatives of grape growers in the Napa Valley. But more relevant to the Italian Swiss Colony empire are its enormous $16-million glass factory, bottling plant, wine and champagne cellars, and shipping facility in Madera in the San Joaquin Valley, from which emerge wines not only of the Italian Swiss Colony but of Inglenook, Lejon, Petri, Annie Green Springs—and more.

As far as the consumer is concerned, the last few years have brought some improvement to the wines under the Italian Swiss Colony label: the list of wines has been shortened and the overall image upgraded, with better generic and varietal wines. John Powers, Italian Swiss Colony's president, made an impact on the popular-price market with the release of a screw-cap Cabernet Sauvignon at $1.69, which, for the price, had remarkable varietal distinction. Bob Rife, the winemaker since 1969, produced the wine largely from North Coast counties grapes, with sufficient aging to concentrate an undeniable Cabernet bouquet. Consumers accepted it as intended—for immediate consumption.

At present the Italian Swiss Colony label is in the competition among producers of volume wines which have no regional designation beyond California as an appellation of origin. But even those ordinary table wines today are an unusually good value, possessing a finish and finesse far ahead of Europe's *vins ordinaires*.

Colony French Colombard. Fresh and fruity, brilliant

MENDOCINO AND SONOMA WINE LABELS

straw-yellow; good acid balance and soft finish.

Colony Ruby Cabernet. Pronounced varietal bouquet and aroma from this hybrid developed for warm valleys.

Colony Cabernet Sauvignon. The best wine under the ISC label and an excellent value for daily table-wine use.

Colony Zinfandel. Fine color, good vinous bouquet. Well-blended wine, ready to drink, of zesty, balanced complexity.

JOHNSON'S ALEXANDER VALLEY WINES

8333 Highway 128, Healdsburg, California 95448

Since 1952, the Johnson family has been farming grapes and pears in the Alexander Valley on 111 acres of an old Spanish land grant. Planting of top-flight varietals—Pinot Noir, Cabernet Sauvignon, Johannisberg Riesling, Chardonnay, Gewürztraminer, and Chenin Blanc—was begun in 1967, and the small winery and tasting room emerged from a refurbished barn in 1975. Picnic and camping facilities amid the vines on the bank of the Russian River aided the winery's growing popularity. Two of the brothers—Jay, the vineyardist, and Tom, the winemaker—now have a silver medal for their Chenin Blanc, and a bronze medal for Pinot Noir, won at the Sonoma Harvest Fair, giving official recognition to their development of fine wines in the Alexander Valley. With the 1976 harvest they also produced what is probably the first and only estate-bottled Bartlett-pear wine in California; light, delicate, and sweet, it is called Alexander Valley Gold.

SAMPLER SELECTION

Pinot Noir (Alexander Valley). Vintage and estate-bottled. Chewy, oak-aged. Modestly priced. Good varietal character.

Chenin Blanc (Alexander Valley). A very fresh and fruity wine, for early enjoyment. Vinted from their own grapes.

THE JORDAN VINEYARD & WINERY

1474 Alexander Valley Road, Healdsburg, California 95448

"You have to have a dream when you're playing the wine game to win," mused young Michael Rowan, the graduate viticulturist and general manager of the newest multi-million-dollar prestigious vineyard in the Alexander Valley. "It's the visionary people who can sniff the possibilities." With his fortune made in oil explorations, Thomas Jordan, the sole owner, now only in his early forties, retains the ambition and drive to achieve through practical application. "We've spent a fortune here, but we haven't wasted a nickel. We chose our rootstock correctly from virus-free Cabernet and Merlot. Our program involves five years of aging, which will not permit us to market our first wine until 1981 . . . and no maybe about that date."

The large winery is scaled for an annual production of 100,000 gallons of wine. Jordan will make Cabernet Sauvignon only, with 35,000 cases per vintage. The architecture as well as the focus on a single wine follows the classic pattern of Bordeaux châteaus. No expense has been spared in the creation of this model enterprise, either technically, from vineyard to winery, or aesthetically, with the high-ceilinged fermentation, aging, and storage rooms and the public grand salons.

A battery of tall stainless-steel fermenters were specially designed to leave the wine in contact with the pomace for full extraction. The pomace is removed and pressed to obtain the rich essence of the grape that resides next to the skins, an essence not found in the free-run juice. The first taste of the first wine, from the wood, confirms that it is a gutsy wine that will indeed require five years of aging. To borrow a Burgundian expression that tests the measure of a young wine, it "upholsters the mouth with tannins."

André Tchelistcheff is consultant to the project. The glint in those Slavic eyes when he talks about it is further assurance of impressive achievement when these wines make their debut in 1981. Currently there is some talk of adding a Chardonnay to complement the Cabernet Sauvignon offering.

KENWOOD WINERY

9592 Sonoma Highway, Kenwood, California 95452

Jordan Winery's battery of stainless-steel tanks in which their Cabernet Sauvignon undergoes its fermentation

The evolution of this humble board-and-batten winery, established by the Pagani family of Italy in 1905, and acquired by six enthusiastic winelovers from San Francisco in 1970, follows penciled observations found in Jack London's "Confessions": "The stairway of Time is ever echoing with the wooden shoe going up, the polished boot descending." From gnarled old Zinfandel and Sauvignon Vert vines to bulk wine aged in redwood for local jug-wine buyers and noble varietals finished in classic oak, a transformation is under way here. The setting remains rustic. The new owners —Martin Lee, a former San Francisco policeman, and his sons Mike and Marty; Bob Kozlowski, research chemist and winemaker; and Neil Knott and John Shella—make up a crew that is taking the renamed winery into fine winemaking with positive strides.

While the emphasis is upon red wines—Pinot Noir, Zinfandel, and Cabernet Sauvignon—vintage-dated fine white wines of Chardonnay, Johannisberg Riesling, and Chenin Blanc are produced with equal finesse. Gold medals from the Sonoma Harvest Festival Fair were awarded to the 1973 Sonoma Valley Pinot Noir and 1974 Sonoma Zinfandel.

Kenwood's system of fermenting each varietal separately and later marrying the vintage casks in a blend accenting the desired style, with a minimum of fining or filtering, has come to mark their red wines as *vins de garde*, good to lay away for added bottle age.

SAMPLER SELECTION

Zinfandel (Sonoma Valley). Vintage wine of fine ruby depths, almost harsh tannins, needing time for maturity.

Petite Sirah (Sonoma Valley). Vintage wine of exceptional promise in its full body and notable bouquet and breed.

F. KORBEL AND BROS.

Guerneville, California 95446

Redwood stumps among the vineyards are reminders of the lumbering business that brought Joseph Korbel and his two brothers, Anton and Francis, from Bohemia to this bend in the Russian River in 1862.

The present winery was built in 1886 with great timbers cut from the Korbels' domain and red brick fired in their own homemade kiln. A round tower with a conical roof, topped with a gargoyle holding a banner, served originally to house a distillery for brandy making. Legend has it that one of the Korbels designed it from his memory of a jail in Czechoslovakia in which he had spent some time, but today, masked with ivy, it stands only as a picturesque trademark of one of California's finest champagne houses.

Frank Schoonmaker was one of the first to recognize the superior merits of Korbel California Champagnes, and through his effective writings and Korbel's merchandising the brand was established among the more knowing American wine consumers. In 1954, Anton Korbel sold the winery to another family of winemakers, Adolph Heck of Alsace and his three sons, Adolph, Jr., Paul, and Ben. The elder Heck had been the champagne master at Cook's Imperial Champagne Cellars in St. Louis.

Among the table wines added to the list of Korbel offerings in the last few years are two outstanding white wines, Grey Riesling and Johannisberg Riesling, from grapes planted on well-drained slopes overlooking the Russian River. A light, delicately translucent Pinot Noir is produced from long-established vines growing within a few feet of the old brandy tower. While Korbel Brandy is no longer distilled here, it is still aged and blended by the Heck family to their own mellow ideal.

SAMPLER SELECTION

Korbel Natural California Champagne. Subtitled "Extremely Dry," this brilliant wine has a beguiling softness.

Korbel Brut California Champagne. The most popular wine, accounting for 60 percent of the output. Crisp, clean, dry.

Korbel Sonoma Grey Riesling. A wine to enjoy young, when the bouquet is opulently fruity, the taste crisp and clean.

Korbel Johannisberg Riesling. Now carrying a Sonoma appellation. Delicate as a Moselle wine. Sweet-edged.

One of California's oldest wineries, Korbel first won fame for its bottle-fermented champagnes

MARTINI & PRATI WINES, INC.

2191 Laguna Road, Santa Rosa, California 95401

While most of the wine produced by Elmo Martini and Edward Prati, descendants of pioneer Sonoma wine dynasties, is sold in bulk to other wineries, a memento of earlier times remains in the Fountain Grove label, acquired when that historic winery of the last century was closed. Visitors to the tasting room can buy Fountain Grove Cabernet Sauvignon and also some quite fine Burgundy at modest prices, making the stop worthwhile.

MILL CREEK VINEYARDS
(CHARLES KRECK WINERY)

1401 Westside Road, Healdsburg, California 95448

More than ten years ago, the Kreck family planted their first vineyard of Cabernet Sauvignon in the green, tree-clad Russian River region. Next would come Merlot, Chardonnay, and Pinot Noir. Charles Kreck manages the winery operation today, with the help of his sons Bob and Bill. Wives work right alongside, keeping this an almost 100 percent family-operated winery.

All the vineyards of their Mill Creek Ranch, in cool Region II, ride alluvial slopes to the hills overlooking Dry Creek. The 6,200-square-foot winery, housing stainless-steel fermenters and French, American, and Yugoslavian oak barrels for aging, is close enough to the vines to permit crushing within minutes of harvesting. The family intends to produce only 100 percent varietal wines, using only grapes grown under their own supervision.

Pinot Chardonnay (Sonoma County). A rich vintage edition with well-balanced hints of oak.

Cabernet Blush (Sonoma County). The idea began as a Blanc de Noir of Cabernet, but evolved a strawberry-pink rosé.

Pinot Noir (Sonoma County). A remarkable wine, even in its less-than-mature release. Full, true varietal nose.

Cabernet Sauvignon (Sonoma County). Certain to become a wine in demand by connoisseurs for its breed and character.

Surrounding Parducci's winery are some of the 30-year-old varietal vines with which Adolph Parducci pioneered in Mendocino County

PARDUCCI WINE CELLARS

501 Parducci Road, Ukiah, California 95482

In December of 1973, the Parducci family—Adolph and his two sons, John and George—concluded an arrangement which brought in the more than seventeen hundred California schoolteachers of the Teachers Management & Investment Corporation as financial partners. The educators wisely chose to leave the responsibility of winemaking with the Parducci family, who had established the vineyard and winery at Ukiah in 1931. That decision had effects reaching far beyond capital expansion and the costly goals of introducing a small winery to the technological advances of the day. With cellarmaster Joe Monostori, Hungarian-born winemaker and experienced wine lecturer, an extensive and comprehensive three-year correspondence course in the related sciences of winemaking and wine appreciation was launched for the new teacher-partners. The course has given the winery an academic aura transcending the goals of Adolph Parducci's initial modest hopes of producing 100,000 cases of wine annually. A third Parducci generation is growing up directly in the traditions of contemporary winemaking techniques.

The distinction of Parducci varietal wines, beyond the technological nurturing from field to cellar, derives mainly from two related influences: adherence to strict appellation of origin for vineyard sources (Home Ranch, Talmage Vineyards, Largo Vineyards, and some Cabernet Sauvignon purchased from Philo in the Anderson Valley), and John Parducci's strong belief that it is the grape, not wood, that should sing a wine's tune. One has only to follow John into the winery, climb the metal stairs, and taste, from stainless-steel tanks, a Pinot Noir, a Cabernet, a Petite Sirah, or even a Carignane to know the reason for his passionate belief. The separate characteristics of each wine are sharply differentiated, and the wines will later acquire a gentle finish in wood—some redwood, but never the overriding oak. Little, if any, cellar fining or clarification is given the vintage-dated wines.

French Colombard (Mendocino County). From free-run juice. Crisp and well-balanced. Very fruity. A medal winner.

Pinot Noir (Mendocino County). Rich, elegant, true to Burgundian aroma; bouquet reminiscent of dried rose petals.

Carignane (Mendocino County). A big, bold wine, robust, with garnet depths of color and savor. Requires aging.

Eh bien malin! comment le trouvez vous celui-la! — Oui, oui..
mais enfin — Oui ... oui ... oui !

"Very well! How do you like this one?" Lithograph by Honoré Daumier from *Charivari* (The Christian Brothers Collection)

J. PEDRONCELLI WINERY

1220 Canyon Road, Geyserville, California 95441

No one can tell the Pedroncelli story better than Jim Pedroncelli: "Where we are geographically is a key part of our story. Dry Creek originates a couple of miles over these foothills. The fog in late summer follows the Russian River up and curves into Dry Creek. It runs into a headwall there, and then begins backing down and burning off. We get the fog, just a lovely amount of it, then we get blue sky and sunshine, and we get them sooner than places below, for a balance of chill and warmth and moisture that is quite all our own. We find our wines have a mini-character to them. In essence, that's why we started bottling our own wines. In the early days we sold all our wines in bulk for blending, and my dad always felt it was a shame to blend them away, they were so distinctive."

With wit and modesty his brother John completes the honest legend: "Grapes make wine more than human beings. I often wish I could take a lot of the people I meet in the tasting room out into the vineyards in September and put a grape in their mouth from this first hill, and then take them just a few miles down the road or up the road at random and give them a grape from the same variety and let them notice the difference. Sometimes I must admit this makes me feel a little useless in my role as winemaker. Jim and I frequently refer to 'non-winemaking.' Every time you put a wine through a procedure, you take something out of it. We're definitely non-procedure types. We *tend* wine more than we make it. Incidentally, we try to tend it quite elegantly; many of our oak barrels come all the way from Bordeaux."

The humble old barn of their father's day, with its vats of redwood now replaced with more elegant oak and stainless steel, continues to serve as a winery. All the wines, both red and white, have an intensity of flavor that is as welcome as the modest pricing. From their 135 acres, doubled since their father's day, and with some of the old vines replaced, there has been sufficient wine (50,000 cases per year) for most of the better wine merchants in California, with enough to allocate in 14 states across the country.

SAMPLER SELECTION

Gewürztraminer (Sonoma County). A golden-yellow wine of spicy, racy bouquet and silky softness. Not wholly dry.

Zinfandel Rosé (Sonoma County). One of the first editions in California. Dry, crisp, almost brittle.

Cabernet Sauvignon (Sonoma County). The breed is very apparent in nose and aroma. A vintage wine, to lay away. Great value.

A. RAFANELLI WINERY

4685 West Dry Creek Road, Healdsburg, California 95448

Winemaker and grape grower Americo Rafanelli, with his wife, Mary, as co-owner and chemist, has transformed an old barn building on their vineyard-ranch into a modern winery of technological efficiency. But there are hints of old-fashioned Italian style. Rafanelli punches down the cap on his fermenting Zinfandel and Pinot Noir himself, over and over, for the extraction of all the wealth of color and flavor his grapes contain. The first vintage to carry their label, as

yet unreleased, is of 1975. The Rafanelli unfiltered red wines are certain to be one more reason for a growing sentiment in favor of a regional appellation for the Dry Creek area.

SAMPLER SELECTION

Zinfandel (Sonoma County). Grown, produced, and bottled in Dry Creek. Big, unfiltered wine, of impressive complexity.

Pinot Noir (Sonoma County). Rich in body and color, of an earthiness indicating further promise in the area for the varietal.

SEBASTIANI VINEYARDS

389 Fourth Street East, Sonoma, California 95476

In 1893, among the many immigrants was a fourteen-year-old boy from Tuscany who spoke no English and had no money left after paying for his steerage-class ticket. Samuele Sebastiani went to work and eventually earned enough money to buy a run-down winery in one corner of the original Mission San Francisco Solano. Now known popularly as Sonoma Mission, it was the last of the chain founded by Padre José Altimira in 1823. With it came a 501-gallon redwood tank. Samuele Sebastiani was in the wine business.

Today the Sebastiani winery has a storage capacity of over 2 million gallons and is still growing. August Sebastiani inherited the full measure of his father's intense drive. Though his sons, Sam and Don, show marked evidence of ability to take over the reins, Gus, now in his sixties, forever in striped bib overalls, remains in daily command.

In 1972, Sebastiani inaugurated the custom of making a *nouveau* wine in Beaujolais style for release only weeks after the harvest. However, he selected the Gamay Beaujolais, a descendant of Pinot Noir, rather than the more berry-like French original, thus setting the Sebastiani *nouveau* apart from its prototype. The treasures of the cellar, to be had currently only at the winery, include several old vintage Cabernet Sauvignons and a most extraordinary Angelica, an all but forgotten remnant of an altar wine made long ago and

The tasting room at Sebastiani

stored away in oak by Gus. Now almost an amber liqueur, it is titled Angelica Antigua.

In addition to vintage varietals, many from grapes bought from vineyards near and far, the winery's enormous facilities are also given over to the production of generic and varietal jug wines for mass distribution.

SAMPLER SELECTION

Barbera (North Coast Counties). The vintage selection is a hallmark of the winery. Big, fragrant, dark, dry.

Zinfandel (North Coast Counties). The label carries a subtitle calling attention to a "bramble" flavor, a berry-like taste.

Amore Cream Sherry. A well-aged solera of barrels in the sun ripens this wine to its sweet, mellow softness.

SIMI WINERY

16275 Healdsburg Avenue, Healdsburg, California 95448

The Alexander Valley takes its name from Cyrus Alexander, who moved from the Rockies in 1840 to manage the great Sotoyome Land Grant rancho for Captain John Fitch of San Diego. His pay for overseeing the livestock range after four years was two leagues of land. Not only do these 9,000 acres of an obscure valley today bear his name; with a mean climate approximating that of Napa Valley's Oakville Experimental Station, which in turn is said to have a temperature range equivalent to the Médoc of Bordeaux, Alexander Valley is an official appellation of origin for fine California wines. This came about in 1973, largely as the result of Russ Green's one-man crusade.

The Simi Winery dates from 1876, when Giuseppe and Pietro Simi, who had come from Montepulciano, Italy, thirty years earlier, paced off the dimensions of a knoll just north of Healdsburg whose slope would facilitate the flow of grape juice and fermenting wine from a top-floor winery to aging and storing rooms below. After Carignane, Zinfandel, Cabernet Sauvi-

gnon, and Riesling vines were planted, the Simis began gathering local stone to raise walls for the winery building. With nostalgic pride they lettered a long sign over the canopy of their railroad shipping dock: Montepulciano Winery. But few of the locals could pronounce that mouthful of syllables. The winery became known instead by the brothers' name, and as the Simi Winery it brought fame to the Healdsburg area in pre-Prohibition days.

When Russ Green, president of Signal Oil Company, came to the area in 1958 in search of a second home, he had no winemaking intentions, and he bought an old sheep-grazing ranch in the Alexander Valley. Simi was barely existing as a winery at that time. By 1970, when Green's 50-acre ranch had been planted to vineyard, the acquisition of the winery from Giuseppe Simi's elderly daughter seemed a logical step.

From here on, the story is one of quick changes (three owners in six years), with Russ Green in the background transforming the area, the winery's reputation, and even the winery itself. André Tchelistcheff was signed on as consultant and helper to Mary Ann Graf, a UC–Davis enology graduate with experience in three wineries.

Grapes arrived from the Alexander Valley vineyards to be crushed in new imported Willmes presses. Tchelistcheff revived the Burgundian techniques of open fermentation, in seasoned redwood vats, and the upper floor of the winery became the barrel-aging loft, with trim rows of French oak holding Chardonnay and Cabernet. The wines developed with new and distinctive character.

In August 1974, Scottish & Newcastle, one of Europe's leading brewing companies and whiskey exporters, joined the trend for conglomerates to acquire wineries. They allowed Green to remain as grape grower, with high hopes for moving the Simi Winery closer to its new 90,000-case potential. In May 1976, they sold the winery to Schieffelin & Company of New York, importers of fine wines and spirits, whose dynamic merchandising abilities coincide with Green's own desire to bring Simi Winery out of the past and into present importance in the California wine roster.

Montepulciano, birthplace of Simi's founders, is memorialized above the winery's loading platform

SAMPLER SELECTION

Gewürztraminer (Alexander Valley). One of my favorite California wines for its rich and languid yet spicy charms.

Johannisberg Riesling (Alexander Valley). From Russ Green's acreage, a flowery and fruity wine.

Cabernet Sauvignon (Alexander Valley). A wine of deep ruby color, made to mature to great potential, given sufficient age.

SONOMA VINEYARDS

Old Redwood Highway, Windsor, California 95492

Sonoma Vineyards is a thriving and handsome ornament of Sonoma County's renaissance as one of California's finest wine regions. The concept began modestly when Rodney Strong and his wife, Charlotte, both with Broadway credentials in theater and dance, established a winetasting facility in a 20-room Victorian house in Tiburon, where they sold the wines they bottled themselves. The business was successful, and a decade later a million-gallon winery had been built at Windsor, near the Russian River; 5,000 acres of choice varietal vineyards were in bearing; and the $10,000 annual sales had zoomed to $2 million.

"Each year we plotted recklessly the spread of our varietal vineyards, each in its own proper climate/soil environment," says Strong. Today, with the Renfield Corporation joined to Sonoma as shareholders and national distributors and with expediency dictating less expansive and distant vineyards, Sonoma has 2,000 acres remaining. Strong could write *the* book of the winemaker's travails.

"In any artistic form," Strong says, "one has a right to expect subtle differences. So we have different vines, different soils, different woods—Yugoslavian, Nevers, Limousin, and American oak—to age our wines. Plus all those doodads considered essential,

Rodney Strong, chairman of Sonoma Vineyards, with a model of his winery, a revolutionary design

including the centrifuge. Some people have been so enamored of the centrifuge they've spun the bejesus out of the juice. I like my Chardonnay to be a nice golden wine, *some* oak, not too much, with style, not just a little dry, acid wine. Oak must be used with a great deal of discretion."

Rod's approach to champagne is also unique. "I'm trying to get some *wine* back into the champagne," he said of his vintage Blanc de Noir Champagne, produced in the *méthode champenoise* tradition. "Too often you don't get the *seat* of the wine because of the effervescence. The bubbles should be the smallest part of champagne."

The handsome winery designed by Craig Roland, a disciple of Frank Lloyd Wright, rises from the earth in four wings, surrounded by vineyards of true Burgundian Pinot Noir vines. One wing holds more than 4,000 barrels of imported oak, aging the fine vintages that are certain to fulfill Strong's original dreams.

SAMPLER SELECTION

Chardonnay (Sonoma County). This estate-bottled, vintage wine is comparable to a fine French white Burgundy.

Johannisberg Riesling (Sonoma County). From Strong's River East vineyard, touched with botrytis. No wood, silky, gentle.

Pinot Noir (Sonoma County). Exceptionally fine. Aged in Nevers oak to wood/grape balance in bouquet and taste. Classic style.

Cabernet Sauvignon (Alexander's Crown). This Sonoma County jewel made its debut with a stunningly fine 1974 vintage of nonirrigated grapes from a 51-acre plot of volcanic soil. It will unquestionably become one of California's greatest wines from the French claret grape.

Zinfandel (Sonoma County). Vintage, estate-bottled wine from 30-year-old vines. Similar to claret in style and texture.

SOUVERAIN OF ALEXANDER VALLEY

Independence Lane/Souverain Road, Geyserville, California 95441

When the Pillsbury Company of Minneapolis joined the corporate rush to the California wine fields in the early seventies, patience was left out of their ambitious plans. Even though numerous medals had been awarded the Souverain wines in June 1976, the landmark winery was sold to North Coast Cellars. North Coast is an association of grape growers comprising 150 vineyardists from Napa, Sonoma, and Mendocino, said to represent almost 80 percent of the growers of those areas. Under the new ownership Souverain will concentrate on selecting the best grapes from the finest vineyards for each type of wine, the winery becoming a showcase for the resulting products. Particularly outstanding lots, under winemaster Bill Bonetti's plans, will be aged and bottled separately and sold with the designation Vineyard Selection; this policy was inaugurated with a 1973 Cabernet Sauvignon of extraordinary merit. Souverain of Alexander Valley, designed by Sausalito architect John Marsh Davis, is certainly among the outstanding examples of winery architecture. Davis drew inspiration from the few remaining old hop kilns that can still be seen off the byroads of Sonoma County.

SAMPLER SELECTION

Chardonnay (North Coast Counties). Modestly priced vintage wine of outstanding value. Oak-aged to

Souverain's winery borrows the distinctive shape of the old hop kilns still seen in Sonoma County

September 25th harvesting. The retired Western Airlines captain was using both arms for the task. A heady scent of fermentation filled the winery, but visible action had subsided in this vat. The pomace of skins and seeds, with the wine, had become a deep, dark reddish-purple gruel, thick as pudding. "I think it will be a fine wine," he said with quiet modesty, and I knew he was pleased with his wine at this stage of its extended contact with the skins. Together we tasted the '75 from the wood. Its elegance and breed told me why Tchelistcheff had suggested my visit here. California has reason to be proud of these wines.

Joseph Swan's wines are sold largely through mail orders from a roster of enophiles who have discovered the sturdy excellence of each custom-made varietal.

SAMPLER SELECTION

Chardonnay (Sonoma County). Vintage, estate-bottled wine, French-oak-aged to a well-balanced fruit-and-wood richness.

Zinfandel (Sonoma County). The Swan style is always intense, with maximum varietal bouquet from long fermentation.

Pinot Noir (Sonoma County). In the opinion of many expert winemakers, this is one of California's finest

Joseph Swan punches down the cap of pomace on top of a vat of Pinot Noir

crisp, balanced elegance.

Cabernet Sauvignon (Vineyard Selection). Winemaker Bonetti's pride among the red wines. Full breed and character to enjoy now, or to age.

Moscato Bianco (North Coast Counties). A newcomer bound to enchant lovers of dessert wine with its delicate sweetness.

JOSEPH SWAN VINEYARDS

2916 Laguna Road, Forestville, California 95436

It was André Tchelistcheff who suggested I track down Joseph Swan because of his success with the true Burgundian Pinot Noir grape, which has defied so many winemakers in California. I found Swan in his tiny, unpretentious cement-block winery, punching down the cap of his '76 Pinot Noir that had been in its open redwood fermenter for two weeks after its

red wines. Always estate-bottled, vintage, from a true Burgundian clone of the temperamental grape variety.

TRENTADUE WINERY

19170 Redwood Highway, Geyserville, California 95441

Encroaching subdivisions in 1959 moved Leo Trentadue and his family from a Santa Clara County ranch to the Healdsburg–Geyserville area of Sonoma County. Along with Bernard Fetzer and Russ Green, he was among the first to plant fine varietal vineyards in commercial quantities in this northern area of Sonoma County. This was no doubt a part of the attraction that drew Pillsbury to the area for their Souverain venture, and Trentadue sold them 20 acres of his original 160 for the splendid winery, completed in 1973, which now stands near his own more modest facility. There is a gold medal for his Napa Gamay and genuine enthusiasm for his big, robust, and fragrant Petite Sirah. Each of his labels carries the number 32—*trentadue* being the Italian word for thirty-two.

SAMPLER SELECTION

Merlot (Sonoma). A vintage, estate-bottled wine, of full ruby color and intense flavor. Bottle-aging suggested.

Gamay (Sonoma). This is from the Napa Gamay grape of the true Beaujolais variety, of substantial vinosity here.

Petite Sirah (Sonoma). Even when young this estate-bottled vintage wine has gutsy swagger; for serving with game.

ZD WINES

20735 Burndale Road, Sonoma, California 95476

ZD stands for the names of the owners and winemakers, Gino Zepponi and Norman de Leuze. Both partners share the belief that exceptional wines can be made only from exceptional grapes given intensive care and personal attention. The tiny winery, not much bigger than its name, with a fermenting capacity of only 6,400 gallons, is fortunately near the source of the two varieties that interest the owners most—Chardonnay and Pinot Noir. Located just north of San Francisco Bay, at the southern junction of Napa and Sonoma counties, the Carneros district is cooled by early morning fog and breezes off the bay. Several Napa Valley wineries pioneered this location, originally thought to be too cool for proper ripening of grapes. But when it was realized that Burgundian varieties thrived in such a climate, Carneros began to garner praise as an area well suited to the growing of Chardonnay and Pinot Noir.

Zepponi and de Leuze frequently extend their devoted winemaking attentions to grapes from other areas: Zinfandel from the Sierra foothills, Chardonnay from Tepusquet Vineyards of Santa Maria, Cabernet Sauvignon from Paso Robles, and even a Pinot Noir from the Umpqua Valley of Oregon.

SAMPLER SELECTION

Chardonnay (Sonoma). From the Zepponi Vineyard, an intensely flavored varietal, well-balanced. Big enough to age well.

Gewürztraminer (Winery Lake Vineyard). Rich and clean, with full measure of the spicy bouquet and aroma of the grape.

Pinot Noir (Napa). From the Winery Lake Vineyard of Carneros, a dark, garnet-red, 100 percent varietal; enhanced with aging.

Zinfandel (Amador). Made in the same style as the Pinot Noir; dark, rich, full-flavored, and long-lived.

NAPA COUNTY

Napa, the proudest name among California's wine districts, refers to the county, which lies just east of Sonoma, separated from it by the Mayacamas Mountains, but more specifically to the Napa Valley, a 35-mile stretch from San Pablo Bay northwest to Mount St. Helena, where many of California's most illustrious vineyards flourish.

The Napa Valley today has more than double the vineyard acreage it had in 1919. Ten thousand acres of

Visitors are welcome at Beaulieu, known familiarly as BV, one of the oldest vineyards in Napa

vines, preponderantly the noble vinifera, were in cultivation when the Eighteenth Amendment struck like a plague. Some of the vines survived, but many were uprooted or grafted to vulgar "juice grapes" that could withstand shipment to the East for the making of home wines during Prohibition. When Repeal came, in 1933, Chardonnay was all but unknown, and even by 1965 only a scant 942 acres of Cabernet Sauvignon were in bearing.

Inexpensive jug wines carrying a Napa Valley appellation and generic name will soon become a thing of the past. Although many a famous Napa winery owes more than a little of its present prosperity to the Mountain Burgundy and Mountain Chablis blendings from Carignane, Crab's Black Burgundy, Alicante Bouschet, Burger, Sauvignon Vert, and Golden Chasselas vines, those varieties are now being replaced with fine Pinots, Rieslings, Cabernet Sauvi-

gnon, and Chardonnay. The land is too expensive for any but premium varieties today.

Harvest from the present 22,000 acres in fine grape varieties remains insufficient for the demand created by the magic word Napa. The larger wineries based in Napa must reach out to other regions, other appellations, to fill the demands for their wines. Meanwhile the small winemaker, producing on the basis of his own grape supply from limited local plantings, gains enthusiastic patronage as he makes his small lots of expensive quality wines. They cannot help but be costly, and to the connoisseur they are often worth their premium pricing.

Winemaking remains an intimate thing, despite the dominance today of impersonal stainless-steel tanks. For these fermenters are holding living wines safely and securely—and also the hopes and dreams of the most creative farmers of our land. The profile of

124

the land remains much as it was in centuries past, but the patchwork design of vineyard plots is more lush than yesterday's landscape, and the wines are ever finer.

BEAULIEU VINEYARD

1960 St. Helena Highway, Rutherford, California 94573

The prestige of California wines following Repeal depended principally on those wineries whose vineyards were maintained for the legal production of sacramental wines. Preeminent among them was Beaulieu Vineyard, established by Georges de Latour, a native of the Périgord region of France, who came to America in 1883 and, with his wife, established at Rutherford in 1900 a vineyard, winery, and gracious home. The enterprise was sold to Heublein by Fernande de Latour's daughter Hélène, the Marquise de Pins. The family has retained the founder's country house and its sunken gardens, rose arbors, vegetable and herb plots, and, most important, Cabernet Sauvignon plantings. This is the "beautiful place"—Beaulieu —for which the vineyard was named, a word so difficult for Americans to pronounce that the initials BV have become its most familiar designation.

The question is often asked, what is the difference between the regular Beaulieu Vineyard Cabernet Sauvignon and the Georges de Latour Private Reserve Cabernet Sauvignon? Both are 100 percent Cabernet wines, but the Private Reserve is produced from the grapes of the family estate on the west side of Highway 29, these well-established vines being responsible for the subtle difference (which the late founder ascribed to "Rutherford dust," a whimsical reference to variation in soil).

While a nucleus of 745 acres of Beaulieu vineyards remains, grapes are also bought from other Napa Valley vineyards. But particular credit is due to the Chardonnay and Pinot Noir plantings in the cool Carneros region pioneered by André Tchelistcheff during his tenure as enologist and winemaster, from 1937 until 1973.

Tchelistcheff's admired cellarmaster, Theo Rosenbrand, remains at the helm of winemaking; Legh Knowles, Jr., is general manager. In 1977 Beaulieu Vineyard '71 Champagne de Chardonnay emerged in first place in an open competition with all other leading sparkling wines of California. Even the generic Beaulieu Vineyard Napa Valley Chablis and Burgundy are accorded uncommon acceptance among winelovers everywhere.

SAMPLER SELECTION

Pinot Chardonnay (Napa Valley). Also known as Beaufort. Grapes from the Carneros region. Crisp, clean.

Chateau Beaulieu (Sauvignon Blanc). In French Sauternes style, 73 percent Sauvignon, with a touch of Muscadelle. Sweet.

Cabernet Sauvignon (Private Reserve). Aged in French oak in the Tchelistcheff-established tradition. Always outstanding.

Champagne de Chardonnay. Produced in classic *méthode champenoise* on the Beaulieu estate. Breed and high style.

BERINGER/LOS HERMANOS

2000 Main Street, St. Helena, California 94574

In 1970 the golden wand of Nestlé of Switzerland touched the Napa Valley with the $6-million purchase of the Beringer/Los Hermanos winery and vineyards. (Beringer Brothers was the original name of the winery, while Los Hermanos—"The Brothers" in Spanish—was the name of the vineyard owned by the family before Prohibition. The winery now uses Beringer for the estate wines and Los Hermanos for jug wines and less expensive labels.) The transformation, almost immediate, was beneficial and lasting. The landmark winery established by Jacob and Frederick Beringer, German immigrants from Mainz, in 1876, had been the oldest continuously operating winery in the Napa Valley, but after 1950 it was in decline, though the old limestone caves were a continuing tourist attraction.

Today, thanks to excellent renovation, Beringer is a model of winery design. The Beringer wine production business is today controlled by the Labruyère family of France, who lease the distinguished winery

facility from Nestlé. Richard L. Maher, experienced wine merchandiser, is president and in residence, assisted by William T. Ryan, an E. & J. Gallo marketing alumnus. Myron Nightingale continues as winemaker, adding a further note of distinction to this highly competent organization.

From Beringer vineyards in the Napa Valley, the Carneros and Yountville regions, and Knights Valley in nearby Sonoma, and from Tepusquet Vineyards of Santa Maria, Nightingale has produced a succession of magnificent wines. Perhaps the most outstanding have been the Chardonnays—the '73 a huge wine from the Yountville vineyards, suggesting an equally rare Musigny Blanc, the '74 impressive for intense character, breed, and 13.5 percent alcoholic strength, assuring long, developing finesse. The Cabernet Sauvignon released in 1976, like the Chardonnay of the same year, celebrates the centennial of the winery.

Two proprietary wines deserve mention: Barenblut ("Bear's Blood"), an old Beringer wine that Nightingale has revived in a fragrant marriage of Napa Gamay and Zinfandel grapes, and Traubengold, Nightingale's sumptuously fragrant, very fruity white Riesling with an undeniably sweet edge. For value hunters—which includes us all—the Los Hermanos 1.5-liter jug decanters of Chablis, Chardonnay, Johannisberg Riesling, Chenin Blanc, Gamay Beaujolais, Zinfandel, and Burgundy are everyday wine winners.

SAMPLER SELECTION

Chardonnay (Napa Valley). Rivals the finest white Burgundy of France. Judiciously aged in Yugoslavian oak. A big wine.

Johannisberg Riesling (Napa Valley). Look for the late-harvested editions, touched with botrytis.

Malvasia Bianca. A most extraordinary semisweet dessert wine of liqueur richness and classic grape fruitiness and delicacy.

Cabernet Sauvignon (Napa Valley). Rich wine of lasting potential, kept long on the skins, touched with Merlot.

BURGESS CELLARS

1108 Deer Park Road, St. Helena, California 94574

In the early forties, J. Leland Stewart, an executive of a national meat-packing firm, decided to seek a new life in the Napa Valley on a 60-acre tract of land that had a small vineyard, a prune orchard, and a tiny winery. He called his new enterprise Souverain Cellars.

In 1970, he sold the house, the winery, and the name to a group of investors, who in turn sold the entire estate in 1972 to Tom Burgess, a young jet pilot.

The winery facilities have been enhanced with a centrifuge for the fresh juice of select grapes, most of which are purchased from premium vineyards in the valley. The 22 acres of Burgess's vineyard supply choice, nonirrigated Cabernet Sauvignon, Zinfandel, and Petite Sirah. Burgess has added three stainless-steel fermenters with cooling jackets, but he and his winemaker, Bill Sorenson, share the belief that white wines emerge softer and silkier when fermented in the European manner, in white-oak casks. His Chardonnay and Johannisberg Riesling substantiate that belief.

SAMPLER SELECTION

Chenin Blanc (Steltzner Vineyard). A completely dry version, given subtle complexity and color through oak aging.

Johannisberg Riesling (Winery Lake). Cold-fermented techniques give an intensely flavored, full, rich wine.

Cabernet Sauvignon (Napa Valley). Complex aroma and deep color and flavor. From Burgess's own and Rutherford grapes.

Chardonnay (Napa Valley). Winery Lake Vineyards are the source of this huge, oak-aged, golden dry wine. Expensive but worth the price.

CARNEROS CREEK WINERY

1285 Dealy Lane, Napa, California 94558

It is not likely that the proliferation of "boutique" wineries in the premium winegrowing regions of California will abate. Not as long as there are enthusiasts like Balfour and Anita Gibson who know that dedication and knowledge, plus choice, select grapes, are a route to fine wines, bound to win recognition. Their first wine, a 1973 Napa Valley Pinot Noir, made from a vintage blend of Carneros grapes balanced with some from the fine Trefethen Vineyards of Napa, is full-bodied, aged in French oak, unfined, and certain to age with splendid bouquet. Francis Mahoney is the wine-maker.

SAMPLER SELECTION

Cabernet Sauvignon (Shenandoah Valley). Expensive vintage wine for the collector; well worth the price.

Zinfandel (Sutter Basin). Fans of California's "big Zin" find this full-bodied wine a prize.

Petite Syrah (Napa Valley). Big and almost exotic wine needing added age to round out its complexity.

CAYMUS VINEYARDS

8700 Conn Creek Road, Rutherford, California 94573

A tub-thumping viticulturist of the eighteenth century declared, "Fine wine is made in the vineyard." There's not a grape grower alive who wouldn't agree with this sentiment. Charles Wagner, a longtime Napa Valley grape grower, finally could not resist the temptation to bond the barn near his home and vineyard into a winery. He owns 70 acres of magnificently attended vines and buys choice lots of grapes from as far away as Amador County, in the foothills of the Sierra, an area noted for exceptional Zinfandel. With his son to help him, there will surely be winemakers' wines with the Caymus label—not in great quantity, but characteristic of the vintner who knows his grapes and makes his wines without compromise. The 1974 Cabernet Sauvignon quickly claimed California connoisseurs' attention, sending them scurrying for a share of this richly endowed, heavy-bodied varietal wine, a rival of fine French clarets—a worthy *vin de garde*.

CHAPPELLET VINEYARD

1581 Sage Canyon Road, St. Helena, California 94574

A peaceful domain was what Donn and Molly Chappellet of Beverly Hills were seeking as an alternative life-style for themselves and their six children. Donn, like many other capitalist dropouts mentioned in this book, looked to the land, and in 1967 his explo-

rations of the Napa Valley were rewarded with this site—sloping, with a westerly exposure for terracing, almost entirely new to vines.

The 100 acres of vineyard were planted to four varieties: Johannisberg Riesling, Chenin Blanc, Chardonnay, and Cabernet Sauvignon. The handsome triangular winery building, designed by an artist friend and constructed by an engineer, was ready for the first harvest in 1969. Chappellet is now well on its way toward its 20,000-case yearly goal.

With the 1969 Cabernet Sauvignon, it was obvious that with this vine in this setting the winery was destined for continuing greatness, and as the vine roots go deeper into the reddish, iron-rich soil on this mountain, the wines grow in complexity.

SAMPLER SELECTION

Chardonnay (Napa Valley). Vintage, estate-bottled wine of pale, straw-yellow brilliance. Crisp, clean, elegant.

Johannisberg Riesling (Napa Valley). Like the Chenin Blanc, which is fermented dry, this is of noteworthy delicacy.

Cabernet Sauvignon (Napa Valley). Wine of singular depth and rich-textured complexity, assuring long, unfolding life.

CHATEAU CHEVALIER

3101 Spring Mountain Road, St. Helena, California 94574

Jacob Beringer planted his first vines in the 1870s on the curving knolls surrounding this great estate. It was acquired in 1884 by the Fortune Chevalier family, San Francisco wine merchants. Even before Prohibition, the difficult and steep vineyards suffered neglect, and like the fairy-tale castle of "Sleeping Beauty" the Chateau Chevalier, its grandeur all but obliterated, had to wait for its moment of awakening—until September 1969.

The prince of this engaging history is winelover Gregory Bissonette, a disenchanted stockbroker seeking a new life in the wine country. Today, with Greg, his wife, Kathy, and their six children in residence, the

Chappellet's terraced vineyards on Pritchard Hill overlooking the Napa Valley

reconstruction continues: the grand stone staircase to the gardens leading to the mountainside vineyards has been cleared; 54 acres of new vines, 65 percent Cabernet Sauvignon, some Merlot, and 30 percent Chardonnay, were planted in 1970 and 1971, with a few acres of Johannisberg Riesling and Pinot Noir "to play around with." The basic hope is to make Chateau Chevalier essentially a two-wine venture, with the stained-glass-window label reserved for wines from the Bissonettes' own grapes, while the "Mountainside" label is used for wines produced here from selected grapes purchased from other vineyards.

SAMPLER SELECTION

Johannisberg Riesling (Napa Valley). Carrying the Chateau Chevalier label with pride for its nectar-sweet, luscious zing.

Chardonnay (Napa Valley). Early versions carried only the Mountainside label; the estate label indicates greater depth.

Cabernet Sauvignon (Napa Valley). There is little need to go abroad for big clarets, with California wine as rich as this.

CHÂTEAU MONTELENA

1429 Tubbs Lane, Calistoga, California 94515

Château Montelena burst upon the American wine scene like a skyrocket, without advance notice and with only modest distribution of its new label, when its Napa & Alexander Valleys Chardonnay scored a stunning victory over illustrious white Burgundies of France in a tasting by a French jury of experts in Paris on May 24, 1976. It was a well-earned award, underscoring modest but positive determination to produce fine wines at a historic location.

The 100-acre vineyard was established in 1882 by Senator Alfred A. Tubbs, whose travels to the château wine country of Bordeaux inspired him to establish traditions no less elegant on his own vineyard estate.

In 1968, industrialist Lee Paschich and his wife, Helen, amateur winemaking enthusiasts, bought the 142-acre property, converting an upper portion of the old winery to a country house. In May of 1972, the

Jade Lake, with its oriental bridges and red pavilions, was part of the original Château Montelena estate nearly a hundred years ago

owners, well aware of the greater potentials, formed a partnership with attorney James Barrett, administrative financier Ernest Hahn, and winemakers Jerry Luper and Miljenko ("Mike") Grgich, whose qualifications included nine years with the legendary André Tchelistcheff at Beaulieu.

Winemaking at Château Montelena, a marriage of European methods with California's modern style, is focused upon four wines: Johannisberg Riesling, Chardonnay, Zinfandel, and Cabernet Sauvignon. The château label is reserved for wines of outstanding excellence. Silverado Cellars is the secondary designation, for wines from grapes purchased from other growers, and for vintages of good wines of more modest value.

SAMPLER SELECTION

Johannisberg Riesling (Napa & Alexander Valleys). Flowery, full-bodied wine, suggesting citrus and peaches.

Chardonnay (Napa & Alexander Valleys). Big, creamy, rich, in Meursault style, golden from judicious aging in oak.

Zinfandel (Napa Valley). Unique and zingy, the berry taste modified with oak. Dark, deep, highly enjoyable.

Cabernet Sauvignon (Napa Valley). Needing age to bring out the potential of its plentiful tannins.

THE CHRISTIAN BROTHERS

Mont La Salle, Napa, California 94558

There is a stunning contrast between the humble beginnings of The Christian Brothers as winemakers in 1882 and their position today as the largest Church-owned producer of wine in the world. The 300-year-old teaching order maintains 600 teaching centers in 80 countries, partially supported by revenues from their winemaking. The first Christian Brothers in California made their first wine at Martinez in a horse-watering trough, crushing the grapes with a wooden club; their present circular stainless-steel fermenting facility at St. Helena looks more like a "Star Trek" launching pad than a grape-receiving station. The con-

trast sums up an unparalleled success story.

By 1937 production at a big vine-clad brick winery at Mont La Salle stood in need of marketing assistance. Fromm and Sichel of San Francisco was chosen to market and distribute Christian Brothers wines and brandies and champagnes and has made them a household name not only in America but in forty-five countries abroad as well. Today, The Christian Brothers own and operate three major wineries in the Napa Valley, two in the San Joaquin Valley, and 2,400 acres of fine varietal vineyards, 1,400 of them in the Napa Valley.

From the beginning, Brother Timothy, the distinguished cellarmaster at Mont La Salle and a one-time chemistry teacher, has had an abiding belief in blending for the production of the finest table wines, nonvintage and ready to drink. The red wines go from the fermenting tanks into a diversified library of cooperage that includes American oak as well as the fine varieties from European forests. They are given two to five years before they enter the blending program. Further aging marries the blend in wood before bottling, and six months later it arrives in the market.

The estate-bottled wines are made entirely from grapes grown in the Mont La Salle Monastery vineyards in the Napa hills. Each bottle indicates a special *cuvée* on the neck label, giving the number of the blending lot. The wines designated as Brother Timothy Special Selections have additional aging in a variety of wood cooperage for a minimum of two years. Dessert wines and brandies come from the two wineries and vineyards in the San Joaquin Valley, in Reedley and Fresno.

SAMPLER SELECTION

Pinot Chardonnay (Napa Valley). Always an outstanding value. Buttery soft; wood has accented the grape's breed.

Napa Fumé (Napa Valley). Dry-finished Sauvignon Blanc, rich in fragrance and with an enticing, refreshing fruitiness.

Pinot Saint George (Napa Valley). Estate-bottled from the Mont La Salle vineyard. Ruby-red, dry, softens with aging.

At the Napa Valley property of The Christian Brothers, Mont La Salle, the novitiate is surrounded by flourishing vineyards

Gamay Noir (Napa Valley). Of the true grape of Beaujolais, the Napa Gamay. Dark, soft in the mouth, berry-like taste.

CLOS DU VAL WINE COMPANY

5330 Silverado Trail, Napa, California 94558

It was barely rumored that Bernard Portet, son of the winemaster of Château Lafite-Rothschild, had selected the Napa Valley for his career in winemaking before eagerness to taste his wines began to mount. Astute wine merchants vied for their quotas of the only two wines he would make, the Cabernet Sauvignon and Zinfandel. The first releases were of the 1972 vintage, and while nowhere near the peak of their potential, they satisfied the most critical that here indeed was a small winery deserving a more honorific description than "boutique," for there was nothing diminutive about the stature of the wines. The goal of 15,000 cases has already been achieved, with distribution in thirty-two states at this writing.

"Of all the wine-growing regions in the world that I had visited," Portet said, "this California region seemed the most favorable spot in which to launch a premium winery enterprise." A 120-acre site was bought just off the Silverado Trail, below the rocky pinnacles of Stag's Leap on the valley's eastern slopes. A small winery, completed in 1974, is equipped with stainless-steel fermenters, upright oak tanks for early aging, and, of course, French-oak 50-gallon barrels for the traditional Médoc finishing before bottling. "Substantial" best describes both the Portet wines. Long on the skins and therefore rich in texture and loaded with tannin, they demonstrate the importance of cellar aging.

SAMPLER SELECTION

Zinfandel (Napa Valley). Dark, full-bodied wine of rich balance; needs longer age in bottle for full enjoyment.

Cabernet Sauvignon (Napa Valley). Vintage; estate-bottled. In Bordelais style, rounded with Merlot.

CUVAISON

4560 Silverado Trail, Calistoga, California 94515

Set back of and above the Silverado Trail, this trim new winery among its 30 acres of Pinot Noir, Gamay, and Riesling vines is a monument to trial and error. Established by Dr. Thomas Cottrell, a physicist, and his fellow scientist Thomas Parkhill, it was christened with the French word for the fermentation of red wines on the skins—*cuvaison*. The first vintage, in 1970, was made in stainless-steel fermenters installed just in time for the arrival of the first grapes.

After producing eighteen wine varieties, none of stellar quality, Cottrell recognized the need for capital and professionalism. He invited Oakleigh B. Thorne of New York's C T Corporation System to assume ownership and control, and engaged Philip Togni as winemaster. Togni, whose brilliant, peregrinating career had included Montpellier, Chile, Bordeaux, Alsace, and finally California (Gallo, Inglenook, Mayacamas, Chalone, and Chappellet) came to Cuvaison in January of 1975. The original inventory was sold off to visitors to the handsome tasting room, and a new policy, in the French estate tradition, of making only three wines—Chardonnay, Cabernet Sauvignon, and Zinfandel—was adopted by merchandising manager Winston Wilson.

In Togni's opinion, the Calistoga area is too warm for Pinot Noir. Cuvaison now buys 100 percent of its grapes from choice hillside lots, including the first Cabernet Sauvignon in eighty-five years from a vineyard with northwest exposure in Marin County, yielding a rich 1 1/2 tons per acre. The '75 Cabernet has grapes from six different Napa Valley vineyards, including a significant 15 percent blending of Merlot from the picturesque grape-growing estate of René di Rosa in the Carneros district.

Togni, well remembering his winemaking days at Château Lascombes, in Margaux, makes big, chewy red wines. His time with Hugel in Alsace taught him the subleties of dry white wines, with no need for excessive dependence on wood for taste. His first Chardonnay at Cuvaison was the '75 vintage with a .7 total acidity and with 13.8 percent alcohol. It will

The stained-glass window in Cuvaison's Spanish Colonial winery is featured on their wine labels

go far in accomplishing for Cuvaison a reputation to match the distinction of the handsome label.

SAMPLER SELECTION

Chardonnay (Napa Valley). Winemaster Philip Togni selects premium grapes for his charming French-oak-aged banner wine.

Cabernet Sauvignon (Marin County). Limousin-oak-aged wine out of stainless-steel fermenters. Egg-white fining and classical care give promise to each vintage.

DIAMOND CREEK VINEYARDS

1500 Diamond Mountain Road, Calistoga, California 94515

In his own words, after a "hectic, punishing business career" in the beauty-aid business in southern California, Al Brounstein was ready for a sylvan retreat. He found it on Diamond Mountain, due west of Sterling Vineyards and minutes away from Schramsberg. Twenty acres of the 79-acre estate are planted with 90 percent Cabernet Sauvignon and 10 percent Merlot. They produced the first vintage in 1973.

The arable tracts were of such dissimilar geological natures that Brounstein determined to make three different wines whose names would reflect the differences: Volcanic Hill, Gravelly Meadow, and Red Rock Terrace.

An old-fashioned basket-press is used, with equally old-style open wooden fermenters. The aim is for big wines, long on the skins, to be aged in Nevers, Limousin, and Yugoslavian oak barrels. All the wines have a cedar tinge to the bouquet. While the Red Rock Terrace Cabernet Sauvignon, in Brounstein's opinion, is softer than the other two, each of the three has its adherents who would give it top rank.

SAMPLER SELECTION

Cabernet Sauvignon (Napa Valley). Three vineyard designations, each a big wine, not overly tannic, but requiring aging.

DOMAINE CHANDON

California Drive, Yountville, California 94599

When in February 1973 the late Count Robert de Vogüé of Moët-Hennessy, producers of Dom Pérignon Champagne, bought 875 acres of prime vineyard land in the Napa Valley, the question greeted him everywhere, what would he call his California sparkling wine? Champagne? Heresy for a Champenois!

The debut of the wine occurred in December 1976, and it was named Domaine Chandon Napa Valley Brut. Moët-Hennessy's finest champagne master, Edmund Maudière of Épernay, commuted between France and California to assure the excellence of the first American sparkling wine to carry the name of Chandon, a name synonymous with Dom Pérignon. Moët-Hennessy even sent Lucien Dambron to instruct the Domaine Chandon employees in the art of turning the bottles, known as "riddling," which maneuvers the sediment of wine in secondary fermentation onto the corks, a technique dating back to the time of Dom Pérignon. Dambron can turn 50,000 bottles per day; his apprentices are already up to 20,000 per day.

Domaine Chandon Napa Valley Brut is approximately two-thirds Pinot Noir and one-third Chardonnay, with an undeclared amount of Pinot Blanc. "California Chardonnay," Maudière says emphatically, "it is too strong. It's more a Burgundy Chardonnay than a champagne Chardonnay, but we need Chardonnay because it gives a particular sparkle and zest to our wine." The *cuvée* has a kinship with Dom Pérignon, not only sharing the same champagne master but also being made from similar grape varieties. "It would be a mistake to try to make a French champagne here," Maudière concluded. "It should be Californian." It will always be nonvintage, and this indicates the importance of blending for that elegant *cuvée*.

In 1977, Domaine Chandon began the harvest of their own vines on the Mount Veeder ranch, in addition to taking grapes from Carneros and the 50 acres surrounding the new winery in Yountville. A second wine, a Cuvée de Pinot Noir, will have a frankly pale-apricot blush from its 100 percent rich black-grape origins. Both wines take about eight years to ascend to

Domaine Chandon, newly launched with two bottles of its own wine, flies the flags of the United States, California, Champagne, and France

their peak of perfection, largely because of the dominant role of Pinot Noir. The Moët-Hennessy $12-million investment in California, shared with Californians, is a boon whose promise is just beginning to reach fulfillment.

SAMPLER SELECTION

Napa Valley Brut. Nonvintage sparkling wine of a bold and round richness of taste. A silvery-bronze blush of color.

Napa Valley Cuvée de Pinot Noir. Long, silky, and elegant. Pale-apricot color, dry, classic fruit and yeast bouquet.

FRANCISCAN VINEYARDS

Highway 29 at Galleron Road, Rutherford, California 94573

One of the handsomest new winemaking facilities in the center of Napa Valley had a sad beginning. The original investors, in a last-ditch effort at salvation, had to sell Franciscan Vineyards' bottled goods at discount prices to weekend tourists. Now Franciscan Vineyards has been restored by a former Christian Brother, the rugged and genial Justin Meyer, in association with a Denver financier, Raymond Duncan, with Leonard Berg of Christian Brothers as production manager.

The winery's storage capacity—367,000 gallons of stainless-steel fermenters and oak cooperage—is more than adequate to handle the harvests of the 500 acres of prime vineyards in Napa Valley, plus 250 acres in the Alexander Valley and 300 in Lake County.

The new management is realistic. It knows that the foundation of the California wine business is in volume sales of half-gallon jugs of generic Chablis and Burgundy. These are the Friar's Table selections, a secondary label that pays the freight for the fine wines under the Franciscan Vineyards label.

SAMPLER SELECTION

White Riesling (Napa Valley). A crisp vintage wine of tart acidity balanced with only a token residual sweetness.

Chenin Blanc (Napa Valley). The sweetness level is

Justin Meyer, every inch the genial friar, savors the bouquet of a Franciscan Cabernet Sauvignon

right at the threshold of awareness—1 percent—assuring popularity.

Burgundy (Napa Valley). A vintage generic blend of Charbono and Petite Sirah. A wine drinker's wine, dry, gutsy, fine.

Cabernet Sauvignon (Napa Valley). A vintage wine of modest price and substantial value. Aged in American oak.

FREEMARK ABBEY

3022 St. Helena Highway, St. Helena, California 94574

The only association of a religious nature that can be linked with the name of Freemark Abbey (coined from those of its three founders) is the devout faith in its wines held by an ever-growing number of eno-

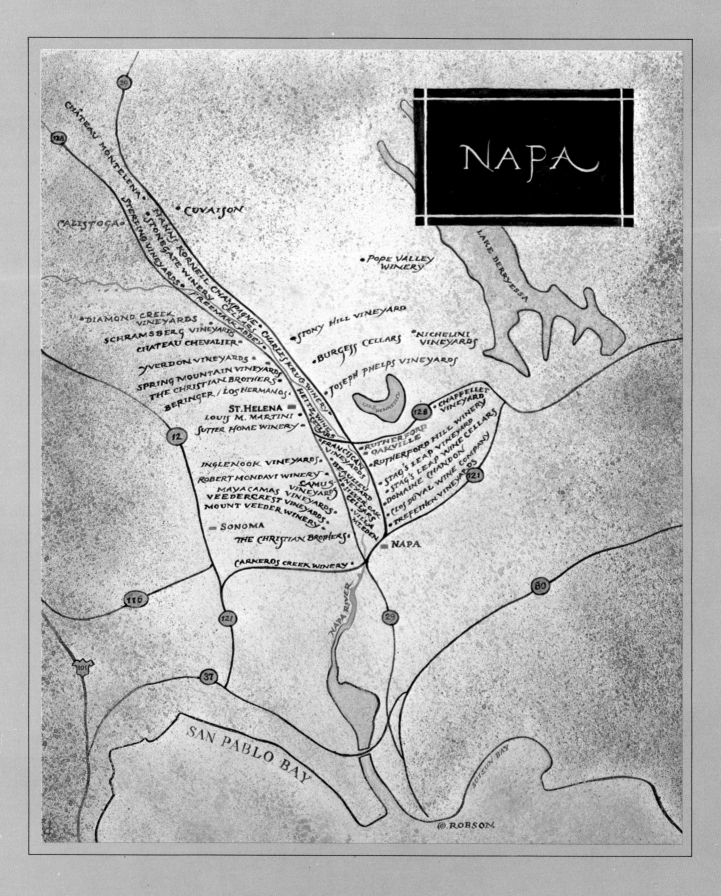

philes who seek their share of its modest 25,000-cases-per-annum production.

The owners of the present Freemark Abbey include Charles A. Carpy, of a pioneer Napa Valley family; vineyardist Laurie Wood; William Jaeger, Jr., also of Napa; and R. Bradford Webb, one of the state's leading biochemists, who had been the creative operator of Hanzell for the late Ambassador Zellerbach.

Production was and is essentially limited to four varietal wines: Pinot Chardonnay, Johannisberg Riesling, Cabernet Sauvignon, and Pinot Noir. Of particular interest to many winelovers are the Cabernet Sauvignon grapes from the John Bosche vineyard, a Rutherford neighbor of the famed Beaulieu Vineyard, where the Georges de Latour Private Reserve wine is made. The Freemark Abbey Cabernet Sauvignon from these grapes always carries the Bosche designation on

At Freemark Abbey: checking the sugar content of Johannisberg Riesling

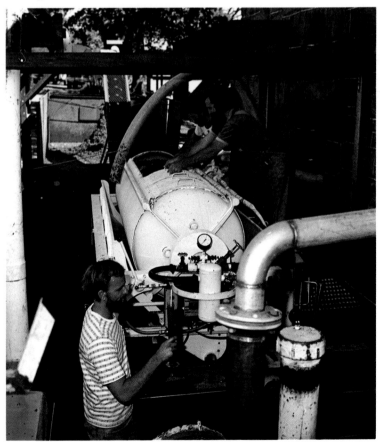

its label. Select lactobacillus strains are added to the crush of red wines to assure the malo-lactic fermentation, with its subsequent reduction of total acidity. New wines are held in stainless steel for racking, with fining and filtration at a minimum. The Cabernet Sauvignon, with 10 percent Merlot, the Pinot Noir, and the Chardonnay are aged in Nevers oak, the Johannisberg Riesling kept softly and gently fragrant in the large American-oak casks.

In 1973, by dint of the skill of Brad Webb and winemaker Jerry Luper, gondolas of Johannisberg Riesling grapes with fully developed *Botrytis cinerea* produced the incredible Edelwein not incorrectly likened to a fine German *Beerenauslese*. In 1976, a difficult harvest year, luck smiled again and Edelwein II began its life in the crusher with an incredible refractometer reading of 35 sugar and a total acidity of .95.

Every year, approximately 600 cases of Petite Sirah are produced from York Creek Vineyard grapes from Spring Mountain. Connoisseurs stand in line for it, and know that further bottle aging will develop rounded bouquet and description-defying depth.

SAMPLER SELECTION

Johannisberg Riesling (Napa Valley). Released after one year in wood, one year in glass. Rich, dry, elegant.

Pinot Chardonnay (Napa Valley). Each vintage more firmly establishes this as one of California's greatest white wines.

Cabernet Sauvignon (Napa Valley). Like the Cabernet Bosche, these dark, big, tannic wines need time to become drinkable.

Petite Sirah (Napa Valley). York Creek grapes from nonirrigated mountain vineyards build an enormously rich wine.

HANNS KORNELL CHAMPAGNE CELLARS

Larkmead Lane, St. Helena, California 94574

Hanns Kornell is a third-generation winemaker who began his career in Upper Silesia at the age of four, helping to clean bottles for his grandfather in the family winery. Academic education in enology began at Geisenheim, with on-the-job training in Épernay, Burgundy, and finally in Italy where he learned the secrets of vermouth's aromatic infusion. Before returning home to Germany, there was practical experience with bottling techniques in England.

After fleeing Germany in 1939, Kornell got his first significant break with his appointment as champagne maker for the memorable Fountaingrove Winery of Santa Rosa. With scrimping and saving, by 1952 he had accumulated just enough to lease the Sonoma Wine Company in Sonoma. "Bottle by bottle, I built the business, taking orders for wine by day, filling them by night. I lived on six hundred dollars that first year. I ate a lot of salami."

In 1958, with an inventory of 5,000 bottles, he was ready for his own winery. He found it on Larkmead Lane—a fine old stone winery built in 1845 and operated in the post-Repeal era as Larkmead Cellars.

There was a time when many of the leading California champagnes were brought up to their sparkling finish in the Hanns Kornell Champagne Cellars. But today, the more than two million bottles in those stone cellars are exclusively Kornell wines. Kornell has an abiding affection for Johannisberg Riesling, and his *cuvées* often run a maverick course. Sehr Trocken is just such a maverick wine, having no *dosage* and, unlike most California champagnes, being made primarily from Riesling. Honored with gold-medal awards from tasting competitions at home and abroad, it is a connoisseur's selection—dry, dry, dry, and pungent with the yeastiness of the true "champagne nose." Kornell utilizes Pinot Blanc and Sémillon as well as Riesling. All his sparkling wines are bottled, fermented, aged, then shipped in their original bottles in the classic *méthode champenoise* tradition,

SAMPLER SELECTION

Hanns Kornell Sehr Trocken. Often as much as six years "on the yeast," an intensely dry, crisply brilliant wine.

Hanns Kornell Brut. Drier than many California champagnes of this *dosage*. A beautiful golden straw color and fine bead.

Hanns Kornell Extra Dry. To many, the favorite for its more gentle mien and fruity roundness, barely edged with sweetness.

HEITZ WINE CELLARS

500 Taplin Road, St. Helena, California 94574

From the day that he received his master's degree in enology from UC–Davis, Joe Heitz has moved toward his winemaking goals with uncomplicated simplicity, uncompromising and, ultimately, highly rewarded. Today his name is synonymous with the finest of California wines. His vintage Cabernet Sauvignons are favorably compared with the finest growths of Bordeaux, and his multi-lot Chardonnays frequently with the best *grand cru* growths of the Côte de Beaune, Meursault, or Montrachet.

Before establishing his own winery, there were significant years in the fifties with André Tchelistcheff in the lab at Beaulieu, and a few years of giving courses in enology at Fresno State College. In 1961 Joe and his bride, Alice, bought a small winery surrounded by 8 acres of Grignolino grapes which the former owner had vinted for his "Only One" winery. With the tenacity for which he has become famous, Joe quickly developed an attachment to Grignolino, giving the Piedmontese variety a Napa Valley distinction the grape has not known before or since. Vintage Grignolino Rosé at a modest $3 is always on the Heitz list of offerings, along with the more noble and expensive varieties that are collectors' items. One example of the interesting wines he has cellared is featured on his list as Cellar Treasure Angelica, a wine too often scorned by wine snobs who don't know what they're missing.

Joe has an answer for critics of the pricing of Heitz wines, many of whom will pay as much or more for European growths of lesser quality. "The wines are limited, require minute attention and long-term aging. I work long, hard hours to make a fine wine, and so I feel I am entitled to a fine price. Our pricing is not

Joe Heitz makes beautiful wines no matter what the weather

based on supply and demand alone, but actually on the kind of quality that I try to get into my wine."

In support of his theory, there is a waiting list of wine merchants all across the land hoping they'll have even a token supply of Heitz wines.

SAMPLER SELECTION

Pinot Chardonnay (Napa Valley). Each vintage lot carries its code number, and each is dry, golden, wood-aged, distinguished.

Grignolino Rosé (Napa Valley). Characteristically orange-pink in hue, fragrant of its fruit, dry, surprisingly silky.

Cabernet Sauvignon (Martha's Vineyard). Among the finest clarets of the world, each vintage a cellar treasure.

Cellar Treasure Angelica. Rich wine of golden amber color, luxuriously sweet and mellow—music by candlelight.

INGLENOOK VINEYARDS

Highway 29, Rutherford, California 94573

No winery in California has a more romantic history than Inglenook. Its founder, Finnish sea captain Gustave Ferdinand Niebaum, bought the young vineyard in 1879 from the Scotsman who gave the property its name, which means "cozy corner," an apt description of this property tucked protectively into the Mayacamas foothills.

In his corner of the foothills, Captain Niebaum built a grand mansion in 1879, and he spared no expense in building the winery, completed in 1887. The years have softened the majestic exterior with vines that turn a glowing red in autumn. Fermentation is no longer conducted as it was in Niebaum's day, on the top floor, but the raked gravel corridors which tunnel into the shelter knoll still hold 1,000-gallon oak oval casks filled with aging red wines.

A corner of the baronial Inglenook tasting room

Shortly after Repeal, ownership of Inglenook had passed to John Daniel, Jr., a grand-nephew of the founder. Speaking of his red wines, he once told me, "Wines, you know, are like children. Each one develops differently. The wines in all these casks, as you can see from these chalked scribbles, are Cabernet Sauvignon. No two of them are identical. We could blend them all together, of course, but some of them are just too outstanding to lose." Daniel's feeling for the casks of Cabernet Sauvignon resulted in "cask bottling" at Inglenook, a practice which was started in the late thirties and continues today.

In 1964 John Daniel, Jr., sold the winery (but not the mansion and its adjacent vineyard) to Heublein. The mansion was used in a television movie, "Killer Bees," starring Gloria Swanson as the mysterious bee-loving matriarch of a wine dynasty. I played the role of the Episcopal priest summoned for the heroine's last rites. In late 1976, the great mansion became the home of Francis Ford Coppolla, director of "The Godfather."

In 1971 a change of policy brought young Thomas Ferrell to Inglenook as winemaker. A graduate of UC–Davis and a member of the American Society of Enologists, he brings uncompromising standards as well as talent to the broad spectrum of wines bearing the Inglenook label. A newly constructed and expanded fermentation and aging facility, completed in 1974, provides Ferrell with deluxe equipment for fine winemaking.

Inglenook table wines are now grouped into four distinct bottlings: (1) Inglenook Navalle (a contraction of Napa and Valley) are modestly priced generic and varietal wines from California-grown grapes; (2) Inglenook Vintage wines come from grapes of Napa, Mendocino, and Sonoma counties carrying vintage dates; (3) Inglenook Estate Bottled wines are vintage-dated, from the Napa Valley, all top varietals including the famed Cabernet Sauvignon and Charbono, plus exciting new white wines from Chardonnay, Johannisberg Riesling, and Gewürztraminer; (4) Inglenook Cask Bottling, in limited production of Cabernet Sauvignon, Red Pinot (Pinot St. George), and Pinot Noir.

Estate Bottled Chardonnay (Napa Valley). Held on the skins eight hours, fermented at 45° F. A big, oak-aged, virile, white poem.

Estate Bottled Johannisberg Riesling. Allowed two months to complete fermentation. Flowery, fragrant, essentially dry.

Estate Bottled Gewürztraminer. As freshly pungent and fragrant as nasturtiums in a summer garden. Beautiful wine!

Estate Bottled Cabernet Sauvignon. Soft and velvety wine with an intriguing pepperiness. Cask editions worth long holding.

CHARLES KRUG WINERY

Highway 29, St. Helena, California 94574

The Charles Krug Winery was established in St. Helena in 1860 by Prussian-born Charles Krug, who had come from Germany to San Francisco in 1852. There, working at the U.S. Mint under the dynamic Agoston Haraszthy, he was infected by his enthusiasm for winemaking possibilities in California. In 1860, Krug married General Vallejo's grand-niece, Caroline, and, fired by ambition, moved to the Napa Valley, where his bride owned land. The Charles Krug Winery became a great estate of far-reaching fame, but at the time of Krug's death in 1892, phylloxera had devastated his vineyards, and he was deeply in debt.

In 1943 the sadly neglected winery facilities and ranch, owned then by James K. Moffitt's family, were sold to Cesare Mondavi. The $75,000 purchase price included two houses, a dilapidated winery, and 150 acres of land. With enormous energy, thrift, and skill, the Mondavi family made a net profit of $77,000 that first year, solidly establishing this immigrant family as worthy inheritors of the Charles Krug wine traditions. Despite the deplorable conditions of the winery equipment, Cesare Mondavi, with the assistance of his sons, Robert and Peter, bottled bulk wines that at once found a demand in the market.

Cesare Mondavi died in 1959, leaving his widow, Rosa, as the head of the family corporation and Robert

NAPA WINE LABELS

and Peter as the winemakers. Innovations by Robert, trained in enology after graduation from Stanford in 1937, emphasized longer, cooler fermentation of white wines than was common practice at the time. Glass-lined tanks, purchased from breweries, were used to hold wines before bottling, preventing excessive woodiness. In 1955 a wine called White Pinot was rechristened Chenin Blanc after its 100 percent varietal source. With notable brilliance, fresh perfume from cool fermentation, and a certain residual sweetness, it not only won a gold medal at the Sacramento Fair but was the first California white wine to become so popular that its makers had to place it on allocation to dealers.

Differences began to arise between Robert, who tended to pioneer new enological frontiers, and Peter, who held to more traditional ways. In 1966, Robert left the family firm to establish his own winery at Oakville, while Peter and their mother, Rosa Mondavi, administered the operation of the Charles Krug Winery. The August Moon Concerts, since 1965 a popular tourist attraction, are conducted on the lawn beneath the great oaks of the Krug Estate, where members of the Mondavi family live in their own houses within the flower-bordered compound.

The Charles Krug Winery owns 1,200 acres of vine but much of the wine in their 3 1/2-million-gallon storage space is made from grapes bought from other growers. The finest wines, such as the Vintage Selection Cabernet Sauvignon, honoring Cesare Mondavi, and the immensely popular Moscato di Canelli, are listed as "when available," but the regular varietals and CK jug generic wines are sufficient to supply retail customers and the nation's restaurants with dependably excellent house wines of fine value at a moderate price. The Chablis, with a significant percentage of Chardonnay press wine, is in my opinion one of the state's best buys in this much-abused category; it is crisp, dry, and with enough Chardonnay character to warrant a Chablis title. And Charles Krug Napa Valley Chenin Blanc is a popular standard, essential on any wine list across the land.

SAMPLER SELECTION

Napa Valley Chablis. Nonvintage wine, always dependable, dry, crisp, clean, inexpensive.

Napa Valley Blanc Fumé. A vintage wine carrying the flowery and fruit charms of its Loire namesake.

Napa Valley Chenin Blanc. When well-chilled, the apparent sweetness seems to add to the pleasing silkiness of the wine.

Napa Valley Cabernet Sauvignon—Vintage Selection. Oak-aged to soft maturity in 50-gallon barrels before release.

LOUIS M. MARTINI

Highway 29, St. Helena, California 94574

Both wine and wisdom were in the heritage from the late Louis M. Martini, who was born in 1887 on the Italian Riviera at Pietra Ligure, and died in California in 1974. "Industry without art is brutality," he once told me. "Infallible grace of instinct makes a winemaster of one man, while avarice makes an industrial brute of another."

In one of the winery's brochures is the statement "Wine is a food beverage intended to make our meals more enjoyable each and every day." In the wide range of wines offered under the Martini label, from the least expensive generic jug wine to the aged Special Selection varietals and richly mellow dessert wines, the dominant consideration has been the pleasure-giving potential of wine to enhance food.

In 1937, Louis acquired a large vineyard 1,000 feet above the Napa Valley floor, extending across the Napa–Sonoma line in the Mayacamas Mountains. Since it was in both Napa and Sonoma counties and was truly a mountain vineyard, where nonirrigated vines struggled with the elements to produce grapes rich in concentration, low in tonnage yield, it was logical for the Martini labels to read neither Napa nor Sonoma but California Mountain. The phrase moved into the American wine vocabulary quickly after Louis bottled a good red and a good white wine, popularly priced, and labeled the red, California Mountain Red Wine (or Mountain Burgundy) and the white, Mountain Chablis. Today, "California Mountain" means "inexpensive" but the Louis M. Martini Mountain Cabernet Sauvignon is properly named not because it is a low-priced

Louis M. and Louis P. Martini, father and son, relaxing in front of their rock-solid winery

wine but because it does indeed come from one of the Martini mountain vineyards.

The Martini vineyards now total more than 1,000 acres, including acreage in the cool Carneros region, a ranch in the Healdsburg area, as well as Monte Rosso, and a new acquisition in Chiles Valley.

It is the red wines of the Louis M. Martini vineyards and winery that connoisseurs treasure: the Cabernet Sauvignon, Zinfandel, Barbera, and Pinot Noir. The Private Reserve labels are the wines regularly offered which have been given added bottle aging, while the Special Selection labels are wines from outstanding years, produced in small lots and having greater quality and aging potential. Louis P. Martini, the son of the founder and now the head of the company, has made some experimental lots, available at the winery only, where the celebrated Moscato Amabile is still enchanting winelovers with its gentle effervescence and delicate perfume.

The Martini white wines, particularly good accompaniments for food, are dry, crisp, and brilliant, always to be enjoyed young. The Gewürztraminer is unique among California examples for its dryness, and in its 100 percent varietal composition, aromatic, spicy, and appetizing. The Johannisberg Riesling is subtle,

soft, almost fragile in its delicacy on early release, suggesting a Moselle wine.

Ever since Louis P. Martini graduated, in 1940, from the University of California at Berkeley—in the banner class that included agriculture and enology majors Myron Nightingale, winemaster today at Beringer, Charles Crawford, chief enologist at Gallo, and Zev Halperin of Christian Brothers—he had been unobtrusively active in extending the range and reputation of the Martini name. There is a measure of true greatness in Louis P. that kept him working quietly in the shadow of his father's genius until the older man was ready, at the close of his life, to surrender the reins of management. There are no more highly respected wines made in California today than those of the winery that continues to bear the Martini name.

SAMPLER SELECTION

Mountain Folle Blanche. Vintage wine, uniquely tart, crisp as lettuce, ideal with shellfish.

Mountain Gewürztraminer. Produced dry in the tradition of Alsace. Spicy and fruity; vintage, and in limited supply.

Mountain Merlot. Pure Merlot of distinctive tartness and familial relationship to Cabernet Sauvignon.

Mountain Cabernet Sauvignon. A wine of consistent elegance and breed from the finest grapes, all mountain-grown.

MAYACAMAS VINEYARDS

1155 Lokoya Road, Napa, California 94558

In 1889 a sword engraver from Stuttgart, Germany, turned pickle merchant in San Francisco, made his way up through the tangled scrub and rocky dells of Mt. Veeder to establish a small vineyard and winery at an elevation of 2,000 feet. This is the kind of terrain that the Roman poet Ausonius called the "land Bacchus loves." Though difficulties—such as swarms of locusts, marauding birds, mountain thunderstorms —abound, when the sun shines bright the vines, nourished by the volcanic soil and natural rainfall, yield grapes that concentrate a wonderful richness.

In 1941 petroleum engineer Jack Taylor and his

wife, Mary, acquired the 400-acre property with its old graystone winery and distillery and its gnarled Zinfandel vines. They renamed it after the mountains that the Indians called Mayacamas ("cry of the mountain lion"), and even today the howl of the cougar is not unknown in this wilderness paradise.

In 1968, Bob Travers, another young petroleum engineer from Stanford, turned to wine production, and, after an apprenticeship with Joe Heitz, he took over Mayacamas Vineyards with a small group of investors. That September the Travers's first child arrived just when the Zinfandel grapes were ready to be harvested. By the time Bob got around to picking them, the must reading registered a dismaying 27.5 sugar, which zoomed to a Balling reading higher than 35°, attributable to some raisined grapes. By rule-of-thumb conversion, this indicated that the alcoholic

The Late Harvest Zinfandel of Mayacamas, with the terraced vines on the upper slopes of Mt. Veeder in the background

content of the wine might be higher than 17 percent. Any reading higher than the critical 15 percent suggests a "stuck" fermentation, that is, the annihilation of the yeasts by the alcohol before all the sugar is converted. "We kept our cool . . . and prayed a lot," Bob Travers remembers. When with ears pressed to the casks they discerned no more sounds of bubbling within, a reading was taken. The wine was bone-dry, and registering a 17-plus percent alcohol. Impossible! Obviously those yeast cells didn't know they couldn't go on converting grape sugar at over 15 percent alcohol, so they did it anyway!

After many complications, including the payment of higher taxes because of the alcohol content, and a refusal to call the big Zinfandel Port, the wine emerged as "Mayacamas Vineyards 1968 Late Harvest Zinfandel—Alcohol 17 1/2 Percent by Volume." I dubbed it "the Miracle at Mayacamas," and all the world beat a track to the Travers's cellar doors. In 1972, Travers produced another Late Harvest Zinfandel, and again in 1974, but the wines are too big to serve with anything but cheese and fruit after dining. They served primarily to call winelovers' attention to the Chardonnay from the terraced vineyards established by Jack Taylor and to the rich Cabernet Sauvignon developed by Bob Travers. All the Mayacamas wines are 100 percent varietal and emphasize only these three titles.

SAMPLER SELECTION

Chardonnay (Napa Valley). Big wines of true varietal character, aged one year in American oak, six months in French oak.

Zinfandel (Napa Valley). "Late Harvest" editions are not regularly produced. (Sometimes a Zinfandel Rosé is added.) The big robust wines are intensely flavored to last a lifetime.

Cabernet Sauvignon (Napa Valley). Each vintage edition needs at least five years before its stature can be adequately judged.

ROBERT MONDAVI WINERY

Highway 29, Oakville, California 94562

When he broke away from the family winery in

Michael Mondavi at work filling barrels of wine

1966 to put his own winemaking theories into practice, Robert Mondavi's career had its real beginning . . . at age fifty-four. Today the Robert Mondavi Winery, with its grand archway and tower in the California mission style of architecture, is a Napa Valley landmark, housing the equipment for this century's most exciting developments in California winemaking. The proliferation of storage and fermentation capacity to millions of gallons is a minor accomplishment compared with the advances in wine quality brought about by the creative drive of Robert Mondavi. He was assisted in no small measure by his talented sons Michael and young Tim in the formulation of these new trend-setting methods that have influenced the winemaking industry.

To the layman the dazzling stainless-steel fermentation equipment, the horizontal rotating tanks, the centrifuges, the pyramids of French oak, German oak, and Yugoslavian oak barrels, the glass-enclosed laboratories seem implements of modern alchemy. All serve to bring added dimension to the wines, to extract ever more and more from the potential in the grape, to aid in achieving wine's main purpose—its harmony with food at table. There is not a wine country in Europe or Australia that has not been visited by Robert Mondavi. It is as if two thousand years of winemaking, all the techniques developed since Noah, were as nothing before what can be done now. "Unfiltered" or "Unfined," like "Reserve," on a Mondavi label is a signal to the ardent collector that these bottlings are in some way superior, the wines more whole and natural; like so many Mondavi ideas, these bottles lead the way to better wine.

From 600 acres of their own vines Robert and Michael Mondavi make 40 percent of their wines, and they have contract arrangements for additional grapes. The facility is used to produce more wines than those emerging under the Robert Mondavi label; only the premium production carries their name.

SAMPLER SELECTION

Johannisberg Riesling (Napa Valley). Soft, flowery, dry, clean; centrifuged nectar. A mere touch of oak.

Chardonnay (Napa Valley). Full, round, with varietal depth and fragrance even after 15 months in oak. A big, intense wine.

Fumé Blanc (Napa Valley). Light, dry, golden wine of the Sauvignon Blanc grape. Long, silky, ideal with fish.

Cabernet Sauvignon (Napa Valley). A "paprika dustiness" edges this always superb wine toward distinctive merit.

Pinot Noir (Napa Valley). Each vintage moves toward a greater realization of the grape's true, full, dry dignity.

MOUNT VEEDER WINERY

1999 Mt. Veeder Road, Napa, California 94558

Originally this was a summer home in the Mayacamas Mountains, nestling among the trees and rocks, with a prune orchard but no vineyard. Eventually the aura of the Napa Valley and its winemaking traditions moved Arlene and Michael Bernstein to replace the orchard with grapevines and to build a pocket-size winery. "We're a two-man operation," Michael told me. "I dug the holes, Arlene planted the vines, and I make the wine." Today, there are 13 acres of Cabernet Sauvignon vines, plus token representations of Cabernet Franc, Merlot, Malbec, and Petit Verdot to complete the claret spectrum, plus 2 acres of Zinfandel and 2 acres of Chenin Blanc. The San Francisco lawyer-turned-winemaker, having done a brief stint as apprentice at the Robert Mondavi Winery, is now making wines of exceptional merit as he faces the new challenge which he created.

SAMPLER SELECTION

Chardonnay (Napa Valley). Vinted from purchased premium grapes, fermented in French-oak barrels. Of classic mien.

Cabernet Sauvignon (Napa Valley). Deep, dark, red-purple wine of pure Cabernet richness with tannins for long life and balance.

NICHELINI VINEYARDS

2349 Lower Chiles Rd., St. Helena, California 94574

Winemaking has been going on almost without interruption here ever since 1890, when Anton Nichelini came to the valley from Switzerland. Then as now, good, sound table wines from good, sound grapes brought customers to the cellar doors. At 900 feet above sea level, with its own microclimate and soil complexity, the Chiles Valley is attracting more and more attention from vineyardists of Napa, below.

James and Rosemary Nichelini put the welcome mat out in an engaging way, and winelovers may sit on the open terrace and sample wines at leisure, so the detour is worth the effort.

SAMPLER SELECTION

Chenin Blanc (Napa Valley). Fresh and fruity, the zing of the earth giving substance to the dry white wine.

Sauvignon Vert (Napa Valley). Long one of the Nichelini specialties. Crisp, clean, dry; not great, but good.

JOSEPH PHELPS VINEYARDS

200 Taplin Road, St. Helena, California 94574

Driving north on the Silverado Trail, the casual tourist cannot miss the freshly painted green-and-white schoolhouse topped with a belfry. It is a part of the 670-acre former cattle ranch that Joseph Phelps has adopted as a temporary home. An interior valley of gentle knolls is now ribbed with 120 acres of Cabernet Sauvignon, Merlot, Cabernet Franc, Zinfandel, and Syrah, the last a stock—distinctly different from the more common planting of Petite Sirah—imported to California from the Rhône by Professor Olmo.

Phelps, the president of the Hensel Phelps Construction Company, of Colorado, came into wine with innocent inadvertence. On vacation in Italy he became fascinated with both the taste and the production of Italian wines. His company's commission to build the two Souverain wineries, one in Napa and the other on a multi-million-dollar scale at Geyserville in the Alexander Valley, reinforced his desire to build a winery of his own. Phelps located his double-winged winery, built from recycled lumber, on a rise of land above the

The old schoolhouse at Joseph Phelps Vineyards, a landmark on the Silverado Trail

oak-shaded meadow, without losing a single tree.

As winemaker, Phelps secured young Walter Schug, a graduate of the famous center for the study of viticulture and enology in Geisenheim in the German Rheingau. It is not surprising that the first wine released from the winery was Johannisberg Riesling of the 1973 vintage. Under full production, the goal is 40,000 cases of wine annually by 1979.

On my first visit I tasted the 1975 Special Selection Johannisberg Riesling, which remains in my memory as perhaps the finest vinification of this grape I have ever experienced in California. Statistically, it had 10 percent residual sugar, which is very sweet, but the sweetness was balanced with .94 total acidity, while a light 10 percent alcohol by volume allowed a delicacy hauntingly reminiscent of fine *Beerenauslese* of the Rhine. But the color, a brilliant lemon yellow, was equally striking. Totally botrytised grapes were used, and the slow, cool fermentation was conducted by Schug with the care of a conscientious baby-sitter for four and a half months at 58° F. Any cooler and fermentation would have stopped.

Already available in eighteen states, Joseph Phelps wines are bound to become highly prized members of California's growing family of premium wines.

SAMPLER SELECTION

Johannisberg Riesling (Napa Valley). A 100 percent flowery varietal wine of delicacy and clean brilliance.

Gewürztraminer (Yountville). Aged briefly in Schug's style—in German-oak ovals, with 1 percent residual sugar.

Chardonnay (Napa Valley). A generous, big wine of full bouquet with its oak aging not overshadowing the fruit.

Cabernet Sauvignon (Stanton Estate). Blended with 5 percent Merlot; ready in the early eighties. Aged in French-oak barrels.

POPE VALLEY WINERY

6613 Pope Valley Road, Pope Valley, California 94567

In 1972 the James Devitt family undertook to restore this gravity-flow winery, built into the side of a slate hill in 1910. Wine is being made here as it was early in this century at almost every winery: grapes are delivered to the crusher on the top (third) floor; the juice flows naturally to the fermenters on the second floor; the finished young wine flows, still by gravity, to aging and storage tanks on the cool ground floor. Devitt, an electronics engineer (as are many other California winemakers), began his alliance with vines and wines as an avocation. Now it is a full-time, rewarding occupation. Making fine wine has become his primary ambition, leading to the acquisition of new stainless-steel fermenting tanks, modern presses, and European-oak barrels for aging. None of the rustic charm of the place has been lost, and visitors may enjoy picnic lunches under giant oaks while delighting in the rural quiet of old California.

In line with the goals of fine winemaking, James

and Robert Devitt (the latter is in charge of winemaking) supplement the grapes from their own 65 acres of vines with premium grapes from the Dry Creek area of Sonoma.

SAMPLER SELECTION

Sauvignon Blanc (Pope Valley). Light, dry, soft wine of modest price; pleasing with shellfish and trout.

Cabernet Sauvignon (Napa and Sonoma). One of the finest wines produced by the James Devitt family; richly complex.

RUTHERFORD HILL WINERY

Souverain Road at Silverado Trail, Rutherford, California 94573

"Wineries used to be perennials, with dependable flowering each new vintage season," an astute observer of the California wine scene remarked to me. "Now, they're row crops . . . in and out!" Tucked away in the hills just east of the Silverado Trail, this handsome, modern winery designed by John Marsh Davis was built in the early 1970s after Pillsbury of Minneapolis had bought the property then known as Souverain Cellars. Pillsbury sold their interest in 1976 to a group of seasoned vineyardists and winemakers that included William P. Jaeger, Jr., Charles Carpy of Freemark Abbey, Brad Webb, who brought his considerable skills in wine technology, and Phil Baxter, their winemaker.

The inventory of existing wines was sold off in 1976, emerging under several old and new labels of other wineries. The new company releases their wines under the Rutherford Hill Winery label. Pure varietal wines, Gewürztraminer, Johannisberg Riesling, Pinot Noir, Cabernet Sauvignon, and Zinfandel, are featured. An exceptional Zinfandel from the Giles Mead vineyard on Atlas Peak, one of the highest Napa Valley regions where the vine grows, is also an exclusive source of great promise. The production goal is 40,000 cases annually. Drawing upon splendid vineyards for its grapes, Rutherford Hill would seem to be on the road to greater stability and lasting achievement.

Jamie and Jack Davies enjoy a private tasting of
Schramsberg champagnes

SCHRAMSBERG VINEYARDS

Schramsberg Road, Calistoga, California 94515

Jack Davies and his wife, Jamie, came to Calistoga as young wine enthusiasts. When they found Schramsberg it was all there, not only the tradition and the history, but the house, the caves, some old vines—a relic of the great winemaking days a century or more ago. The Davies's transformation began in 1965. The caves hewn from the rocks by Chinese laborers in the last century would henceforth house only sparkling wines. New vineyards of Chardonnay, Pinot Noir, Pinot Blanc, and Napa Gamay were planted; an additional 25 acres have been acquired and an additional 3,500 square feet of winemaking room added, as the goal of 12,000 cases yearly nears realization.

In champagne making, there is a special marketing formula: for every bottle you market, you must have as many in reserve as the number of years you age each bottle marketed. For Davies at present that is a costly three years, which translates into space for 36,000 cases, or 432,000 bottles. In short, it means filling those caves with an expensive resting inventory.

André Tchelistcheff became the first consultant at Schramsberg, and he recalls well the day of their first harvest, when the automatic press failed to work. "Madame," he announced to Jamie, "your duty is clear!" The slight, bewildered mistress of the house gasped, "Not me!" But there was no denying the gallant winemaster, who insisted, "Oui, madame!" and escorted her into the grapes . . . minus her stockings.

Twelve years have added luster to the wine named Schramsberg, and it is found today on all the great wine lists of the country.

All Schramsberg champagnes are produced by the classic *méthode champenoise* technique, the secondary fermentation occurring in the same bottle that goes to market, after hand riddling, racking, and disgorging have removed the claw of sediment. The Blanc de Noirs, an absolute *tour de force* of brilliant pale-gold wine without a tinge of color from the black skins, often appears daringly in a clear bottle.

There are six Schramsberg wines: the Blanc de Blancs, predominantly from Chardonnay; Blanc de Noirs from free-run Pinot Noir, with a little Pinot Blanc for silky body; Cuvee de Gamay, a salmon-pink wine of free-run Napa Gamay grapes with some added Pinot Noir; Blanc de Blancs Reserve Cuvée, select lots of each vintage left "longer on the yeasts"; Crémant, a demi-sec dessert champagne from the hybrid Flora; and the newest wine, Cuvée Nature, a still wine from the Blanc de Noirs *cuvée*, very dry, high in acid (on sale at the winery only). Like the still champagne of France, it is delectable, in rare supply, and therefore super-chic.

SAMPLER SELECTION

Blanc de Blancs (Napa Valley Champagne). Two years on the yeasts. Substantial fruit in the bouquet. Dry, crisp.

Blanc de Noirs (Napa Valley Champagne). Three years on the yeasts. Classic richness and elegance. Improves with age.

Crémant (Demi-Sec Napa Valley Champagne). California's most distinguished dessert sparkler. Fragrant, sweet, golden.

Cuvée de Gamay (Napa Valley Champagne). Pale salmon-pink in color, recommended for fine luncheon service.

SILVER OAK CELLARS

915 Oakville Crossroad, Oakville, California 94562

With their 1972 vintage 100 percent Cabernet Sauvignon, aged three years in 50-gallon oak barrels, plus two years in the bottle, Justin Meyer and Raymond Duncan pioneered: they may possibly be the first winery in the valley offering only this one wine.

Approximately one half of their 1,000 acres of vineyards in Napa, Sonoma, and Lake counties is in Cabernet Sauvignon, in Meyer's opinion the finest grape variety of the region. It is not unreasonable to believe that both Silver Oak Cellars and the Franciscan Winery, which they acquired in 1976, can offer exceptional bottlings of this popular red-wine varietal.

In 1972 heavy rains that turned the vineyard rows into muddy sloughs diluted the grape's concentration and diminished its complexity. This debut wine shows evidence of that weakness, but wines from the more

A Victorian stained-glass window in the Tiburcio Parrott house, home of Spring Mountain's Michael Robbins

substantial harvests of both '73 and '74 will be a better measure of this winery's achievement.

Cabernet Sauvignon (North Coast). Vintage blending of grapes from three counties, always five years old before release.

SPRING MOUNTAIN VINEYARDS

2805 Spring Mountain Road, St. Helena, California 94574

If it is true that every man at some time would like to have a yacht, an oil well, a mistress, or a restaurant (not necessarily in that order), a winery with a mansion would also fit into this inventory of Walter Mitty fantasy. In 1968 Shirley and Michael Robbins of southern California found a small but stately mansion with a terraced vineyard just north of Beringer and its Rhine House, bought it as a second home, began restoration, and found themselves entering the wine business, as it were, by the back door. At first the trim cellar lined with oak barrels was merely an elegant appurtenance. The next step, bonding that cellar as a winery called Spring Mountain, added a new dimension to the "double" life of Michael Robbins, a lawyer who was commuting regularly between Los Angeles and St. Helena. The first wine was a Sauvignon Blanc, bought from Wente Bros. and cellared in St. Helena. A small cameo-etching of the little house became the trademark on the Spring Mountain label, which was soon to appear on spectacular vintages of Chardonnay and blends of Cabernet Sauvignon. By now, the real-estate-lawyer-turned-winemaker was deeply into the business of premium winemaking.

In 1974 Shirley and Michael found an even grander house—the Tiburcio Parrott home—with a winery including hillside caves. There are 110 acres of hillside vines, now replanted. This final step of the project brought Robbins's double life to an end: he has become a full-time vintner.

SAMPLER SELECTION

Sauvignon Blanc (Napa Valley). A vintage selection, always bone-dry, crisp and golden, suggesting a Graves of Bordeaux.

Chardonnay (Napa Valley). Each successive vintage has rated high in critical esteem. Aging in French oak. Soft, splendid.

Cabernet Sauvignon (Napa Valley). Grapes from contracted acres produce wine in the French tradition, requiring long aging.

Cabernet Franc (Late Harvest). An unusual wine, of 16.8 percent alcohol and 6 percent residual sugar. Ideal with cheese after dining.

STAG'S LEAP VINEYARD

6150 Silverado Trail, Napa, California 94558

A private road leads from the Silverado Trail to a small secluded valley just below the stony peaks of the mountains on the eastern border of the Napa Valley. A great sixteen-point Roosevelt elk once fell or leaped to his death from those stone cliffs to the slopes below. For years the great set of stag horns ornamented the stone manor house built in the last century by Howard Spencer Chase for his bride, Minnie Mizener, sister of the legendary Wilson and Henry Mizener. Hard times became Chase's master and in 1909 he sold the entire place to Clarence and Frances Grange.

Carl Doumani and a small group of investors purchased the property from widowed Frances Grange in 1970, and have slowly begun restoration of the manor house and replanting of the vineyard and gardens. From the 100 acres of vines replanted in Pinot Noir, Cabernet, and Merlot, some fine wines may emerge. From the existing Petite Syrah and Chenin Blanc vines, a token production already gives reason for great expectations.

SAMPLER SELECTION

Chenin Blanc (Napa Valley). Lovely, silky wine, not bitingly dry, tinged with residual sweetness.

Petite Syrah (Napa Valley). A big, beautiful wine of great substance; a wine of majestic quality, after long airing.

Wines aging in wood in the cellars—a veritable Fort Knox of Chardonnay and Cabernet Sauvignon—of Joe Heitz

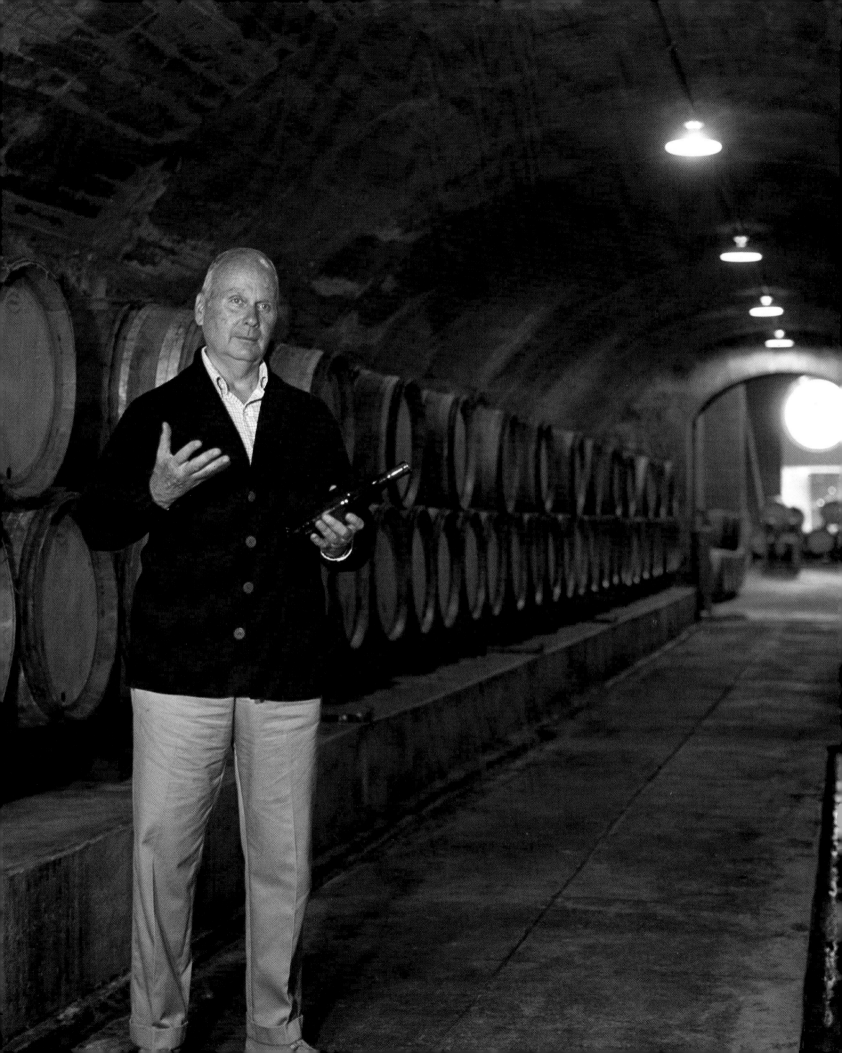

Warren Winiarski of Stag's Leap Wine Cellars

STAG'S LEAP WINE CELLARS

5766 Silverado Trail, Napa, California 94558

The legendary stag's leap of this area is enshrined in the names of two separately owned and operated wineries, a circumstance sometimes confusing to consumers. It is Stag's Leap Wine Cellars, purchased by Warren Winiarski in 1973, whose esteemed bottles are eagerly sought—and all too rarely found—by wine-lovers in all parts of the United States.

Winiarski completed his first crush in his new winery in 1973, a Cabernet Sauvignon that dazzled the wine world at a Paris tasting in May 1976. A completely French jury placed it first over a clutch of stellar First Growth clarets of Bordeaux. Shock waves from that event are still rippling in the sea of controversy surrounding California/French wine comparisons. In Winiarski's own estimation, and that of many,

including myself, his 1974 edition was even better.

After years of apprenticeship, at Souverain with Lee Stewart, at Beaulieu with André Tchelistcheff, and at the Robert Mondavi Winery in Oakville, Winiarski, with his wife, Barbara, their children, and a group of partners, operates his own vineyards and winery, where he can produce wines according to the highest ideals of winemaking. The 45-acre property contains his Cabernet Sauvignon and Merlot vines. White Riesling grapes come from the Birkmyer Vineyard of Wild Horse Valley. Fermentation of the Riesling is in oak tanks (for a softer wine), Cabernet Sauvignon and Merlot in stainless steel. A Chardonnay, his first, was made in 1976, and, released in 1978, rounded out the offerings of intense varietal wines.

SAMPLER SELECTION

Johannisberg Riesling (Birkmyer Vineyard). A long wine of delicate complexity, masculine in its solidity.

Gamay Beaujolais (Napa Valley). A combination of Napa Gamay for softness and Pinot Noir for intriguing fruitiness.

Cabernet Sauvignon (Stag's Leap Vineyards). So rich in substance you can almost chew it. Velvet-soft, full varietal fragrance.

Merlot (Stag's Leap Vineyards). In keeping with the winery policy, the varietal is emphasized, though touched with Cabernet Sauvignon.

STERLING VINEYARDS

111 Dunaweal Lane, Calistoga, California 94515

It took almost a decade to reach the goals Mike Stone shares with Peter Newton, his partner in the management of Sterling Vineyards. The parent company, Sterling International, which deals in the manufacture, conversion, and sale of paper products, has been unstinting in the funding of these objectives. The trellised vineyards were planted in 1964; the dazzling white winery was completed in 1973.

The first wine from Sterling's own grapes, a 1968 Merlot, was rich and balanced, reflecting the under-cropping techniques, which result in fewer berries of

Cabernet Sauvignon and Merlot vines lined up beneath the high rocks where the legendary stag is said to have made his famous leap

159

more concentrated complexity. The wine inaugurated a period of new importance for Merlot in California.

Winemaker Richard Forman, a UC–Davis graduate, traveled to the Beaujolais district of France to study the involved biochemistry of the *macération carbonique* technique, which might bring a special soft fruitiness to Merlot Primeur. Clusters of grapes, with the whole berries neither crushed nor de-stemmed, go into the stainless-steel vats; this results in fermentation taking place *inside* each berry, changing the sweetness to almost total dryness before the lot is transferred, after some light pressing, into French-oak barrels. The innovative wine won immediate acceptance.

Chenin Blanc, with infusions of as much as 30 percent Chardonnay; a Chardonnay from botrytised grapes that bring a tinge of pineapple to the taste; Cabernet Sauvignon blended with Merlot, undergoing a natural malo-lactic fermentation in 60-gallon French-oak barrels to soften acidity, emerging with a "tealike" tannic delicacy . . . these are a few of the exciting vintages that have earned Sterling the steady patronage of the California wine cognoscenti.

As an architectural gem and as a cultural center presenting grand opera, Sterling can enjoy a certain eminence. But the *raison d'être* of a winery remains wine, and that is being fulfilled magnificently. The winery has already passed the midpoint of its objective of 100,000 cases annually.

In August of 1977, the Coca-Cola Company acquired this distinguished California winery, whose announced plans include the retention of Michael Stone in his executive managerial role and Rick Forman as winemaker. The new ownership has also declared its intention of concentrating on premium estate-bottled wines, with the acquisition of more Napa Valley vineyard acreage toward this goal.

SAMPLER SELECTION

Blanc de Sauvignon (Napa Valley). Golden, dry wine of a balanced acidity and fruitiness. Silky, of rare finesse.

Pinot Chardonnay (Napa Valley). In some vintages, a big, bold wine 13.8 percent alcohol, 100 percent barrel-fermented.

Merlot (Napa Valley). Elegant, dark garnet in color, with tea and cherry fragrance. Pleasant to drink early, yet long-lived.

Cabernet Sauvignon (Napa Valley). With added Merlot for fragrant complexity; requires aging for full appreciation.

STONEGATE WINERY

1183 Dunaweal Lane, Calistoga, California 94515

West of Calistoga, the highway over the mountains to Sonoma curves upward through hillside farming plots which even before the turn of the century were planted to orchard and vine. On these steep slopes in 1969 James and Barbara Spaulding planted Cabernet Sauvignon and some Chardonnay and Merlot in place of gnarled old Mission vine stumps. Grape growing led naturally to winemaking. In 1973 they bonded a very small winery adjacent to a bungalow on Dunaweal Lane. On an outside concrete pad stands their compact, modern winemaking plant—crusher and thirteen jacketed stainless-steel tanks for controlled fermentation. Their son David now shares the increased responsibilities that have come with an additional 16 acres of vines surrounding the tiny winery. Annual production is geared to 5,000 cases, with the purchase of choice grapes from independent growers to round out their offerings. Robert Stemmler, who has had German training and California experience, is consultant.

SAMPLER SELECTION

Sauvignon Blanc (Napa Valley). Aged in Limousin-oak barrels, the estate-bottled wine has eloquent varietal bouquet.

Chardonnay (Napa Valley). The first from their own winery and hillside grapes was produced in 1975. Big, racy, fine.

Petite Sirah (Maryroy Vineyard). From a nearby vineyard on the Silverado Trail, purple-black; a huge wine with peppery finish.

Cabernet Sauvignon (Napa Valley). Aged in Nevers oak. Estate-bottled production of a rich wine of complex varietal bouquet.

Grand opera against a backdrop of vineyards, one of Sterling's summer attractions

STONY HILL VINEYARD

P.O. Box 308, St. Helena, California 94574

The annual supply of Stony Hill Napa Valley Pinot Chardonnay is the equivalent in cases of half of the entire production of Montrachet in a good year. The excellence of Le Montrachet and of Stony Hill's Pinot Chardonnay cannot be denied, though in most instances the argument must rest upon faith...faith in those lucky few whose tasting experience permits them to report on the glory of those wines.

In January 1977, Frederick Hoyt McCrea—the founder, with his wife, Eleanor, of Stony Hill Vineyard—died at the age of seventy-nine. He was among the first of the city dwellers to move into a second career of winemaking from a corporate boardroom, having retired to the Napa Valley in 1943 from McCann-Erickson of San Francisco. A thrifty man of pragmatic intelligence, he aimed at having his small winery make nothing but the finest product. He and Eleanor produced their first wine in 1952, and twenty-five succeeding vintages proved his decision to be right.

With the family and Michael Chelini, the vineyard and winery manager, Eleanor is continuing the noble legend of Stony Hill. "Because of the two-year drought, we may have to strip the vines of their fruit to save the life of the vines," she told me recently. "Last year you could *feel* the lack of rainfall in handling the bunches of berries, they were so light in weight." Even those lucky enough to be on the Stony Hill mailing list (the only way to buy their wines) will be strictly rationed in the amounts they can purchase.

In the lowest part of the vineyard is a tiny plot of Sémillon grapes, cuttings from the Sauternes vines pioneered in California at the Wente vineyards in Livermore. Eleanor and Fred embarked upon an experiment not unrelated to the *vino santo* techniques of Tuscany or the *recioto de Soave* using the loft-dried grapes of the Veneto. Picked at 26° Balling of sugar, the grapes were laid out on prune-drying trays for five to ten days in the sun, after which the sugar content would soar to 36°. (The first year the raccoons found these trays a marvelous buffet set out just for them!)

Cool fermentation, stopped at 8 percent residual sugar and 13 percent alcohol by volume, produced a straw-gold wine of extraordinary richness not unlike a Château d'Yquem. Wine merchant Darrell Corti of Sacramento is the fortunate and exclusive purveyor of this wine, which Fred declared "a curiosity, not commercial" even though Corti customers gladly pay $6 a tenth, when they can get it.

No man can have a greater monument to his memory than his created works. As such, the Stony Hill Vineyard wines maintain Fred McCrea's ideal of perfection for winelovers everywhere.

SAMPLER SELECTION

Pinot Chardonnay (Napa Valley). Subtle differences exist with each vintage. All long-lived, full-bodied, glorious.

White Riesling (Napa Valley). First editions were made dry, later with slight residual sugar. Very fruity, intense flavor.

Gewürz Traminer (Napa Valley). Fresh, clean wine of spicy bouquet from 100 percent varietal fermentation.

SUTTER HOME WINERY

277 St. Helena Highway South, St. Helena, California 94574

In 1946, the Trinchero family purchased the large, barnlike winery building constructed in 1874 and later bought by Jacob and John Sutter, cousins of the gold-rush pioneer of Sutter's Fort. Access to the streams of tourists on the central highway of the valley gave the Trincheros reason to buy the old building. To qualify them as dealers in bulk wine were six generations of winemaking in the Asti region of Piedmont. Bring a container and John or Mario Trinchero would fill it with almost any kind of wine in the book, at a bargain price. But the story changed when Mario's son Louis, known as Bob, entered the picture. Risking his father's scorn, in 1968 he bottled a fine Zinfandel with a Sutter Home label, and priced it well above the winery's going price. At $1.25 a fifth it sold out quickly, because it was fine wine.

The 1968 Sutter Home Deaver Vineyard Zinfandel became the fulcrum, turning and lifting Sutter Home into the ranks of front-line attention from winelovers. Sutter Home Zinfandels are produced with as little cellar treatment as possible. They are among the most sought-after Zinfandels of California today, of great depth of flavor, fruitiness and spice, capable of lasting ten to twenty years.

SAMPLER SELECTION

White Zinfandel (Amador County). From the white juice of black grapes; 2 percent residual sweetness.

Zinfandel (Amador County). Vintage selections from vines growing at 1,500-foot elevations. Always dark, rich, fragrant.

Moscato Amabile. A dessert wine produced from the Muscat grape. Popular, but a pallid pretender to this noted title.

TREFETHEN VINEYARDS

1160 Oak Knoll Avenue, Napa, California 94558

An old 1886 winery has been saved from oblivion and returned to its early prestige by industrial executive Eugene Trefethen, who acquired the 600-acre ranch in 1968. The eighty-year-old vines and the apple and walnut orchards were uprooted, and, under the direction of viticulturist Anthony Baldini, Cabernet Sauvignon, Merlot, Chardonnay, Pinot Noir, White Riesling, Gewürztraminer, and Zinfandel were planted. The microclimates of the property, previously determined by careful weather-station findings, were found to be well suited to those varieties. The new concrete flooring and modern winemaking equipment were in place literally only moments before the first grapes came in from harvesting in 1973.

The first Trefethen wine, a 1974 Napa Valley Chardonnay, produced under the direction of enologist David Whitehouse, made its debut in February 1977 as a 100 percent varietal. With son John as general manager and daughter-in-law Janet in charge of marketing, Trefethen Vineyards is a family enterprise, strongly dedicated to the respected European concept of making wine only from the estate's own vineyards.

John and Janet Trefethen, one of the many young couples who have found winemaking in California an attractive way of life

In this château tradition, all the wines will be 100 percent Trefethen grapes, and production will be limited to but three wines: Chardonnay, White Riesling, and Cabernet Sauvignon blended with some Merlot. Our tasting has been limited to the first two.

SAMPLER SELECTION

Chardonnay (Napa Valley). Two examples were assayed, one with and one without oak aging. Both are clean, dry, fruity, and fine.

White Riesling (Napa Valley). With just the lightest kiss of oak, this delicate wine aims properly to be a good accompaniment to food.

VEEDERCREST VINEYARDS

1401 Stanford Avenue, Emeryville, California 94608

This small winery, managed by A.W. Baxter and owned by a group of partners, has a larger winemaking facility projected for completion in 1980. In the meanwhile, wines are being produced from choice lots of grapes from René di Rosa's Winery Lake Vineyard in the Carneros district in the southern part of Napa Valley, some exceptional botrytis-touched White Riesling from the Steltzner Vineyard in Yountville, and Merlot, White Riesling, Chardonnay, Malbec, Petit Verdot, and Cabernet Franc from Veedercrest's own vineyard in the Mayacamas Mountains, where the vines grow in the volcanic soil of Mt. Veeder.

Considerable international fame accrued to the relatively new Veedercrest label with the triumph of the 1972 Chardonnay at a tasting at Maxim's in Paris, where it scored a victory over a fine French white Burgundy. Shades of Robert Louis Stevenson's prediction to his European readers: "The smack of Californian earth shall linger on the palate of your grandson."

Johannisberg Riesling (Spätlese). Rich wine, with a unique touch of Gewürztraminer.

Chardonnay (Cask designation). Very well balanced, with hints of vanillin from the wood mingled with the fruit.

Cabernet Sauvignon (Gamay Acres). Label legends, as with all Veedercrest wines, are explicit as to origin and content.

VILLA MT. EDEN

Mt. Eden Ranch, Oakville Crossroad, Oakville, California 94562

Two Stanford graduates, Anne and James Mc-Williams, have joyously undertaken the vintner's profession, bringing back into productive use a frame winery built on their Napa Valley property in 1881. Young Nils Venge, a UC–Davis graduate in viticulture and enology, is their winemaker. With previous experience at Charles Krug and Sterling Vineyards, Venge has worked at Villa Mt. Eden since early 1973.

The 80 acres of fine varietal vines grow on an alluvial fan that slopes gradually toward nearby Mt. Eden. Temperature-summation studies show this slightly rising land to be cool, with varying microclimates favorable to the planting of Chardonnay and Pinot Noir as well as Cabernet Sauvignon. Field-crushing, to bring full fruitiness to the must, is well exemplified in both the Chenin Blanc and the Gewürztraminer.

Chardonnay (Napa Valley). The second-leaf wine, aged in Nevers oak, already indicating the great potential of this label.

Gewürztraminer (Napa Valley). In true Alsatian style, bone-dry, golden, long on the palate; appetizing character.

Cabernet Sauvignon (Napa Valley). Estate-bottled from second-leaf vines, showing intensive varietal character.

Napa Gamay (Napa Valley). Field-crushing of the Beaujolais grape brings an almost raspberry freshness to the wine.

YVERDON VINEYARDS

3787 Spring Mountain Road, St. Helena, California 94574

Yverdon is the name of the village at the southern tip of Lake Neuchâtel in Switzerland where Californian Fred Aves's grandparents were winegrowers. Aves's desire to make wine as his family had, asserted itself, so he sold his automotive business. With his son Russell, he moved in 1970 to a vineyard at a 2,000-foot elevation on Spring Mountain in the Napa Valley.

The two men engaged in more than one new trade as they became their own builders, stonemasons, carpenters, coopers—all essential to being self-sufficient vinegrowers and winemakers. The Yverdon house, which is pictured on the label, was designed by Fred after a château with mansard roof remembered from travels in France. An additional 90 acres of vineyard on Tubbs Lane near Calistoga now provide Gamay, Johannisberg Riesling, Chenin Blanc, and Cabernet Sauvignon. All the Aveses' wines are 100 percent varietal, made exclusively from their own grapes.

Johannisberg Riesling (Napa Valley). A wine of stunning flower-freshness, full varietal bouquet; sweet-edged.

Cabernet Sauvignon (Napa Valley). Vintage, estate-bottled wine of bold varietal character, needing considerable aging.

VINEYARDS AND WINERIES: BAY AREA AND CENTRAL COAST COUNTIES

"There is no link with the past as eloquent as an ancient wine, and its impact on the senses is intensified by the historic climate in which it was born."

—H. Warner Allen

On the morning of April 5, 1806, a stanch copper-bottomed 206-ton sailing vessel, the *Juno*, flying the Russian flag, sailed into San Francisco Bay. Under the command of Baron Nikolai Petrovitch Rezanof, accompanied by the naturalist George Heinrich von Langsdorff, the *Juno* had sailed southward from Sitka with a cargo of merchandise which the baron hoped to barter for much-needed grain. California's great historian Hubert Howe Bancroft explains: "The contrast between sunny California and the dreary Sitka with its storms and starvation introduced discontent to the *Juno*'s crew. Life in California—where to eat, to drink, to make love, to smoke, to dance, to ride, to sleep, seemed the whole duty of man —must have seemed to these cold, sea-salted men a pleasant dream." When four members of the crew asked to remain and were denied permission by Governor Argüello, they were put onto an island in the bay, an early Alcatraz, until the time of departure, lest they run away and remain in California illegally. In 1816 an English seaman, Robert Livermore, not unlike some of the *Juno*'s crew, found this area of New California such a paradise that he deserted ship. Ultimately, he found his way to the coastal valley and its golden hills, the Valle de Oro, married the daughter of a Spanish grandee, and, from money saved from a variety of endeavors, acquired ownership of the Rancho Los Positas, which he renamed Livermore Valley.

Naturalist Von Langsdorff accepted the invitation of Franciscan Father Cueva to visit the Mission San Jose. It would be the first time a foreigner would navigate the difficult and winding channels of the South Bay approach to the mission or see the fertile development of that region southeast of the bay.

Mission San Jose had been founded on June 11, 1797, by Father Fermin Francisco Lasuen. Von Langsdorff found the splendid mission, with its fine buildings, its extensive fields of corn, barley, wheat, and beans, its kitchen gardens, and its vineyards and orchards of vegetables and herbs, "extremely well laid out, and kept in very good order; the soil is everywhere rich and fertile, and yields ample returns."

In the Mission San Jose area today, where from the steel scaffolding surmounting the outdoor fer-

menters of the Weibel Champagne Cellars one can look to the west and see the winding channels of Von Langsdorff's approach, the early-nineteenth-century naturalist's observations remain significant and true. "Some vineyards have been planted within a few years, which yield excellent wine, sweet, and resembling Malaga. The situation of the establishment is admirably chosen, and according to the universal opinion this mission will in a few years be the richest and best in New California. The only disadvantage is that there are no large trees very near. To compensate for this disadvantage, there are in the neighborhood of the mission chalk-hills and excellent brick-earth, so that most of their buildings are of brick." Today's visitors to Weibel will step inside brick walls housing the winery begun by Leland Stanford.

Very near Mission San Jose, natural warm springs served Spanish colonial settlers as a place for washing linen. By the 1860s Rancho Agua Caliente had become a fashionable watering place for wealthy San

Stony fields are surprisingly hospitable to vines—in California as in Bordeaux

The Weibel Champagne Cellars and vineyards near Mission San Jose

Marker commemorating English-born Robert E. Livermore, who settled in the valley that bears his name

Franciscans. In 1870, only a few decades after Von Langsdorff's visit, railroad tycoon and former governor of California Leland Stanford acquired a square mile of orchards and vineyards surrounding the warm springs. He assigned ownership of the property to his brother Josiah, who tripled the vineyards' acreage, enlarged the brick winery, and inaugurated a brandy distillery.

Alameda County does not have the scenic charm of green, tree-clad hills found in Napa and Sonoma, so alluring to casual tourists. Its treasures consist in the all but invisible qualities of the land. The vines flourish in stony fields where little else could thrive. During the day the rocks become reservoirs of the sun's heat, and they hold the ripening warmth through the cold nights. Drainage, equally essential to the vine's well-being, is provided by the stones and pebbles in the earth, producing an environment for vine roots similar to the gravelly soil of Graves and Sauternes in Bordeaux.

It was San Francisco journalist Charles Wetmore who, following a visit to France in 1879, called attention to the area, with reports supporting California wine production. His entry into the fracas between champions of native wines and champions of imports led Wetmore himself directly into winemaking. In 1882 he acquired 480 acres of almost barren grazing land in the Livermore Valley, planted select vines, and built a winery, naming it Cresta Blanca after the chalk cliff into which the aging tunnels were dug. In 1884 he wrote the first ampelography for the benefit of winegrowers, "A Discussion of Vines Now Known in the State Together with Comments on Their Adaptability to Certain Locations and Uses." Even by today's standards, this 22-page pamphlet is a work remarkable for scholarly application and accuracy. Though Wetmore generously attempted to avoid "a pride of opinion," humbly stating his study of vines to be "kaleidoscopic" and "sometimes confusing," his study not only "brought order out of chaos" but set the industry on the path that was to bring it recognition in Europe.

The Marquis de Lur-Saluces, owner of Château d'Yquem, had sent to California cuttings of Sémillon, Sauvignon, and Muscadelle de Bordelais vines, the varieties comprising the classic blending of the famed Sauternes. Planted in Louis Mel's El Mocho Vineyard, which he shared with Wetmore, they were to earn for the pebbly fields of Livermore the sobriquet "Sauternes district of California" and two gold medals for Cresta Blanca from the Paris Exposition of 1889. The once proud property in Livermore is, alas, no longer productive. As a separate subdivision of Guild Wineries and Distilleries, a growers' cooperative discussed elsewhere, Cresta Blanca wines are now produced largely from Mendocino County grapes at a winery in that area. But El Mocho is a working part of the Wente vineyard.

Throughout these three counties—Alameda, Contra Costa, and Solano—agricultural land has been encroached upon by industry and housing. In the mid-forties, before legislation could be enacted designating existing farmlands as "agricultural preserves," many California wineries disappeared, virtually confiscated through taxation. Rezoned from low agricultural tax rates to prime residential rates, wineries and vineyards had but one alternative—relocation. With tract homes and industrial plants crowding the borders of their vineyards, including the famed El Mocho Vineyard, Wente Bros. acquired acreage in Monterey County. The Cadenasso Winery of Fairfield in Solano County, famed for fine Pinot Noir and Zinfandel, is almost a solitary holdout.

The vineyard domain south of San Francisco is as rich and colorful in its vintage history as the more celebrated regions north of the Bay Area. During the gold-rush days, when more than seven hundred ships swept through the Golden Gate in nine months, passengers and crews scrambled ashore, asking only for directions to the goldfields. Many, finding no gold, stayed on to plant vineyards and make wine on land that had already been proven suitable by Mission Period colonials. In 1850 the price of wine in San Francisco was as high as a king's ransom. Thirsty miners

San Francisco Bay divides the North Coast from the other wine areas of California

The 3,500-acre Almadén empire at Paicines

At Paul Masson: an old basket-press, now retired to the inactive list

3 acres of the famed La Questa Vineyard, planted by Emmett Rixford in 1883, remain and may endure. In the high folds and slopes of the Santa Cruz Mountains, nourished by subterranean springs, forested with trees, young Paul Masson in 1905 planted his own vineyard of Petit Pinot vines for champagne making. At 2,000 feet, free from fog, with double the rainfall of the valley floor, facing eastward toward the morning sun, the *chaîne d'or* (golden ridge), as Masson called it, was an ideal terrain. It remains so today for a small group of winemakers as dynamic and intense as was Masson. Urban encroachment is not likely to displace them.

ALMADÉN VINEYARDS

1530 Blossom Hill Road, Los Gatos, California 95118

Almadén's reputation as the largest of the premium wine producers often troubles the budding enophile, who tends to wonder how the company can make truly fine wines and at the same time satisfy the consumer of good, inexpensive table wine. The answer is to be found in the conscientious administration of a wine empire whose range of products was scarcely dreamed of by its founders more than a century ago.

Stand in the shoes of Étienne Thée in 1847, as he acquired a dominion of 350 acres of fertile land near Mission San Juan Bautista. The humble Bordelais vigneron had survived the rough sea voyage around the Horn to arrive in a new world that seemed patterned after Paradise. In Bordeaux, Talleyrand's Château Haut-Brion had but 92 acres, Château Margaux 155, while Thée now owned more than the two combined. The neighboring Franciscan friars gave him vine cuttings with which to establish more than a home—a small winemaking kingdom.

Similar visions drew another Frenchman to plant a vineyard in the area in 1852. Charles Lefranc, a tailor from Passy, brought with him, besides a determination to make wine, a large basket-press and some white-oak puncheons coopered from German oak. The young immigrant, a bachelor, took great delight in the company of Thée's daughter. Within a short time, they were married and the properties joined. Lefranc chose

consumed 60,000 gallons of California wine, mainly from Los Angeles and Santa Barbara counties. The wiser immigrant vignerons, eschewing the unfamiliar and chancy labor of goldmining, wanted vineyards near the city instead, where a cask of wine would bring them a good-sized bag of gold.

It was inevitable that the swift growth of San Francisco and its environs would crowd agriculture, including the vineyards, on the peninsula. San Francisco is still given as the place of origin on the labels of many wines, although the vineyards just south of the city long ago headed for the hills.

Green-belt legislation did not come soon enough to Santa Clara County to save the Almadén vineyards surrounding the original homestead of the founder, Étienne Thée. The winery still stands, with a few token vines around it, as a historical landmark, but the rest of the vineyards are now real estate subdivisions and tract homes. On the peninsula in San Mateo County,

The president of Almadén, John McClelland, Mrs. McClelland, and winemaker Klaus Mathes try one of the firm's fifty-eight wines

171

for their vineyard the name Almadén ("The Mine"), which the Spanish had given this region because of its quicksilver deposits. Ambitious to produce better wines than Thée was making from the Mission grapes, Lefranc acquired cuttings of choice European varieties. This was the beginning of finer winemaking in Santa Clara County.

In 1878, at the age of nineteen, Paul Masson emigrated to California because of the phylloxera devastation in his Burgundian homeland. He was hired as a bookkeeper by his fellow countryman Lefranc, and with his knowledge of vines and wines the arrangement was a felicitous one. In 1888, Masson married Lefranc's daughter, Louise, and in 1905 he struck out on his own, to the hills above Saratoga, with the intent of making champagne. In this early history can be traced the common background of today's two rival companies, Almadén and Paul Masson, both sharing the original vineyard's founding date of 1852.

The present status of Almadén Vineyards as a winemaking empire had its true beginning in 1941, when the Los Gatos property was acquired by Louis Benoist of San Francisco. A 1,400 percent increase in land taxes forced Benoist to establish new vineyards about 80 miles to the south, where he bought 3,000 acres at Paicines in San Benito County. Early in the 1940s Benoist had called upon Frank Schoonmaker to guide Almadén's winemaking policies. Schoonmaker brought in as winemaker Oliver Goulet from the Novitiate of Los Gatos. Peter Jurgens, as director of merchandising, increased the sales of Almadén wines from thousands of cases to millions, statistics that still boggle the mind.

In 1967 Benoist sold Almadén to National Distillers. Now Almadén's new president, John McClelland, together with Klaus Mathes, his winemaker, is involving Almadén once again in the intimately personal challenge of winemaking, absent since the departure of Louis Benoist. All fifty-eight wines produced by Almadén have improved remarkably. Grenache Rosé, Frank Schoonmaker's innovation a quarter of a century ago, as dry as its inspiration from Tavel, is sold in greater quantities than all the vin rosé of that Rhône region put together. But be sure the

In the La Cienega barrel house, part of Almadén's 23,000,000 gallons of cooperage seems to stretch to infinity

bottle you are buying or pouring is young. An old rosé is a dead rosé, even if it's Almadén's Grenache Rosé.

Once more Almadén Vineyards, expanded from its 350 acres of 1852 to 15,000 acres in four counties—Alameda, Santa Clara, Santa Cruz, and Monterey—is moving ahead. Under the auspices of the new team of McClelland and Mathes a·brilliant new sparkling wine, Eye of the Partridge, has made an impressive debut. The Cabernet Sauvignon still marches to a different drummer, possibly as a result of its aging in those 35,000 American-oak charred whiskey barrels at Cienega. Look for richly improved white wines and a growing program of vintaged varietal wines.

SAMPLER SELECTION

Blanc de Blancs Champagne. Vintage; the *cuvée* from the largest Chardonnay vineyard in California. Crisp, clean, dry.

Gewürztraminer (Monterey). Produced in vintage or nonvintage examples; exceptionally big, spicy wine.

Pinot Noir (Mountain). From the tiny, classic clusters, a pungent, regal wine true to Burgundy in bouquet.

Flor Fino Sherry. Its 17 percent alcohol and lightness nominate it as an ideal aperitif, served icy cold, in the Spanish tradition.

BARGETTO WINERY

3535 North Main Street, Soquel, California 95073

Philip Bargetto, hearing the good report of California as a wine country, came from Asti, in Piedmont, to work with the pioneer viticulturist Antoine Delmas of San Jose in 1887. He was joined by his brother John in 1929, and together they planned their rustic creek-side winery in anticipation of Repeal. Today, John's son Lawrence and his family maintain the winery in this cool coastal region above the north rim of Monterey Bay.

While he is capable of translating the pure, fragrant essence of raspberries, apricots, peaches, plums, strawberries, cherries, and even olallieberries into extraordinary, prize-winning fruit wines, Lawrence Bargetto's training and skill as a winemaker really shine when choice varietal grapes arrive at the red-barn winery. Inside these humble walls there is all the sophistication of first-rate winemaking procedures, with careful aging in Yugoslavian and Nevers oak for Pinot Blanc, Sylvaner, Johannisberg Riesling, and Chardonnay produced from grapes grown in the Santa Cruz Mountains. When warm Indian summers allow full ripening in the 17-acre Vine Hill Vineyard (saved from subdividers by comedian Dick Smothers), these white wines are worth journeying far to taste. The lower-than-2-tons-per-acre yield limits the availability even in the best years.

With distribution planned for select markets on the Eastern seaboard, from Maine to Florida, and representation in Ohio, Wisconsin, Washington, Oregon, and Colorado, Bargetto is a label to look for.

SAMPLER SELECTION

Chardonnay (Vine Hill) Santa Cruz Mountain vintage wine, oak-aged, long, soft, silky, balanced, superb.

Johannisberg Riesling (Vine Hill). An incomparable, silky subtlety sets this wine apart. Very little available.

Raspberry Wine. The berries cost more than premium grapes. Try this instead of Cassis with your next Kir. Jewel-toned.

Chaucer's Mead. Classic golden honey wine, fragrant as clean straw in the sunlight. A sweet touch out of medieval times.

DAVID BRUCE WINERY

21439 Bear Creek Road, Los Gatos, California 95030

On a hot summer day in the 1950s, dermatologist David Bruce, then a young intern, joined in the search for a small boy lost in the Santa Cruz Mountains. In the house of the vineyardist to which he brought the rescued child, Dr. Bruce, hot and thirsty from negotiating the rugged terrain, had his first taste of wine—and became a convert. One day, in a wine shop, Bruce found a bottle of Martin Ray's Pinot Noir that had

Dr. David Bruce holds his unfiltered, unfined vintage Chardonnay to the light

come from those same Santa Cruz Mountains, high above Los Gatos and Saratoga. He paid the extravagant price for it, out of curiosity.

"It was a wonderful wine," he told me. "I decided right then that we'd start looking for some acreage, and plant some vines!" In 1961 he found just what he was looking for, high on a ridge overlooking the whole *chaîne d'or*, fog free at 2,000 feet, complete with an old farmhouse and a few ancient vines. The family project now embraced all the chores of planting, attending, and nurturing 25 acres of Chardonnay, White Riesling, Cabernet Sauvignon, and Pinot Noir. Office hours in San Jose had to compete with the long hours of study and research demanded by the new career in the vineyard and winery. All the skills of the laboratory scientist merged with the devotion of the ardent enophile. Bruce bottled his first Chardonnay unfined, from the wood, accepting a slight cloudiness for fear any further racking might diminish the majesty of the flavor and bouquet.

Today, in his 6,000-square-foot, two-story winery,

completed in 1968, with rows of European-oak barrels, plus some mechanical contrivances of his own devising, the unique and individual winemaker is creating some of the best wines in the mountains. A handsome new label proclaims on its sidebar, "David Bruce wines are distinguished by their out-of-the-ordinary properties and ranges of tastes." You can count me among those who revel in the huge dimensions of his oak-ribbed Chardonnays and extraordinary deep and dark Amador County Zinfandels, so fat they can be chewed. I also subscribe to his own expressive descriptions of his wines, sent out to a loyal mail-order clientele. David Bruce wines require palates prepared for big adventure and, more often than not, for rich excitement.

SAMPLER SELECTION

Chardonnay. Always vintage, never filtered or fined. Requiring long rest and careful decanting. Oaky overtones, big and dry.

Zinfandel. Deep purple-black, sometimes with traces of residual sugar. Intense flavor suggesting chocolate. Aged in Limousin oak.

Cabernet Sauvignon. Vintage wine, 100 percent varietal, aged two years in new and used Nevers oak. Big, powerful.

Pinot Noir. Mouth-filling wine of extraordinary darkness of color and long-lasting aftertaste of fruit. Requires aging.

CONCANNON VINEYARD

4590 Tesla Road, Livermore, California 94550

Four wines currently produced by the third-generation descendants of the founder of Concannon Vineyard—Petite Sirah, Zinfandel Rosé, Muscat Blanc, and Rkatsiteli (from the Russian *Vitis vinifera* pioneered here)—bring renewed attention to the role of the winemaker as it transcends the scientific technology that appears, today, to dominate wine production. These are wines indicative of the young Concannons' creative individuality.

Joseph S. Concannon, Jr., the administrative vineyardist, with his brother James, the winemaker,

Gateway to historic Concannon, now operated by third-generation descendants of the Galway winemaker

inherited a winery chiefly known for its altar wines, although the sacramental production was balanced by many fine generic and varietal wines appreciated by a loyal and steady clientele. The dynamic founder, James Concannon, was a son of Erin from County Galway. When he was twenty-seven, in 1874, he took his bride to San Francisco, working at whatever offered the most promising returns. From Archbishop Joseph Alemany he learned of the Church's need for altar wines. In 1883, he purchased 47 acres of land in the Livermore Valley. It was here that Robert Livermore had planted the first vineyards of the area and that in 1882 Charles Wetmore had drawn attention to the great potential of the deep gravel soil and established his famous Cresta Blanca winery. Following the lead of these pioneers, Concannon built a frame-and-brick winery which still

endures. Vineyard and family both expanded. There were five boys and five girls, and eventually 300 acres of vineyard. Joseph Concannon assumed management of the winery upon his father's death in 1911, and continued to produce altar wines during Prohibition. In 1965, with Joseph's death, ownership-passed to young Joe and Jim. Today emphasis is on a few wines that are aesthetically far beyond the expectations of old James Concannon.

SAMPLER SELECTION

Muscat Blanc (Livermore Valley). Estate-bottled and vintage dessert wine of extraordinary freshness; sweet-edged.

Rkatsiteli (Livermore Valley). Uniquely dry, crisp white wine from a Russian variety, grown here only by Concannon.

176

Petite Sirah (Livermore Valley). For full enjoyment this substantial wine requires long aging. Full, dry, rich.

Cabernet Sauvignon (Livermore Valley). "Limited Bottling" editions have profound varietal character.

ENZ VINEYARDS

1781 Limekiln Road, Hollister, California 95023

Robert and Susan Enz belong to that growing list of city dwellers seeking a better life on the land. In 1966 they found their answer in the Cienega Valley of San Benito County—a 150-acre spread with some vines that had been planted in 1895. In 1970, Robert turned his talents as a civil engineer to transforming an old redwood barn into a twentieth-century winery. With 30 acres newly planted, and with Almadén's winemaster, Klaus Mathes, to guide them, the Enzes hope to make Cienega Valley a significant appellation.

SAMPLER SELECTION

Golden Chasselas (Cienega Valley). The Enzes couldn't resist making a vintage wine of these misprized golden grapes. Dry and clean.

Zinfandel Rosé (Cienega Valley). A beautiful deep pink color, dry, fragrant, almost spicy, with the tang of earth.

Pinot St. George (Cienega Valley). An estate-grown vine of remarkable bouquet and finesse. Needs some aging.

FELTON-EMPIRE VINEYARDS

379 Felton Empire Road, Felton, California 95081

Thirty-five years ago, Chafee Hall, a San Francisco corporation lawyer, set out 5 acres of Cabernet Sauvignon and 9 acres of White Riesling in virgin soil. Hallcrest, the progenitor of today's proliferating boutique wineries, produced some of the earliest of the rare, custom-made wines. Today, a trio of young men have acquired the once-celebrated vineyard and winery—Leo McCloskey, an enologist with experience at Ridge and David Bruce wineries, Jim Beauregard, a viticulturist, and John Pollard, an airline pilot with an M.B.A. degree.

In addition to grapes from the Hallcrest vines, Felton-Empire uses Cabernet Sauvignon, Zinfandel, White Riesling, and Chardonnay from the Vine Hill Vineyard, as well as Riesling from the Robert Young Vineyard of Sonoma County.

SAMPLER SELECTION

White Riesling (Santa Cruz). Made in the German style with late-harvested grapes; soft yet strong, with residual sugar.

Zinfandel (Santa Cruz). Big, dark, rich wines of tannic strength and regional character, expertly made. Full varietal nose.

Cabernet Sauvignon (Santa Cruz). In the tradition of the area, the wine, long on the skins, is full-bodied, fragrant.

GEMELLO WINERY

2003 El Camino Real, Mountain View, California 94040

It is by word of mouth that astute winelovers discover the rich, rugged red wines of Mario J. Gemello. The Cabernet Sauvignons and Zinfandels inevitably end up in high scorings at competitive winetastings. Founded in 1934 by Mario's father, John Gemello, who came from Piedmont, Italy, the small winery on the highway was a family affair until Louis Sarto joined as a partner in 1969. Their search is always for exceptional grapes for exceptional wines, and their quest for the elegance of red-wine grapes has taken them to the Santa Cruz Mountains and into the Carmel Valley.

SAMPLER SELECTION

Cabernet Sauvignon. The 100 percent varietal vintage selections usually stipulate the source of the mountain-grown grapes.

Zinfandel. Earthy, rich, full-bodied, and aged in oak puncheons and barrels to mellow roundness. Wines to last for years.

Barbera. Trust a winery with an Italian lineage to give real meaning to this secondary Piedmontese grape in California.

EMILIO GUGLIELMO WINERY

1480 East Main Avenue, Morgan Hill, California 95037

Emilio Guglielmo established this small Santa Clara Valley winery in 1925, producing unpretentious table wines that, following Repeal, found their way into Italian grocery stores in the Bay Area at modest prices. Today, son George, trained at Fresno State, is the winemaker. A tasting room has been opened, and with considerable expansion some finer varietal wines have been added to the locally popular generics under the Emile's Private Stock label. One of the state's richest and finest Italian-style Vermouths is produced here.

SAMPLER SELECTION

California Chablis. (Emile's Private Stock). In fifths or jugs, one of the best buys in California country wine. Crisp, dry, clean.

Grignolino Rosé. Estate-bottled under the Mount Madonna label, fragrant, fresh, vintage; from Santa Clara Valley grapes.

Petite Sirah. Grandson Gene Guglielmo's pride among the varietal reds under the Mount Madonna label.

Emile's Sweet Vermouth. Too good to waste by mixing with whiskey in cocktails. Superb body; herbs, spices, barks, petals.

KIRIGIN CELLARS

11550 Watsonville Road, Gilroy, California 95020

Instead of retiring, after a full working life as chief wine chemist for such wineries as Almadén, San Martin, Perelli-Minetti in California, and Canandaigua in New York, Nikola Kirigin Chargin decided to start his own winery with his son, Nick, Jr. In December of 1976 they bought the long-established Bonesio Winery, located on the old Spanish land grant Solis Rancho. The house, built in 1827, is among the historic landmarks of Santa Clara County.

Stainless-steel, temperature-controlled fermentation tanks were installed, and an additional 10 acres of white-wine varietal grapes will be added to the present acreage of Cabernet Sauvignon, Pinot Noir, and Zinfandel. With the new professionalism, the modern equipment, and the Croatian winemaking heritage of the Chargin family, there'll be even finer wines.

SAMPLER SELECTION

French Colombard. Produced as a dinner wine. Almost totally dry, it still retains the fruity bouquet of the grape.

Malvasia Bianca. Produced 100 percent from their own vines. Dry, with a bouquet suggesting orange blossoms, apricots.

Pinot Noir. A vintage, estate-bottled wine of light body and pleasing bouquet with true varietal character.

LLORDS & ELWOOD WINERY

Fremont, California 94538

Twenty years as one of the leading wine and spirits merchants of Hollywood and Beverly Hills led the late J. H. ("Mike") Elwood into researching the

Irene Elwood carries on the family wine business with her son Richard

178

BAY AREA AND CENTRAL COAST WINE LABELS

how's and why's of finer wines. By 1955, Elwood was determined to produce good sherries and to blend and bottle nonvintage table wines of superior merit that consumers could enjoy immediately. Since fewer and fewer California houses had anything approximating proper storage facilities for wines, the need for cellar aging was a serious disadvantage. He sold his chain of stores and became a winemaker, producing, blending, and bottling ten wines: a champagne, five varietal table wines, three sherries, and a port. They won many awards and immediate market acceptance. When Elwood died, in 1974, his widow, Irene, and his son Richard carried on the small family business. Their own experienced palates are responsible for the continued reliability of the wines.

SAMPLER SELECTION

Castle Magic Johannisberg Riesling. Mike Elwood was among the first to produce a Riesling with the sweet edge of a German *spätlese*.

Great Day D-r-ry Sherry. Truly comparable to some of the finest dry *fino* sherries of Spain. Full-bodied, smooth.

Dry Wit Sherry. Nutty taste, medium dryness; comparable to solera-aged *amontillado* wines of Jerez de la Frontera.

Ancient Proverb Port. A tawny wine of expanding bouquet, rich body, and ingratiating flavor.

PAUL MASSON VINEYARDS

13150 Saratoga Avenue, Saratoga, California 95070

The overlapping early history of today's rival companies, Almadén and Paul Masson, has been touched on above (see page 171). By the year 1905, young Paul Masson, driven by his consuming ambition to make champagne, was planting his La Cresta Vineyard on the hilltops of the *chaîne d'or* above Saratoga, putting down his "Petit Pinot" vines—Pinot Blanc, Pinot Noir, Pinot Chardonnay, Folle Blanche (for brandy), Cabernet Sauvignon, and Gamay. Masson's Vineyard in the Sky is the well-known locale of the "Music at the Vineyards" weekend concerts and operas presented each summer at the winery.

Wine in the making at Paul Masson's Pinnacles Vineyard in Monterey County

In 1936, in need of money, Masson sold the 350-acre property and its 70 acres of vines to a young Saratoga stockbroker, Martin Ray, keeping only the Vineyard in the Sky. An equally idealistic wine zealot, Ray retained the founder as president until Masson's death in 1940 at the age of eighty-one.

During his brief tenure, which ended in 1941, when fire destroyed the winery, Martin Ray produced some exceptional Pinot Noir and Cabernet Sauvignon and had a brief marketing association with Frank Schoonmaker during which they launched varietal table wines under the Paul Masson Champagne Co. label.

In 1943, through a suggestion made by Alfred Fromm, the winery, which Ray had rebuilt after the fire, was bought by Seagram, and an expansion program was instituted which has continued, successfully, to this day. In 1962, the first of more than 5,000 acres of varietal vines planted on their own *Vitis vinifera* roots were set out at the Pinnacles Vineyard near Soledad in Monterey County. One of the state's finest winemaking facilities was completed, for handling the ever-increasing grapeloads from the Gavilan benchland vineyards. In 1965, the President's "E" award flag came from the United States Government for the

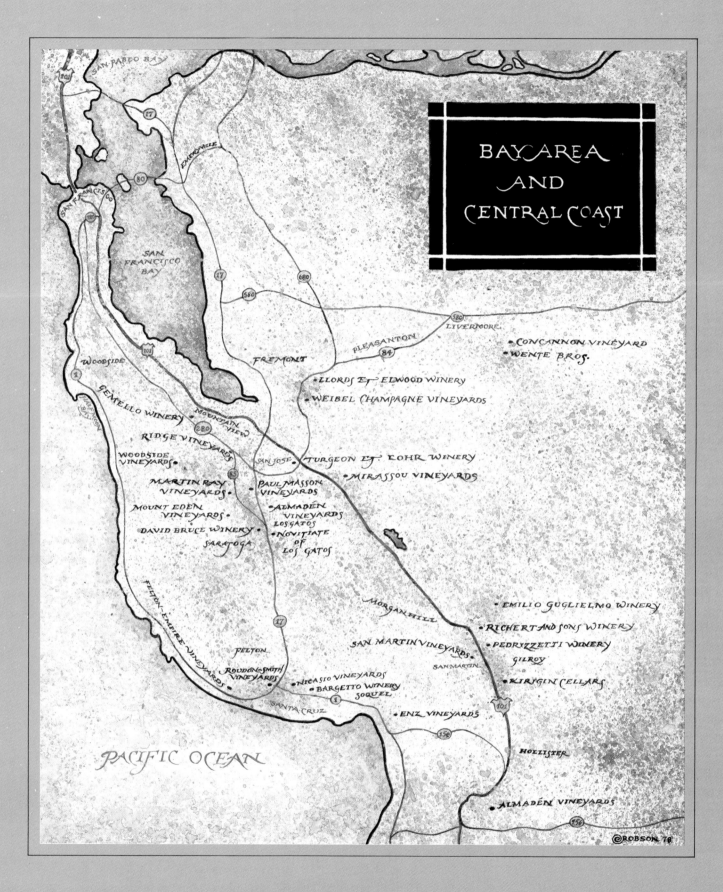

BAY AREA
AND
CENTRAL COAST

SAN PABLO BAY

SAN FRANCISCO

SAN FRANCISCO BAY

EMERYVILLE

WOODSIDE

GEMELLO WINERY

RIDGE VINEYARDS

WOODSIDE VINEYARDS

MARTIN RAY VINEYARDS

MOUNT EDEN VINEYARDS

DAVID BRUCE WINERY

SARATOGA

MOUNTAIN VIEW

FREMONT

PLEASANTON

LIVERMORE

CONCANNON VINEYARD
WENTE BROS.

LLORDS ET ELWOOD WINERY

WEIBEL CHAMPAGNE VINEYARDS

SAN JOSE   TURGEON ET LOHR WINERY

MIRASSOU VINEYARDS

PAUL MASSON VINEYARDS

ALMADÉN VINEYARDS LOS GATOS

NOVITIATE OF LOS GATOS

FELTON-EMPIRE VINEYARDS

FELTON

ROUDON-SMITH VINEYARDS

NICASIO VINEYARDS
BARGETTO WINERY SOQUEL

SANTA CRUZ

MORGAN HILL

SAN MARTIN VINEYARDS
SAN MARTIN

EMILIO GUGLIELMO WINERY

RICHERT AND SONS WINERY

PEDRIZZETTI WINERY
GILROY

KIRIGIN CELLARS

ENZ VINEYARDS

HOLLISTER

PACIFIC OCEAN

ALMADÉN VINEYARDS

© ROBSON 78

excellence of leadership in industry—an export program that sent Paul Masson wines to the principal countries of the world.

Under Seagram's management, the wine merchandising policy at Paul Masson has emphasized non-vintage table wines, in the belief that consumers enjoy wines that are drinkable at the time of purchase and consistent in taste. The shortcomings of one vintage year can be compensated for with artful blending from wines of other years. While this is a boon to steady sales, it limits the potential height that a wine from the wealth of varietal plantings in the Pinnacles Vineyard of Monterey County might achieve. I have tasted the winery's 100 percent varietal Pinot Noir, Chardonnay, and Gewürztraminer, drawn from wood and steel, any or all of which might one day lift the label to more distinguished ranks. A varietal vintage program was initiated in the fall of 1977.

Champagne master Joseph Stillman has developed a sparkling wine *cuvée* of 100 percent Johannisberg Riesling, and another drawn from grapes grown exclusively at the Vineyard in the Sky which might add further luster to the Masson reputation. Paul Masson aperitif and dessert wines, fine, mellow ports and sherries, as well as the proprietary Rhinecastle, the Emerald Dry (from Emerald Riesling), the Rubion (of claret style), and the Baroque, of Burgundy stance, are sound commercial complements to the California Champagnes, which brought the founder up the mountain.

SAMPLER SELECTION

California Champagne (Extra Dry). A *cuvée* of Johannisberg Riesling, Pinot Blanc, French Colombard. Always excellent.

Pinot Noir. Produced almost exclusively from Monterey County grapes. Of excellent varietal aroma and bouquet.

Pinot Chardonnay. Clean, crisp; appetizingly dry, with a slight touch of botrytis adding complexity. No wood.

Rare Souzão Port. One of the finest port wines produced in California from Portuguese varieties. Well-aged, rich wine.

MIRASSOU VINEYARDS

Aborn Road, San Jose, California 95121

Billed as "America's Oldest Winemaking Family," the Mirassous bring more than a touch of showmanship to their sophisticated merchandising. The fifth generation of a family of vintners who first came to California in 1848, the youthful Mirassou clan—Daniel, Steve, Jim, Peter, and brother-in-law Don Alexander—are making up for lost time in bringing the Mirassou name, virtually unknown until 1966, to the attention of American winelovers. For their fathers, Edmond and Norbert, it had been a safe and steady cash business to sell wines in cask and barrel to other premium wineries, under whose alien labels they would emerge. The young Mirassous are interested in building their own name and are prepared to take the risks involved.

Innovation is part of the strategy, as exemplified by Peter's harvester–crusher, which obviates potential oxidation by turning the berries into juice almost instantly while still in the field. Creative merchandising and creative winemaking are exemplified by two of their best-sellers, Monterey Riesling and Fleuri Blanc. No one seems to be attracted to Sylvaner as a wine, but everybody is drawn to Riesling. The fifth-generation Mirassous decided to dub their Sylvaner wine Monterey Riesling and let it have a modicum of sweetness. It has become a star overnight.

Their Fleuri Blanc, a creative blending of 65 percent Gewürztraminer with additions of flowery

Mirassou's first generation: Pierre and Henriette Pellier Mirassou

Johannisberg Riesling and a fruity zing from Pinot Blanc, is one of the most delectable and original white wines to be produced in California. An 8 percent residual sugar is balanced with a sprightly, tart .825 acidity. Served on a warm Indian summer evening with creamy cheese, it will elicit an appreciative response from first-time tasters. You'll need to have a reserve supply chilled for encores.

The Fifth Generation (as they are called on their labels) work closely with their fathers, taking full responsibility for 650 acres in Monterey County and dividing responsibility equally for the homesite acreage near San Jose. With annual sales reaching 126,000 cases in 1975, and still climbing, youth's gamble seems to be winning.

SAMPLER SELECTION

Champagne (Monterey County, Au Naturel). Vintage wine, on the yeasts four years, plus. Superbly crisp, dry, clean.

Monterey Riesling. Vintage wine of the Alsatian Sylvaner in a fragrant, sweet-edged, popularly styled wine.

Chenin Blanc (Monterey County). An almost overwhelming wine of pungent fruitiness and regional distinction.

Johannisberg Riesling (Monterey County). Early editions were of uneven quality. Present vintages are fresh, fruity, silky.

MOUNT EDEN VINEYARDS

22000 Mt. Eden Road, Saratoga, California 95070

"The challenge of trying to make a truly great wine lights a fire in the soul that time won't put out. Time merely fans the flame, intensifies your determination—and humbles you by granting so very few chances for real achievement."

This comment of Martin Ray's explains something of the spell that he cast on California winemakers. The irascible iconoclast realized a boyhood dream on March 15, 1936, when he bought Paul Masson's La Cresta Vineyard and winery for $200,000. The son of a Methodist minister in Saratoga, Ray first worked at

The late Martin Ray, wearing his straw hat like a crown

the famous Vineyard in the Sky earning five cents for every gopher he trapped on the vine slopes. His father, pointing to the windows of the chalet on the hill, brightly lighted late into the night, would call it "the devil's own domain here on earth." This only served to intrigue the six-year-old, who, at his first opportunity, scrambled up the hill to glimpse the famed champagne baron of the mountain. "He was wearing white flannel trousers, white socks and oxfords, a nice jacket, a great big brimmed hat, with his eyeglasses dangling on a ribbon. Standing there beside that château, he was a splendid sight!" In later years, the freckled, red-haired "Rusty" Ray affected a similar wide-brimmed straw hat, his own crowning insigne as ruler of the domain.

In 1945, after he sold the original property to Seagram, he bought the higher hilltops immediately to the north, where old Paul Masson had told him even finer wines might be made. Before Martin Ray's death in 1976, the Mount Eden Vineyards had been sold and the way cleared to produce some great wines from its acres. A small group of investors took over, the M.E.V. Corporation, headed by Robert Nikkel with Dr. Don Alcott, William Hanna, and Dr. Frank Dutra as officers and young Bill Anderson as winemaker.

In the first years, winemaker Richard Graff of Chalone was invited to assist the new group. "I'm convinced," he told me, "that this hill will produce the greatest Cabernet of California!" Superlatives are a normal part of the conversation of those making wines on the *chaîne d'or*. And not without reason.

The first Cabernet Sauvignon of Mount Eden Vineyards was made in 1973, fermented in stainless steel, aged in Nevers-oak barrels, fined with fresh egg whites in the Bordeaux tradition before bottling. The ruby-hued wine has great promise, a subtle peppery undertone, and a body of balanced substance auguring

a good long life. The Chardonnays of '72 and '73, while overpriced, were of a majesty justifying high hopes for the new winery of legendary origin.

SAMPLER SELECTION

Chardonnay. Rich, golden, estate-bottled wine from the 2,000-foot-elevation vineyard. Well-balanced with oak aging.

Cabernet Sauvignon. Expensive. An interesting investment for the connoisseur, bound to be a conversation piece.

NICASIO VINEYARDS

14300 Nicasio Way, Soquel, California 95073

Six miles north of Soquel, in the Santa Cruz Mountains, electronics engineer Dan Wheeler dug a cave into the hillside for storing the wines he produces.

Steel tanks, wooden barrels, and cardboard cartons mark the progress of a wine on its way to the consumer

"Wines by Wheeler" are unfiltered, unfined, and virtually unsulphured. He buys most of the grapes, being careful to retain the recognized regional excellence, and he has developed his own technique for the retention of fruitiness in wine, a secret he is unwilling to share. It accounts for some of the outstanding difference in his white wines, particularly Chardonnay and Riesling, and gives a lilt to his dry Zinfandel Rosé. Because of his own dislike for woody tastes in wine, Wheeler takes his red wines from fermentation in wood into his cave in 5-gallon glass jugs in which they are stored before bottling. Until recently, the loyal customers who consume his 300 cases per year have been accommodated through mail order only.

SAMPLER SELECTION

Champagne of Chardonnay. Vintage champagne, au naturel, aged *cuvée*, no *dosage*, produced in classic bottle-fermentation procedure.

Zinfandel Rosé. Dry pink wine, very fruity, of Santa Cruz Mountain grapes from the Beauregard vineyards.

Zinfandel. Each vintage briefly aged in French brandy barrels and 5-gallon glass jugs before bottling. Big, bold wine.

NOVITIATE OF LOS GATOS

300 College Avenue, Los Gatos, California 95030

Ever since 1888, the fathers and brothers of the Novitiate of the Sacred Heart of the Society of Jesus in Los Gatos have grown and produced the finest sacramental wines of California. Not very many seasons ago, among the novices tending those vines was today's governor of California, Jerry Brown.

There has been some expansion of the vineyard holdings in the San Ysidro district of the Santa Clara Valley. With an 800,000-gallon storage capacity, and 80,000-gallon fermentation facility, Father Louis B. Franklin, the general manager of the Novitiate, has found it expedient to expand the market for their table wines, since the Novitiate has a supply comfortably beyond their needs of altar wines for the Church.

The most famous of the Novitiate wines is Black Muscat, a unique rich liqueur-type dessert wine of the Muscat Hamburg grape. Beyond this renowned and stellar selection, aged in old, dimly lit caves, are some 2,300 oak casks mellowing other prize aperitif and dessert wines, including a rich Angelica, Muscat Frontignan, Cocktail Sherry, Flor Sherry, and varietal Tinta Port. But the focus is now upon Cabernet Sauvignon, Pinot Noir, Chenin Blanc, Johannisberg Riesling, and Pinot Blanc. The wines are modestly priced, with all proceeds going to finance the education and training of Jesuit priests.

SAMPLER SELECTION

Château Novitiate. A rather distinguished blended wine of Sémillon and Sauvignon grapes in the sweet Sauternes style.

Pinot Blanc. Full-bodied, dry white wine in the white Burgundy tradition.

Cabernet Sauvignon. A limited-bottling edition of this claret varietal, wood-aged and ready for drinking.

Black Muscat. From the Muscat Hamburg grape. So rich in body and flavor, it is suggested as a dessert wine-liqueur.

PEDRIZZETTI WINERY

1645 San Pedro Avenue, Morgan Hill, California 95037

The Santa Clara Valley between Morgan Hill and Gilroy is still largely vineyard country. A cooling fog blanket rolls in from the Pacific regularly after sundown, and grape growers in this area are grateful because it makes for a better climate for the better varietals. And it is better varietals that Ed and Phyllis Pedrizzetti are making today.

The winery, with its 60-acre vineyard in rocky riverbed soil, was bought in 1945 by John Pedrizzetti, and from this unpretentious country winery a bulk-wine business was built. Ed and Phyllis Pedrizzetti took over the management in 1963. The Courtyard Tasting Room is in the domain of Phyllis, while Ed is upgrading the wines, made from their own and purchased grapes, that carry the family name.

Padre Junípero Serra was the first of many priests to tend vineyards in California

Pinot Chardonnay. With grapes from Santa Barbara County; a dry, long, and silky wine, free of oak taste.

Chenin Blanc. Monterey County grapes give the intense fruitiness to this pleasing wine of 7 percent residual sweetness.

Barbera. A really distinguished 100 percent varietal from the Pedrizzettis' own mature vines. Beautiful wine, soft and fragrant.

Petite Sirah. Another estate-bottled wine. Deep and dark in color, bold, a little peppery, appetizing.

MARTIN RAY VINEYARDS

22000 Mt. Eden Road, Saratoga, California 95070

On November 14, 1976, Eleanor Ray, Martin Ray's widow, sent out a letter headlined, *Peter Martin Ray Takes Over Martin Ray Vineyards and Brings in a Magnificent 1976 Vintage!* A professor of biology at Stanford, with specialized knowledge of plant physiology, Peter Martin Ray is also a veteran of more than a few winemaking skirmishes with his ebullient stepfather through the good years and the troubled years that divided Martin Ray's empire. Today, five shareholders have formed a corporation to carry on the winemaking traditions in what many people think of as an ivory tower among the vines.

There are only 5 acres of Chardonnay, Pinot Noir, and Cabernet Sauvignon in the Martin Ray Vineyards, but Peter buys select supplementary lots of those varietals. In 1976 the Chardonnay and Pinot Noir came from René di Rosa's Winery Lake Vineyard in the Carneros region of the Napa Valley.

The style of the Martin Ray Chardonnay owes its traditional richness of taste to a triple pressing of the must, which extracts the very essence of the grape. The new wine gains complexity from aging in Burgundian oak barrels acquired from the renowned seigneur of the Côte d'Or, Louis Latour.

A bottle-fermented champagne of Chardonnay and Pinot Noir is contemplated by Martin Ray Vineyards but not yet in *cuvée* blending. It will be called Madame Pinot and will doubtless not only qualify as a successor to the legendary wine of that name but be even finer.

Chardonnay (Winery Lake Vineyard). This first release of the 1976 vintage is a big wine; in current distribution.

RICHERT & SONS WINERY

18980 Monterey Road, Morgan Hill, California 95037

Walter Richert, with his degrees in chemistry and food science from the University of California, and his experience as editor of *Wine Review* and *Wines & Vines*, was a logical candidate for winery ownership in 1953, and he dubbed the budding enterprise Richert & Sons in the strong hope that his three sons, Robert, Eric, and Scott, would ease him into retirement. These hopes have been realized now that Robert and Scott have come home from college with appropriate degrees and with the desire to continue the highly specialized focus of the winery upon port and sherry. Richert chooses his grapes and methods to suit his own positive ideas of good-tasting sherry, and his success is measured by numerous awards and gold medals from competitive tastings. He uses Palomino grapes, of course, plus some Pedro Ximenez for cream sherries, but believes the Flame Tokay of the Lodi area and the misprized Mission grape have valuable roles in contributing their taste to the best sherries. The family label with trademark of four barrels, standing for Walter Richert and his three sons, is familiar to California connoisseurs, and it deserves to be known by a wider audience.

Full Dry Sherry. As the name suggests, it is a wine of full body, golden richness of color, dry on the palate.

Triple Cream Sherry. The medal winner, full-bodied, full-flavored, mellow in the mouth, rich and smooth.

Ruby Port. A glorious jewel-colored wine, with a haunting reminiscence of its grape origins in the full bouquet.

RIDGE VINEYARDS

17100 Monte Bello Road, Cupertino, California 95014

It began quite informally in 1959 as a hobby when Professor David Bennion persuaded some of his Stanford colleagues, electrical-engineering Ph.D.'s, to join him in purchasing a ramshackle old winery 10 miles south of the campus, high on a ridge of Black Mountain at an elevation of 2,300 feet. By 1967 Bennion had become full-time winemaker at Ridge Vineyards. Associates from the university retained their investment and interest, but in 1969 they invited a trained enologist, Dr. Paul Draper, to join them. Industrialist Richard Foster of southern California was invited also, to assist in the shaping of what would certainly become a commercial enterprise.

In 1970 the nucleus of Ridge Vineyards as a

David Bennion, founder of Ridge Vineyards

The big wines of Ridge come, in part, from their vineyards 2,300 feet above sea level on the Monte Bello ridge

winery was moved higher up the mountain to the old stone Monte Bello Winery, which was refurbished and provided with stainless-steel fermenters and a laboratory to accommodate the microbiologist. The legendary primitive complexity of the Ridge Cabernet Sauvignon, Zinfandel, and Petite Sirah was adroitly refined, to keep it satisfying to purist fans appreciating unfiltered wholeness, but possibly to advance the time of drinkability.

Ridge was among the earliest of the California wineries to use wrap-around labels offering each wine's full pedigree, from source of grape to bottling information, for the winelover's cellar book. Zinfandels, made in separate small lots, from as many as ten different vineyard sources, from Mendocino in the north to San Luis Obispo in the south, and from the prized old gold-mining areas of the Sierra, have become collectors' prizes. English wine authority Harry Waugh describes Ridge Cabernets and Zinfandels as "the Mouton Rothschilds or Latours of California." He rightfully adds that "at times they can be too powerful." The names of the Zinfandels have a California ring—Fiddletown, Langtry Road, Jimsomare, Coast Range, Lytton Springs, and Geyserville. The wines also have the individuality and earthy excellence that has earned Ridge Vineyards a reputation for bold purity.

SAMPLER SELECTION

Chardonnay (Monte Bello). The grapes from the original vineyard yield but one ton per acre, for a rich, big wine.

Cabernet Sauvignon (Monte Bello). Classic fining with egg white is used for elegant balance.

Zinfandel (Jimsomare). Every vintage is huge, with almost overwhelming perfume of the grape. An enduring prize.

Zinfandel (Occidental). Another cellar treasure, from a cool Region I area. Strongly built; needs aging.

ROUDON-SMITH VINEYARDS

513 Mt. View Road, Santa Cruz, California 95065

Many of California's new professional "nonprofessional winemakers" are inevitably moved into their second careers with the most ardent devotion. Ignace

Paderewski, the great Polish pianist–statesman, took the greatest pride in the Zinfandel made at his mountain vineyard in Paso Robles. Richard Graff, with a degree in music from Harvard, took enological training at UC–Davis before embarking on his almost monastic existence as a winemaker at Chalone. The founding Stanford professors of Ridge Vineyards were all electrical engineers, and Bob Travers of Mayacamas was trained as a petroleum engineer, as was his predecessor on that mountain, Jack Taylor. Cardiologist Stanley Hoffman of Beverly Hills brought new life to the Paso Robles vineyards by putting down Pinot Noir vines, which face the Paderewski vineyard.

The list is long, and the foregoing few examples are cited merely as preamble to another young winery of laudable ambitions in the Santa Cruz Mountains. Founded in 1972, the winery was to provide an alternate life-style for electronics engineers James Smith and Robert Roudon. Roudon took courses in enology at UC–Davis, expanding on some background in chemistry. Not to labor the point, he is also a musician.

The young 12-acre vineyard surrounding the winery in Scotts Valley is planted in White Riesling, which thrives in the cool region. They are currently buying other grapes: Zinfandel from Lodi, Chenin Blanc, Chardonnay, Barbera, and Pinot Noir, as they work toward a 5,000-case annual goal. At present their small-batch, high-quality varietals are sold directly to consumers and a few local restaurants, but in the near future, as wine enthusiasts spread the good word, Roudon-Smith Vineyards' wines will be appearing in cellars beyond California.

SAMPLER SELECTION

Sauvignon Blanc. A light, graceful, dry wine from grapes grown in the nearby region of Hollister. A hint of oak.

Zinfandel (Lodi). In the tradition of the region, this is a big wine of late-harvest grapes, wholly dry, sturdy.

SAN MARTIN VINEYARDS

1300 Depot Street, San Martin, California 95046

New techniques in the winery are as important as growing conditions in the vineyard for the quality of California's wines

At the height of the wine boom of the 1970s in California, when diversification was the key word in conglomerate structuring, changes of vineyard ownership and direction were the order of the day. Changes at San Martin Vineyards, a fourth-generation family winery established by Bruno Filice in 1892, continue to this moment. A new winemaker of energetic talent and a strong academic background, Ed Friedrich from Trier, Germany, assumed general management for the new owners, Norton Simon's Somerset Wine Company, in the spring of 1977. Somerset's wine affiliates also include the renowned Alexis Lichine. It is reasonable to expect growing national prestige for the San Martin Vineyards label.

The San Martin Vineyards' tasting room on Highway 101 south of San Jose has been a tourists' delight ever since Repeal. There are 45 wines and a brandy to taste—champagnes, ports, sherries, fruit and berry wines, including an extraordinary Santa Clara Valley apricot wine called Aprivette and an equally impressive Satsuma plum wine called Sum-Plum, both of which have my undying support. They translate the essence of tree-ripe fruit into true and brilliant dessert wines, souvenirs of this valley, which was once filled with acres and acres of blossoming trees.

San Martin's Monterey County vineyards are watered by 28 miles of irrigation canals with pump stations like this one

Special mention should be made here of another San Martin exclusive, Montonico, produced from a grape of that name brought to the Santa Clara Valley from Calabria by the Filice family. The present 8.4 acres are believed to be the only planting of this grape on this continent. Winemaker Friedrich discovered aged casks of the wine, a pure varietal made in the Italian *vino santo* tradition, sweet, laced with brandy but not baked as sherry is. Under his guiding hand Montonico has been brought to a mature finish that is nothing short of astonishing in its rich complexity.

San Martin's Monterey County vineyard, whose awesome statistics include 28 miles of irrigation canals, 5 million Malaysian hardwood grapestakes, 90 miles of interconnecting roadways between blocks of vines ribbing the undulating hills, a total of 8,700 acres of bearing vines, known as Viña Monterey, is today owned by a separate corporation called Val-High, the yield being under long contract to Ernest & Julio Gallo with a lesser amount going to San Martin Vineyards.

SAMPLER SELECTION

Johannisberg Riesling (Santa Clara, Santa Barbara County). Friedrich aims for gentle wines of this grape, wins in softness.

Pinot Chardonnay (Monterey, Santa Clara). Through the American oak the taste of the naked grape becomes a striking experience.

Chenin Blanc (Monterey County). A refreshing aperitif wine, long in taste, balanced acidity, 9 percent residual sweetness.

Zinfandel (Amador County). For lovers of the big Zin, this is a collectors' item, of depth and seductive fragrance.

TURGEON & LOHR WINERY

1000 Lenzen Avenue, San Jose, California 95126

Civil engineer Jerry Lohr, with a master's degree from Stanford, and Bernard Turgeon embarked on a multi-million-dollar winery project with twenty-five other partners in 1972. In that year they planted 280 acres of vines in the Salinas Valley, the fabled Steinbeck country near Greenfield. In 1974 they bought a substantial part of the abandoned Falstaff Brewery in downtown San Jose. As winemaker they hired Peter Stern, a UC–Davis graduate in enology with experience at both Gallo and Robert Mondavi. He initiated the layout for the 55,000-gallon winery and the aging facilities, which include American, French, and Yugoslavian oak barrels. Eventually Turgeon & Lohr hope to sell 100,000 cases annually. Stern's scholarly handwritten histories of each released wine indicate his recognition of the present trend·toward enlarging the consumer's technical comprehension of a wine's complexity. For his 1975 Monterey Rosé of Cabernet Sauvignon, the back label reads: "On November 3rd and 4th, 1975, we harvested the first crop from our own-rooted Cabernet Sauvignon vineyards. The grapes were in excellent condition due to the long, cool growing season we experienced this year. This rosé was made entirely from Cabernet grapes averaging 22.9° Brix at the time of crushing. After crushing, the juice remained in contact with the skins for an average of ten hours before pressing. At pressing, the juice was inoculated with a pure yeast culture and fermented at between 50° F. and 55° F. You will find this wine to be slightly sweet with a bright pink-red color. It is distinctly young, having the refreshing aroma of cassis and a hint of yeastiness. It is perfect for immediate consumption. Peter M. Stern, Winemaker, Turgeon & Lohr Winery."

SAMPLER SELECTION

Jade (Monterey County). A delicate, light white wine, predominantly Johannisberg Riesling, blended specially to be served with Chinese food.

Pinot Blanc (Monterey County). A dry white wine of well-balanced acidity, touched with oak; fresh and clean bouquet.

Pinot Noir (Monterey County). The area is cool, and the soil of a nature best suited to this often difficult grape.

WEIBEL CHAMPAGNE VINEYARDS

1250 Stanford Avenue, Mission San Jose, California 94538

Weibel champagnes: Crackling Rosé and Chardonnay Brut Blanc de Blancs

The Wente Bros. tasting room

In 1936 the Swiss family Weibel came to America, where Rudolph Weibel and his son Frederick hoped to produce splendid champagnes. In 1945, when they found the old pre-Prohibition Leland Stanford Winery and surrounding vineyards, this seemed to be the time and place to begin.

Today Fred Weibel heads the company whose champagne cellars remain in the enlarged brick winery built by Leland Stanford near Mission San Jose. The search for grapes took Weibel to the area north of San Francisco, and there in Mendocino County, at Redwood Valley, 6 miles beyond Ukiah, he built a winery for making fine varietals.

"You dig your hands into the soil, smell the rich earth. Live with your grapes day and night. And you pray. And if nature is good to you, the sun, the rain, the cool night air . . . then the winemaker's art can bring out the soul in his wines." Fred Weibel's words tell much about the wines he makes. His delectable Champagne Chardonnay Brut Blanc de Blancs, bottle-fermented in the classic *méthode champenoise*, scored higher than many other California champagnes in a tasting with leading French champagnes of *grande*

marque. But possibly because of its clean fruitiness and softness, purists have been inclined to downgrade its ranking. Less-sophisticated consumers, however, who often find the acid bite and yeastiness of bouquet of brut champagne barely tolerable, enjoy Fred's soft, fine sparkler. The Weibel Champagne Vineyards maintain fine winemaking traditions, including those for their splendid sherries.

Because they have been erratically merchandised, Weibel wines are often hard to find, particularly the excellent, wood-aged Pinot Noir. The champagne cellars produce every kind of sparkling wine— Charmat bulk process, transfer method, and classic *méthode champenoise* bottle-fermented champagnes. Many appear under private labels. The clue is in the bottom line; you will know they are Weibel's if the cellar indicated is Mission San Jose.

SAMPLER SELECTION

Green Hungarian. A popular, very fruity, sweet-edged wine, blended with Chenin Blanc to give it greater appeal.

Chardonnay Brut Blanc de Blancs Champagne. Softer than most brut champagnes. Fruity, clean, silky, charming.

Pinot Noir. The well-aged, vintage selections are well worth seeking for their true varietal depth and complexity.

Solera Flor Dry Bin Sherry. Produced from Palomino grapes with yeast cultures. Comparable to fine Spanish *fino* sherry.

WENTE BROS.

5565 Tesla Road, Livermore, California 94550

Young Carl Heinrich Wente arrived in California from Hanover in 1880. Aware of the winemaking excitement in the state, he determined to make wine his life work. After an apprenticeship with Charles Krug in the Napa Valley, he bought 50 acres of young vines in the Livermore Valley in 1883, and built a modest frame house on Tesla Road. Cuttings of Sémillon and Sauvignon Blanc, the Sauternes varieties imported by Louis Mel, dominated the vineyard when it expanded to 300 acres.

Wente's eldest son, Carl F. Wente, eschewed farming for accounting and in later years became president of the Bank of America; Ernest, after studying at the College of Agriculture at UC–Davis, took charge of the vineyards; Herman, following his studies in enology at UC–Berkeley, became the winemaker. Bulk wines were sold to San Francisco wine merchants until Prohibition, when, through an arrangement with Georges de Latour of Beaulieu Vineyard, production of altar wines was continued. In 1934 the first wines to bear the Wente Bros. label appeared under the proprietary designation Valle de Oro (Valley of Gold), the name the early mission settlers had given the Livermore area.

When Frank Schoonmaker came to California in search of fine wines to augment his imported wine selections, he soon became an ardent advocate of the Wentes' white wines and urged them to differentiate their pure varietal wines from the commonly marketed Sauterne and Chablis. He was convinced that these outstanding wines, of positive individual character, with regional taste distinction, should be marketed without leaning upon European comparison. In the late 1930s, through Schoonmaker's enthusiasm, and with support from winemakers like Louis M. Martini, the Korbels, and even the maverick Martin Ray, varietal labeling of California wines was inaugurated. Wente Dry Semillon and Sauvignon Blanc, among others, became the most popular and dependable wines of California.

Schoonmaker was at the winery on the day the Marquis de Lur-Saluces paid his famous visit to the Wentes in May 1939. Herman set out for him a series of successive vintages of Sauvignon Blanc, a pure 100 percent varietal wine, which is not produced as such in Bordeaux. It was the first time the owner of famed Château d'Yquem had ever tasted California wines produced from cuttings from his vineyard. All of us watched anxiously while he went through the tasting ...silently. Before the Marquis could comment on the bone-dry Sauvignon Blanc, Herman produced a bottle of Semillon. It brought a quick smile to the visitor's face, like meeting an old friend. "These are beautiful wines," he said. "I am delighted to find such splendid work going on here! It makes me happy to see my 'children' doing so well in California in this setting where they are so appreciated."

Herman Wente died in 1961. With the growing popularity of the wines, a cautious expansion of the winery facilities took place, and Wente Bros. wines were distributed to every state in the union. Ernest supervised the changeover into the new technology of both harvesting and winemaking, while his son Karl headed the family winery as president. On my first visit to the enlarged winery, with its new stainless-steel fermenters, representing the investment of millions of dollars, Ernest whispered to me, "You know, Robert, we did this ourselves." It was said with modest pride, underscoring a statement in the Wente Bros. brochure: "Of the many distinguished California wineries established in the 1800s, only a small handful are still owned and operated by the original families. Wente is one of these."

Karl Wente died suddenly at forty-nine, in January of 1977. Under his careful and well-considered guidance, 300 acres of varietal vineyards were pioneered in 1962 in Monterey County at the upper end of the Carmel Valley, 15 miles inland from the ocean.

Karl's sons, Eric and Phillip, with degrees in enology and viticulture, are already at work with Herman and Ernest, all carrying on the family tradition of excellence.

SAMPLER SELECTION

Pinot Chardonnay (California). Of Livermore and Monterey grapes. California's first great Chardonnay. Fruity, dry, noble.

Le Blanc de Blancs. A blend of Ugni Blanc and Chenin Blanc. Semidry, fruity, modestly priced, universally popular.

Grey Riesling. Light, white, dry wine from the Chauché Gris grape; never disappointing, of standard excellence and value.

Chateau Semillon. Once known as "Chateau Wente." In the style of sweet French Sauternes. Among the state's best.

WOODSIDE VINEYARDS

340 Kings Mountain Road, Woodside, California 94062

When Robert and Polly Mullen took up wine-making as a hobby in 1960, they had no idea that they would become not only guardians of a revered legacy, but the mainstays of a community project that keeps residential Woodside alive to the joys of wine. There remain only about 3 acres of the celebrated Cabernet Sauvignon vines of Emmett Rixford's La Questa vineyard, planted in 1883. Some of those ancient vines, of diminishing yield, and newer ones in the same venerated soil, are tended by the Mullens. Their enthusiasm has enlisted six Woodside neighbors, who also grow modest plots of Cabernet Sauvignon, Chardonnay, and Pinot Noir. Even the village church benefits: it has Woodside Vineyards wines for Communion.

The Mullens have their own 3-acre vineyard with 800 vines lovingly cared for. Their Chenin Blanc vines have been grafted over to Chardonnay, which, like Pinot Noir, seems to be better adapted to this moderately cool area. The Cabernet Sauvignon, however, remains the prize and pride of Woodside. It is aged in American oak for two years and spends another two years in bottle before release.

Though in 1973 the Mullens expanded the winery, virtually doubling its size, annual production averages only 1,500 gallons.

SAMPLER SELECTION

Chardonnay. The Burgundian grape is given cool fermentation to capture bouquet, with aging in American oak.

Pinot Noir. Careful handling of the small clusters of tiny black grapes, in open fermentation, brings forth fine wine.

Cabernet Sauvignon. Perpetuating the La Questa label, the wine carries a unique "dusty" bouquet prized by claret lovers.

VINEYARDS AND WINERIES: SOUTH CENTRAL COAST COUNTIES

"Wine opens the heart. It warms the shy poet hidden in the cage of the ribs. It melts the wax in the ears that music may be heard. It takes the terror from the tongue that truth may be said."
—Christopher Morley

MONTEREY, SAN LUIS OBISPO, SANTA BARBARA

Monterey County is a winegrower's dream. Franciscan padres planted the first vineyard at Soledad, but it was not their blue-black Mission grape that sparked today's interest in the famed lettuce-growing region, John Steinbeck's long green valley of *East of Eden*. Reports of a *Vitis vinifera* vineyard planted in the high benchlands of the Gavilan Mountains in the 1880s focused attention on the bleak area called the Chalone Bench. A Frenchman by the name of Tamm had recognized in the geology of the area a similarity to the prized soil of Burgundy and Champagne. Accordingly, he planted grape varieties that prospered in those French regions—Pinot Blanc, Petit Pinot (now known as Pinot Noir), Chardonnay, and some Chenin Blanc. Will Silvear, a mineralogist, patiently tended the Tamm vineyards after 1919. The Wentes bought Silvear's grapes for a number of years and prevailed upon Professors Amerine and Winkler to visit Silvear. The enologists believed that with less than eight inches of rainfall and no possibility of water, the Chalone Bench would not be good for vineyards. Later they advocated the Soledad District, where water was available.

But subsequent studies by Amerine and Winkler in their temperature-summation studies endorsed the region after water wells were constructed and fed from the underground Salinas River. Following the first plantings by Masson, Mirassou, and Wente in 1962, sophisticated overhead sprinkler systems of artificial rainfall were developed: computerized irrigation that could send moisture to those vines that needed it, as determined by sensitized instruments in the ground. Today Monterey County can boast over 33,000 acres of vines, almost as many as Napa and Sonoma combined. The area is classified as Regions I and II. An afternoon breeze blowing in from the broad northern fan of valley that opens to the sea cools the area. The moisture carried by that dependable breeze the "Monterey mistral" has fostered the development of the fungus *Botrytis cinerea*, prayed for by French vineyardists of Sauternes and German viticulturists of the Rhine. The noble rot concentrates sugar in ripen-

An irrigation canal 27 miles long winds through San Martin Vineyards in Monterey County

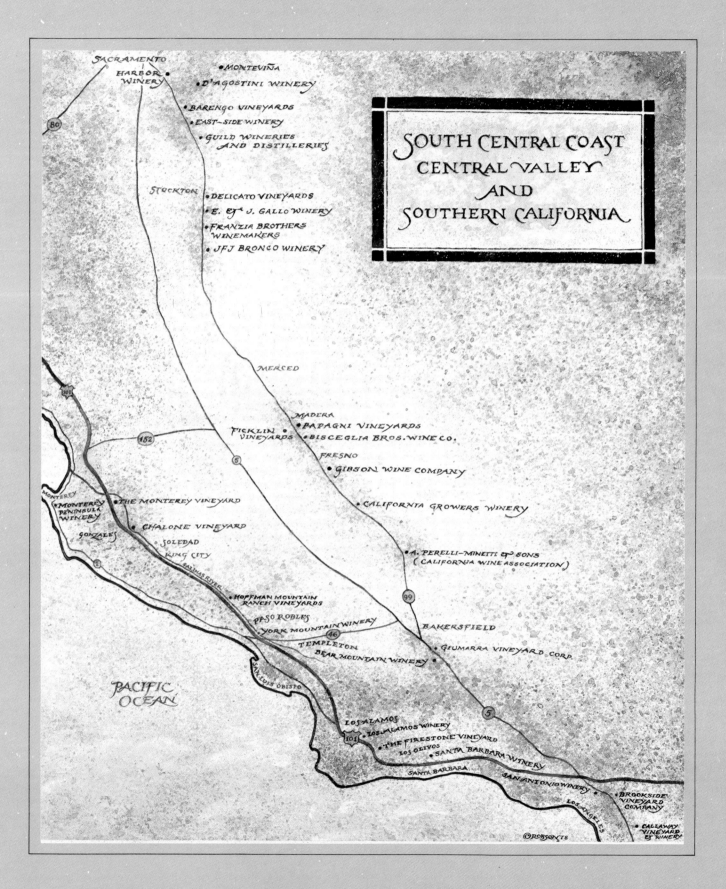

SACRAMENTO
HARBOR
WINERY
• MONTEVIÑA
• D'AGOSTINI WINERY

• BARENGO VINEYARDS
• EAST-SIDE WINERY
• GUILD WINERIES
  AND DISTILLERIES

STOCKTON   • DELICATO VINEYARDS
• E. & J. GALLO WINERY
• FRANZIA BROTHERS
  WINEMAKERS
• JFJ BRONCO WINERY

SOUTH CENTRAL COAST
CENTRAL VALLEY
AND
SOUTHERN CALIFORNIA

MERCED

MADERA
FICKLIN   • PAPAGNI VINEYARDS
VINEYARDS • BISCEGLIA BROS. WINE CO.
FRESNO
• GIBSON WINE COMPANY

• CALIFORNIA GROWERS WINERY

MONTEREY
• MONTEREY   • THE MONTEREY VINEYARD
PENINSULA
WINERY
GONZALES   • CHALONE VINEYARD
SOLEDAD
KING CITY
SALINAS RIVER

• A. PERELLI-MINETTI & SONS
  (CALIFORNIA WINE ASSOCIATION)

HOFFMAN MOUNTAIN
RANCH VINEYARDS
PASO ROBLES
• YORK MOUNTAIN WINERY
TEMPLETON
BEAR MOUNTAIN WINERY

BAKERSFIELD

• GIUMARRA VINEYARD CORP.

SAN LUIS OBISPO

PACIFIC
OCEAN

LOS ALAMOS
• LOS ALAMOS WINERY
• THE FIRESTONE VINEYARD
LOS OLIVOS
• SANTA BARBARA WINERY
SANTA BARBARA
SAN ANTONIO WINERY
LOS ANGELES
BROOKSIDE
VINEYARD
COMPANY
© ROBSON 78
CALLAWAY
VINEYARD
& WINERY

Richard Graff coaxes rich Burgundian wines from his rocky Chalone vineyards

Barely whispered among winelovers is the existence of a Pinot Noir from Chalone Vineyard which, as made by Dick Graff, has all the majesty of a Chambertin or Musigny of Burgundy. The very first pure Pinnacles Selection bottlings of the variety from the Paul Masson plantings gave the same true scent, recalling wines of the Côte d'Or. Monterey County is still young, the full promise yet to be achieved. The same is true of the limestone hills of the Paso Robles area, with new pioneering of Pinot Noir at the Hoffman Mountain Ranch, and in the Santa Ynez Valley, inland from Santa Barbara, at The Firestone Vineyard.

There are 10,000 acres of premium varietal grapes growing in the Santa Maria region, some from Rancho Tepusquet, which has become a highly regarded source of grapes. Scouts from Beringer, Sebastiani, Robert Mondavi, Louis M. Martini, Château Montelena, and ZD of Sonoma have found Chardonnay, Johannisberg Riesling, Gewürztraminer, Pinot Noir, and Merlot from this microclimate worthy of their own more exalted labels.

CHALONE VINEYARD

Stonewall Canyon Road, The Pinnacles, Soledad, California 93960

There is an old Gallic saw that declares: "To produce a great wine, the vine must suffer a little." In many of the world's most renowned vineyards, vines thrive where nothing else will grow. Impossible conditions seem to favor the wine vine. The site of Chalone Vineyard, first planted by the Frenchman Tamm and tended by Will Silvear, was acquired by the Graff family almost twenty years ago. Before that, most people had been deterred by its many difficulties: inaccessibility, lack of water, lack of modern conveniences such as the telephone.

Enter Richard Graff, music major from Harvard, young, sinewy, with some UC–Davis theories clamoring to be tested, plus his father's indulgence for his proposal to make something of the Chalone Vineyard. On my first visit, half a dozen years ago, I followed Dick's pickup truck from the verdant rows of the Paul

ing grapes, giving wines made from botrytised berries richer glycerines and subtle nuances of flavor. While it is a boon for white wines, it is a bane for red-wine varieties, calling for special spray controls.

The superlative early estimates of Monterey County as California's great vineyard bonanza caused cultivation to be extended southward into San Luis Obispo County. The boom of the seventies revived interest in Santa Barbara as grape-growing country.

Regional characteristics of the wines are only now becoming apparent as vine roots penetrate deeper and deeper into the soil, extracting a recognizably different mineral complex. Vinification by Mirassou and Wente is designed to avoid the *goût de terroir*, which can be strong enough to suggest an earthiness tinged with cabbage, garlic, and overwhelming herbal odors in white wines where delicacy is being sought. But balancing this occasional risk is an extraordinary affinity of the Monterey region for those two vines that demand a cool climate, Pinot Noir and Riesling of the Rhine.

The first harvest from Firestone Vineyard is blessed and weighed en route to becoming an elegant wine

Masson Vineyards on the lower slopes, where sprinklers like the fountains of Versailles were showering the vines with water. We wound upward into the hills, the earth growing more and more arid and desolate, the parched red soil a veritable hot waste out of Dante's Inferno. As we turned into an upper valley, I saw some straggling vines, each row with empty spaces where vines had died. We pulled up to a ramshackle cottage with the spavined boards of a porch sagging above a broken stairway. Graff leaped out of the pickup with a merry smile. "We're here!" he said, to which I could only reply, as I vaulted onto the porch, hoping the boards would support me, "We certainly are!"

Once inside, the whole scene changed. A modern Scandinavian iron fireplace held center stage, and as my eyes took in the room, they moved from a three-rank Mason & Hamlin organ to a life-size oil portrait of Dick's grandaunt in flowing silks and taffeta painted in the style of Sargent. In an adjacent dining room a table was set with Baccarat crystal and fresh flowers. Young Graff poured a golden wine into one of the goblets, and from its generous bowl emerged a scent unmistakably Chardonnay, as regal as any Montrachet or Meursault of my tasting experience. In a daze of disbelief, I walked with him to the makeshift winery, a small whitewashed adobe outbuilding, half submerged in the earth. Graff flipped a switch, and a Diesel generator whirred into life, giving electricity to light the interior and also power for fans blowing over blocks of ice trucked up from Salinas to provide the needed air-cooling in the blistering heat of autumn harvest days and nights.

With equal ingenuity, Graff had bought an antique tank truck, made a goat-trail roadway up the side of a hill above the vineyard, installed a redwood storage tank for water hauled up the mountain from Salinas, and, with plastic lines to each of thousands of old and new vines, inaugurated a drip system for irrigation years ahead of other California vintners. In 1975 and 1976, with no help but that of his brothers, he built a two-story winery into the side of the hill. There, with modern stainless-steel equipment plus French-oak cooperage, some of the finest wines of California are being made. A group of investors headed by Richard Graff, assisted by William P. Woodward, with young John and Peter Watson-Graff as winemakers, assures a future for Chalone Vineyard, and, it is to be hoped, greater availability of its wines.

SAMPLER SELECTION

Pinot Blanc (Estate Bottled). In French bottles, from French oak, a substantial wine of woody incense and long-lasting flavor.

Chenin Blanc (Estate Bottled). Made completely dry. A wine of stature, crisp, clean, and with unusual elegance. Oak-finished.

Chardonnay (Estate Bottled). Easily one of the most superb vinifications of this grape in California. French-oak-aged.

Pinot Noir (Estate Bottled). A collectors' prize. Proof that the difficult grape *can* produce elegant, translucent wine here.

THE FIRESTONE VINEYARD

Zaca Station Road, Los Olivos, California 93441

The first crush for the vineyards planted in 1972 by Ambassador Leonard Firestone and his son Brooks

Dr. Stanley Hoffman

was blessed and dedicated on the morning of September 23, 1975. The 75,000-case winery, with its 300 acres of vines, has been an expensive gamble involving an enormous investment. But the first "third leaf" wines affirm the wisdom of the endeavor, in which the Firestones are joined with Suntory, Ltd., of Japan, and André Tchelistcheff, who has been the consultant from the beginning. Winemaker Tony Austin declares: "I try for elegance." He is succeeding.

The labels that launched the first wines, with their sketches of Firestone under construction by California artist Sebastian Titus, will be souvenirs for coming generations. Cellared bottles of the good red wines, for those lucky enough to find the vintages of '75 and '76, might well be laid down for twenty-one years against the coming of age of a fortunate child. They will surely last that long.

SAMPLER SELECTION

Johannisberg Riesling (Santa Ynez Valley). Clean, light, gentle. Late-harvest, botrytised editions are richer, fuller, sweeter.

Chardonnay (Santa Ynez Valley). A big, unique wine of dry-weed scent, classic chalky taste, complex hints of wood and fruit.

Cabernet Sauvignon Rosé (Santa Ynez Valley). Silky and dry, with hints of the noble grape from which it was made.

Cabernet Sauvignon (Santa Ynez Valley). A big wine of deep color and taste, French-oak-aged, logan-berry aftertaste.

HOFFMAN MOUNTAIN RANCH VINEYARDS

Adelaide Road, Paso Robles, California 93446

The first new winery in San Luis Obispo County in nearly fifty years is set on the rolling terrain of a 1,200-acre walnut and almond ranch in the Santa Lucia Mountain range, 1,700 feet above sea level. It borders the ranch that once belonged to the great Polish patriot and pianist, Ignace Jan Paderewski, whose Zinfandel wines were widely praised many years ago.

Winemaking history will be well served for generations to come in a project as carefully planned as Hoffman Mountain Ranch Vineyards. Consultant André Tchelistcheff has described it as "a jewel of ecological elements." One of the first Chardonnays from the 1973 vintage was awarded a Gold Seal diploma by the Club Oenologique in an International Wine Competition at Ockley in Surrey, England.

Dr. Stanley Hoffman planted his first 62 acres of Pinot Noir, Chardonnay, and Cabernet Sauvignon in 1965. It was the first step toward a change from the hectic pace of a successful cardiologist's practice in Beverly Hills to the quieter role of country doctor and winemaker. In the early years, while Dr. Hoffman was in London on a teaching exchange, his two sons, Michael and David, tended the vineyard under the watchful guidance of André Tchelistcheff, making their first wines in a converted garage. When Dr. Hoffman returned to begin his country practice—the only cardiologist for miles around—his sons continued as grape growers and winemakers. The yield from the vineyard showed sufficient promise to build a real winery. Today there are 30,000 gallons of wines resting in fine oak cooperage in a multilevel winery.

There is already great achievement with Chardonnay, and the highest hopes are riding on the fine potentials of the Pinot Noir and Cabernet Sauvignon.

SAMPLER SELECTION

Franken Riesling. HMR wine of the Sylvaner grape has a silky softness, with a well-balanced residual sweetness.

Chardonnay. A round, mouth-filling wine of varietal depth, dry, fragrant, rich, with moderate bouquet in its finish.

Pinot Noir. Vintage, estate-bottled wine from the true clone of Burgundy. Translucent ruby with penetrating bouquet.

Cabernet Sauvignon. Vintage, estate-bottled wine of deep, dark garnet color. Certain to require long aging. Full bouquet.

LOS ALAMOS WINERY

Route 135, Los Alamos, California 93440

Attorney Samuel D. Hale, Jr., is a self-taught winemaker who, like many another city dweller, was

A wind-shaped Monterey cypress at Carmel

caught up in the fascination of grape growing. In the newly developed region below Santa Maria, in Santa Barbara County, Hale planted 330 acres of six choice varietals in 1972, with a sensitivity to the distinctly different microclimates favorable to each. His Chardonnay, Johannisberg Riesling, and Pinot Noir grow in the cool areas, while on the slopes of the back canyons of his estate, where it is much warmer, are his Cabernet Sauvignon, Merlot, and Zinfandel. By his own admission, the "second leaf" wines were a little disappointing. But vines and winemaker had matured for the "third leaf" harvest of 1975: the Chardonnay of that year won a bronze medal at the Los Angeles County Fair; the Zinfandel was allowed to gain a fuller stature by leaving the grapes longer on the vine. With a unique and rather baroque label, gleaming with burnished gold, Los Alamos Winery takes its place among the new boutique wineries worthy of consumer recognition.

SAMPLER SELECTION

White Riesling. A lilting freshness and ingratiating lightness give this wine, too often heavy, indications of fine promise.

Chardonnay. Early editions were made by Dr. Richard Peterson at The Monterey Vineyard before the Los Alamos Winery was completed.

Zinfandel. The late-harvest 1975 wine showed fine potential for the newly planted area to produce this varietal as a big wine.

THE MONTEREY VINEYARD

800 S. Alta Street, Gonzales, California 93926

Twenty-eight Monterey County properties, growing 9,600 acres of choice varietal grapes for a 500,000-case winery, alas came apart at the seams in the first wave of the 1974 recession's effect upon California's wine world. Pay-back schedules for the multi-million-dollar financing were predicated upon the grape prices of the early seventies. When prices fell in 1974, the grim handwriting was on the wall, not only for many marginal grapeland investors but also for such seemingly well-funded enterprises as The Monterey Vineyard.

Winemaker and president of the winery division of the enterprise was, and still is, Dr. Richard Peterson, who left the security of Beaulieu Vineyard to head the challenging Monterey County operation. There was deserving praise for the Grüner Sylvaner, assisted toward its perfection by Dr. Peterson's $100,000 adjustable centrifuge.

In the rapid dissolution of the original corporation, the grape growers had to look elsewhere for support. Many were able to salvage their future through advantageous contracts for their grapes with Gallo. In December 1977 the large winery was bought by Coca-Cola of Atlanta. Dr. Peterson, as winemaster–director, declares that the winery will continue to operate as in the past, producing vintage-dated varietal wines for its own label, and offering winemaking facilities to others, under contract.

Today the winery uses grapes from 600 acres of choice varietals, and operates virtually as a small boutique winery. Among the new titles already in demand is a rich botrytised Sauvignon Blanc, Monterey's golden answer to Château d'Yquem—elegant, honey-sweet, and flowery-clean in bouquet. The first 100 percent Pinot Noir, from the 1974 vintage, is thoroughly Californian in taste, intense in character, like velvet on the tongue. There is an earthy taste, a unique and majestic boldness, that gives credence to the high hopes for this region and is an indication that The Monterey Vineyard will be making wines of marked indigenous character in the years ahead.

SAMPLER SELECTION

Grüner Sylvaner (Monterey County). Wholly dry, with exceptional fruit. To be enjoyed young.

Chardonnay (Monterey County). More time for the vine roots in the ground will bring greater complexity to the wine.

Zinfandel (Monterey County). Unusually late-maturing grapes, harvested in December, produce a wine of lasting promise.

SOUTH CENTRAL COAST WINE LABELS

Johannisberg Riesling (Monterey County). Perky, fresh, and crisp wine; taste suggests grapefruit.

MONTEREY PENINSULA WINERY

2999 Monterey–Salinas Highway, Monterey, California 93940

The rich red wines of the Monterey Peninsula Winery are a magnet to wine buffs seeking the purist approach to winemaking. There is no fining, no filtering. Each wine is produced in a separate small lot. Under winemakers Dick Nuckton and Roy Thomas some huge blockbuster Zinfandel wines have been produced. The small stone winery is the only one in the romantic bayside city of Monterey. In October, music, wine, and good times are to be had at the "Wine Stomp," when 300 people gather to crush 10 tons of grapes with their bare feet.

SAMPLER SELECTION

Chardonnay. A 1974 vintage lot came home with a bronze medal for winemakers Roy Thomas and Dick Nuckton.
Cabernet Sauvignon (Monterey). Gold medals from the Los Angeles County Fair are evidence of the virtues of these small-lot, truly big wines.
Zinfandel (Lodi). The bigness of this dark, deep, mouth-filling wine suggests another decade ahead for its full enjoyment.

SANTA BARBARA WINERY

202 Anacapa Street, Santa Barbara, California 93101

Trained as an architect, a businessman with diversified interests, Pierre Lafond seems to gain a modicum of aesthetic satisfaction from his chores as a devoted winemaker. At the informal cinder-block winery, in the heart of downtown Santa Barbara, Lafond receives choice grapes from Santa Barbara and San Luis Obispo counties, ferments them in stainless steel, and ages the wine in Yugoslavian-oak tanks. Under a Mission label he provides house wines for many of the local restaurants and fruit wines and mead for the Danish colony at nearby Solvang. The premium varietals are modestly priced and a good value.

SAMPLER SELECTION

Pinot Chardonnay. Cool-fermented over four to five weeks at 45° F., the wine retains a fresh fruitiness and varietal character.
Muscat Alexandria. A vintage wine, with residual sweetness and the full, exotic perfume of the grape.
Zinfandel. Substantial red wine with fine varietal berryness of nose and taste. Vintage selections are the choice here.

YORK MOUNTAIN WINERY

York Mountain Road, Templeton, California 93465

In 1970, Max Goldman, an enologist and champagne maker from New York, bought from Wilfred York the historic property founded in 1882 by Andrew York, and with his son, Steven, a University of Colorado art major, has been bringing it back to an aesthetic and practical level commensurate with its potential. The old vines have been replaced with Pinot Noir and Chardonnay, for a possible future champagne *cuvée*, and there are Cabernet Sauvignon and Merlot for classic claret. But as Max Goldman rightly says, "This is Zinfandel territory." (Paderewski used to send grapes from his San Ignacio Ranch to the York Mountain Winery to be made into the ruby Zinfandel that became so famous.) Veteran winemaker Max Goldman is pleased with the varietal character the good earth is lending to his 10 acres of new vines.

VINEYARDS AND WINERIES: CENTRAL VALLEY AND SOUTHERN CALIFORNIA

"Let those who drink not, but austerely dine,
Dry up in law; the Muses smell of wine."
—Horace

SACRAMENTO, AMADOR, SAN JOAQUIN, FRESNO, KERN, MADERA, MERCED, TULARE, LOS ANGELES, RIVERSIDE, SAN DIEGO, SAN BERNARDINO

The Central Valley, which extends about 400 miles from north to south, is best known, in terms of wine production, for its yields of heavy-tonnage wine grapes—quantity rather than quality. Every harvest season truckloads of grapes go from the Bakersfield area to North Coast wineries, to be used for a significant amount of the cheaper wines released from those distinguished wineries, many of which depend for economic survival on the volume sale of jug wines. As wine country the region has suffered in comparison with the North Coast counties of Napa, Sonoma, and Mendocino. At this writing, California winemakers are locked in an emotionally charged battle for legal definitions of wineland boundaries. Regional appellations within narrower boundaries are being urged by small wineries. The larger wineries argue for one blanket designation—North Coast—for the entire coastal region from Santa Barbara to Ukiah, reflecting the elitism that attaches to the North Coast counties as compared to the highly productive Central Valley.

There is reason for a revised and upgraded opinion of the Central Valley as a region of potential for fine wines. Without any question, California's greatest Zinfandels are coming to market today boasting Lodi or Amador County as their birthplace. The San Joaquin Valley has unrecognized pockets of earth where fine wine grapes *can* grow. In the sandy loam, mineral content is high, the soil is well-suited to grape culture, and drainage, a most important factor, is excellent.

In this region, which was once semi-arid desert, healthy and productive *Vitis vinifera* grows as well as in any other wine country of the world. Today Central Valley wines are shipped not only around this country but overseas to Japan and Germany. But the legend of San Joaquin as wine country is just taking shape. I would suggest suspended judgment until some of the wines hereinafter listed are explored.

The great San Joaquin Valley was noted as early as 1772 for its profusion of wild grapevines. This is the heartland of California agriculture. Eighty percent of all the vegetables sold in the United States are grown here. Although Kern County is the largest oil-producing county in California, oil is secondary to agriculture in the economy of the region. Viniculture is a major element in the valley's economic structure, with the largest producing winery in the world, E. & J. Gallo, at Modesto, and the largest continuous agricultural holding in the state, the 280,000 acres of historic Tejon Ranch, which by 1981 may be producing 15 million gallons of wine.

There are many reasons for a changed viewpoint about this hot wine country. Hybrid vines such as Ruby Cabernet and Emerald Riesling produce better-quality wines in a warm climate than was possible heretofore. Mechanical harvesting and field-crushing, properly understood and expertly controlled, bring juice into the wineries with minimal oxidation; it comes not into old frame wineries, where even the coolest shade was withering to man and wine alike, but to refrigerated environments equivalent to the cool Rhineland. San Joaquin Valley varietals, given premium viticultural attention, are characterized by softness and delicacy. The white wines are fresh, fruity, with distinct grape taste. The reds often lack depth and mature rapidly, but they constitute a vast reservoir of pleasant and dependable table wines for daily use. Central Valley gives us an abundant heritage of great value, worth reappraisal and increased appreciation.

In San Bernardino County, at the foot of the Sierra Madre Mountains, there was at one time a vineyard—the largest in the world—that dazzled beholders and delighted photographers. But today, as a result of the inroads of subdivision and the devastating effects of smog, only gnarled stumps remain in the unharvested, untended vineyard that was formerly the pride of the Guasti family. The winery names that dominate the region—Brookside and San Antonio—still produce some local wines, but the best of their production is from grapes purchased outside the blighted areas—from North Coast counties or the new

From December through February, skilled pruners cut away canes, improving both the quantity and the quality of the next harvest

vineland in San Diego County near Temecula and the Rancho California district.

Branch wineries of San Antonio and Brookside are neighborhood tasting centers where, instead of wines, converts to the pleasures of wine are made by the thousands. Across the tasting bars, they learn the charms of wines made from descendants of the Mission vines first planted in San Diego by Padre Junípero Serra in 1769.

BARENGO VINEYARDS

3125 E. Orange Street, Acampo, California 95220

Shortly after Repeal, this brick granary was converted into a 1,650,000-gallon winery by a group of grape growers headed by Cesare Mondavi. When Mondavi sold it in the 1940s, Dino Barengo became the new owner. In 1949, he was the first to make and bottle a Ruby Cabernet from the hybrid developed at UC–Davis, and his wines continued to bring deserved recognition to the variety.

In 1973, the new owners opened a number of Barengo Vineyards retail tasting rooms, new labels were designed, and the winery was off to acquiring a slick new image. There were the good generic wines of modest price and some classic varietals of excellent value under the Barengo Reserve label. The winery was sold again, in 1976, to the present owner, Ira Kirkorian, of Campbell. UC–Davis-trained Brad Alderson is the new winemaker.

If you should come upon it in a food store, the Barengo Vineyards Wine Vinegar will do wonders for your salads.

SAMPLER SELECTION

Pinot Chardonnay. Under the "Reserve" label, this wood-aged wine is light, well-balanced, tart, and good value.

Muscadelle du Bordelais. Fresh, light, delicately sweet; well-chilled, it makes a pleasant summer luncheon feature.

Ruby Cabernet. With the Cabernet perfume, a light claret body, and good ruby color, it makes a bid for daily wine service.

BEAR MOUNTAIN WINERY

Comanche Road, DiGiorgio, California 93217

Few top varietals were being grown in the Tehachapi area until, in the 1950s, Keith Nylander, the manager of the DiGiorgio Wine Company, realized the possibilities of the region for fine table wines. Then, in 1966, when the DiGiorgio Corporation decided to get out of the wine business, the local grape growers joined together and founded the Bear Mountain Winery. Today the co-op, with 130 members, is the fourth-largest winery in the state, harvesting 135,000 tons of grapes each year from more than 16,000 acres. Bear Mountain buys no bulk wine from anyone. "We *sell* it," the marketing manager told me.

Bear Mountain's vice-president in charge of marketing, Karl Thielscher

A vertical still at Bear Mountain Winery

BOTTLING TANK
NO. 501

CAPACITY
55.033 GALS.

GALS.
PER INCH 114

In 1975 the winery's M. LaMont brand Barbera, Semillon, Chenin Blanc, and Zinfandel received gold seals from the Club Oenologique's International Wine Competition in Surrey, England, and their Cabernet and French Colombard received silver seals. For the last two years, 15,000 cases of their varietal wines have been sold to Japan under the Manns California label. These wines are sold in Japanese sake shops, department stores, and supermarkets. Because of Japan's inflation, the Chenin Blanc sells for $5 per bottle.

Winemaker for the medal-winning M. LaMont bottlings is Leonard ("Bud") Berg, who oversees the quarter of a million dollars' worth of centrifuge equipment that cleans the must expressed from freshly harvested grapes. Craig D. Crisman, Bear Mountain's new young president, still has an uphill battle, but from the fermenters and aging casks are emerging wines that should encourage the growers to keep on.

SAMPLER SELECTION

Green Hungarian. M. LaMont, estate-bottled 92 percent varietal wine of round, delightful, soft aromatic charms.

Semillon. Another M. LaMont varietal winner with the same intriguing regional character.

Ruby Cabernet. Estate-bottled, gutsy wine to lay away; good aging potential and pleasing Cabernet bouquet.

Barbera. Estate-bottled wine with an *amarone* finish in true Italian style. Rather light in body, but the nose is complex.

BISCEGLIA BROS. WINE CO.

25427 Avenue 13, Madera, California 93637

In 1888, Alfonse F. Bisceglia came to California from Calabria, to make wine with his three brothers, Joseph, Pasquale, and Bruno. During the Depression, the Bisceglia brothers bought the famed Greystone Cellars of the Napa Valley for the bargain price of $10,000. It proved to be a huge white elephant, as it had been for several previous owners. However, since The Christian Brothers, to whom the Biscegalias sold it, began making sparkling wines there, its worth has escalated into six figures.

But winemaking in the San Joaquin suits the Bisceglia brothers. Operated now by Bruno T., son of the founder, and Joseph, one of the original four brothers, the company makes and sells bulk wine to other wineries. In their tasting rooms, they offer private-label reserves, made in small quantities and handcrafted in Old World style. There are generic wines, fruit and berry wines, sparkling wines, vermouth, and brandy. Their finest wines honor the founder, Alfonse F. Bisceglia.

SAMPLER SELECTION

Grenache Blanc. An essentially dry white wine with the delicate acidity plus the varietal zing of the French grape.

Château d'Or. Billed as "a salute to Château d'Yquem," it is a golden wine of Sauternes sweetness, albeit much lighter.

Château Noir. A blended red wine of deep ruby hue, dry and full-bodied, to accompany lamb, beef, or spaghetti dinners.

J F J BRONCO WINERY

6342 Bystrum Road, Ceres, California 95307

South of Modesto, surrounded by fields of maize, cotton, and corn, and peach orchards, is Ceres, where John, Fred, and Joe Franzia have built a million-gallon winery, not to make wine but to receive and package bulk wine from the excess inventories of other wineries. As "seconds" these wines are often of outstanding quality, with bargain-bin pricing, a bonanza to the alert buyer. The shrewdness and life-long wine experience of the Franzias were rewarded at the end of their first year in business with sales of 1 1/2 million cases. Blending to the Franzias' own style is involved, and that style is unquestionably one reason for their success. They have also pioneered the light metal cap for sparkling wines, a boon to airline flight attendants, for safety and ease of opening, and of course to caterers, since less help is needed for opening champagne bottles during large receptions.

In the early months of 1977 Bronco and the Getty Oil Company announced a joint venture to build and

Bottling tanks at the million-gallon Bronco Winery

operate a wine-grape conversion and storage facility capable of processing 30,000 tons of grapes annually. Bronco will be the sole operators of the winery, with their bulk table wines available to other vintners.

The young Franzia clan—two brothers and a cousin—are the third generation of the Franzia family that had entered San Joaquin Valley agriculture with Giuseppe Franzia's arrival from Italy in 1890. They resigned from the family winery and formed the Bronco company suddenly in 1972, when the Coca-Cola Bottling Co. of New York acquired the family winery. Volatile Fred Franzia says *bronco* is the colloquial Italian term for "grape stump," a likelier definition than "untamed horse." Bronco's quart carafes can be found in fifteen states, and for a good Cabernet Sauvignon, Napa Gamay, or Gamay Beaujolais they are bargains.

SAMPLER SELECTION

Rhinewein. Cellared and bottled by John, Fred, and Joseph. Sold in quart carafes. Brilliantly clear, sweet-edged, and a bargain.

Sangria. Fruit-flavored red wine in handy carafes, ready to pour over ice cubes and be garnished with a slice of orange.

California Champagne. An Extra Dry *cuvée*, modestly priced, clean, well-made, very, very pale, bland, inexpensive.

BROOKSIDE VINEYARD COMPANY

9900 Guasti Road, Guasti, California 91743

The founding date of 1832 makes Brookside Vineyard one of the oldest in the state. In 1916 the original Brookside in Redlands was sold, and the grandsons of one of the founders went to work for Garrett and Company, which included the Guasti winery. One of the grandsons, Philo Biane, in 1952 reestablished the Brookside Vineyard Company at Ontario, and four years later he purchased the historic Guasti property from the California Wine Association. The old Guasti winery, with native fieldstone walls more than 3 feet thick and cellars measuring 600 by 100 feet, affords Brookside underground aging

facilities that are among the largest in the United States.

Though Brookside was sold in 1972 to Beatrice Foods, Inc., a Chicago conglomerate, management remains with the Biane family. Brookside produces some sacramental and commercial wines with the Benedictine monks of Assumption Abbey at Richardton, North Dakota. Some of the Bianes' finest varietal wines, from vineyards near Temecula, are put out under the Abbey label.

A unique aspect of Brookside's operation is their retail outlets, in which they are licensed to serve free samples of wine of their own production.

SAMPLER SELECTION

Saint Emilion (Assumption Abbey). A dry white wine from the Ugni Blanc grape, packaged in a Burgundy bottle! Clean, silky.

Zinfandel (Assumption Abbey). From well-established vines of the Sierra Madre slopes; aged and blended for present service.

Malmsey Madeira (Vin de Biane Fres.). A blending created by Philo Biane; mellow, rich and satin-smooth.

Sherry d'Oro (Assumption Abbey). From well-aged reserves, a medium-dry sherry; modest price and fine value.

CALIFORNIA GROWERS WINERY

38558 Road 128, Cutler, California 93615

California Growers was established as a cooperative by the Setrakian family in 1936. For many years, while it produced bulk wines for sale to other wineries, it specialized in sherries and brandy. Under its own label, Growers Old Reserve Sherry developed a considerable following among discriminating buyers. In the boom years of the early seventies, Robert Setrakian expanded both the winery and the vineyards, planting 800 acres of popular table-wine varieties, adaptable to the warmer growing region, including Chenin Blanc, Emerald Riesling, Ruby Cabernet, and Barbera. Storage capacity, mostly in stainless steel, now amounts to 12,134,000 gallons.

California sherry, port, and Madeira can hold their own with the table wines

Robert Setrakian has his own wineries in nearby Yettem for the production of premium dessert and table wines, sparkling wines, and brandies to be released under the Robert Setrakian Vineyards label.

SAMPLER SELECTION
Pale Dry Sherry. This Growers-label wine with its 99¢ price tag is better than wines at twice the price; comparable to some Spanish sherries.
Cabernet Sauvignon. Also modestly priced, and of more modest quality. Good everyday wine.

A. PERELLI-MINETTI & SONS (CALIFORNIA WINE ASSOCIATION)

Highway 99, Delano, California 93215

In 1969, enologist Antonio Perelli-Minetti, a 1902 graduate of the Conegliano Institute in Italy, purchased the California Wine Association and all its brands and labels: A. R. Morrow and Aristocrat (brandies); Ambassador, Eleven Cellars, Greystone, and Fruit Industries (table wines). There was an inventory of 5 million gallons of brandy alone, a statistic that gives an idea of the scope and scale of C.W.A.'s combined operation.

Antonio Perelli-Minetti died in 1976 at the age of ninety-four. Aside from the company bearing his name, he left a most extraordinary heritage, the discovery of a grape variety (which he named "101" and patented) from which wines will be made for generations to come. It gives character to the Eleven Cellars Burgundy, color and a crisp clean taste to Ambassador Colombard Rosé.

The taste is wholly unique, quite spicy over and above the *goût de terroir* that may be drawn from the ground. It is Antonio's lasting contribution. His sons and family are continuing the large winegrowing enterprise, which, while utilizing local grapes for brandy, dessert wines, and some table wines, brings Cabernet and other cool-region varietals from the Napa Valley. George Kolarovich, from Australia, is the new winemaster.

SAMPLER SELECTION
French Colombard. Under the Ambassador label, a crisp, clean, not wholly dry, but pleasant table wine.
Chenin Blanc. The Pineau de la Loire in a gentle, soft, mellow white wine, ideal chilled as a luncheon wine.
Colombard Rosé. A gold medal from the State Fair's Consumer Reaction Council. The color and piquant taste derive from the maverick 101 grape, added to white Colombard.
Ruby Cabernet. The Ambassador label wine has intriguing and rich complexity from additions of Petite Sirah and Barbera.

CALLAWAY VINEYARD & WINERY

32720 Rancho California Road, Temecula, California 92390

When Eli Callaway, the former president of Burlington Industries, decided to dedicate his autumn years to winemaking in a remote region of southern California, few among his associates, beyond his

Eli Callaway depends on his own weather station to record temperature, moisture, and sunlight

devoted young wife, shared his enthusiasm. Rancho California? Temecula?

In ten years the Callaway Vineyard & Winery of Temecula has become a principal case study for the enological school at UC–Davis and for connoisseurs across the country.

The microclimate of this high plateau, 23 miles inland from the Pacific Ocean, has the advantage of cooling sea breezes almost daily. In his 135-acre vineyard, Ely Callaway has his own weather station to record the all-important moisture affecting the surfaces of the vine leaves and the skins of the grapes. Temperature and sunlight records confirm Callaway's belief that the environmental factors here duplicate those of the more celebrated North Coast winelands. Even the White Riesling of the Rhine thrives here, and has successfully produced wine of extraordinary depth, brilliance, freshness, and complexity.

Callaway brought his administrative thoroughness and perfectionist drive from textiles to winegrowing. His viticulturist is John Moramarco, a tenth-generation vinegrower, who personally does the final pruning on every single vine at Callaway; he also supervises the cluster-thinning, limiting each crop to about two tons or less per acre where others might push the vines to ten tons per acre. His objective is richly concentrated berries, at the peak of their varietal character. Chenin Blanc, Sauvignon Blanc, White Riesling, Cabernet Sauvignon, Petite Sirah, and Zinfandel planted in 1969 brought in their first commercial crop in 1974, when the winery was completed.

The interior of the winery was laid out by Karl Werner, former winemaster of Schloss Vollrads of the Rheingau, and he designed much of the equipment, all, like the Spessart oak cooperage, imported from Germany. At harvest time, small gondolas, deliberately only half-filled, come leaf-free to the crusher within minutes after hand-harvesting in the adjacent vineyards. Fermentation begins with whole populations of yeasts, selected by Werner in Geisenheim and flown to California. A Westphalia centrifuge cleans the white-wine musts prior to fermentation.

Oak aging barrels are steam-leached to remove excess flavor-producing agents. The Callaway Cabernet Sauvignon, Petite Sirah, and Zinfandel are among the very few California red wines aged in German white-oak barrels. They are fined with the whites of fresh eggs, following the European tradition. The white wines are fined with *Hausenblase*—a solution made from the cured, dried bladder of the Black Sea sturgeon, imported from Russia.

All Callaway wines are bottled in one classic Burgundy shape with punt bottom, and made of dark-green glass to protect the wine against light. Full 2-inch corks from Portugal ensure minimal risk in extended cellar aging.

Young Steve O'Donnell, until recently with Beringer in the Napa Valley, is now winemaker, with Werner as consultant. Present production is in the neighborhood of 25,000 cases per year, moving toward 35,000. Distribution is national through leading metropolitan stores and restaurants. André Tchelistcheff, who was Callaway's mentor through the tremulous beginnings, retains his role now that Callaway enjoys enthusiastic acceptance.

One distinguished purchaser in Manhattan, Dr. Grayson Kirk, president emeritus of Columbia University, so enjoyed the Callaway 1974 White Riesling that he suggested it for the luncheon honoring Queen Elizabeth II and Prince Philip held at the Waldorf on July 9, 1976. The sixty cases purchased from an astonished Eli Callaway were shipped by refrigerated truck to New York. Callaway was presented to Her Majesty, who had expressed a desire to meet the producer of this lovely wine.

The big, dark-red wines, of rich, grapy essence, are only now moving to market after aging. There is regional character detectable in the taste of both red and white wines. Temecula can no longer be considered a dry, arid desert region. It is one of California's newly discovered areas for quality wine, much of which is proudly labeled . . . Callaway.

SAMPLER SELECTION

Sauvignon Blanc, Dry (Temecula). Vintage, estate-bottled; silky characteristics of Loire and dry Graves wines—but Californian.

Chenin Blanc (Temecula). "Harvested Late" editions called "Sweet Nancy" honor Callaway's wife. The botrytised wine is highly scented, very sweet. The regular Chenin Blanc is quite dry but not austere.

Petite Sirah (Temecula). A big, dark-garnet wine of powerful nose and mouth-filling body; often 14.7 percent alcohol.

Zinfandel (Temecula). Wholly regional in its own taste; complex, earthy, spicy rather than fruity.

D'AGOSTINI WINERY

Shenandoah Road, Plymouth, California 95669

The label carries the winery's founding date of 1856, although Enrico D'Agostini acquired the historic vineyard and winery in 1911. Following Repeal, his four sons continued the tradition of keeping the beautiful oval oak casks filled with the good country wine from their Zinfandel, Mission, and Carignane vines. The estate-bottled Zinfandel from this pioneer winery of Amador County is well worth a pilgrimage into the Sierra foothills.

SAMPLER SELECTION

Burgundy. The Reserve California Burgundy, modestly priced, is a blend of Zinfandel and Carignane.

Zinfandel. Estate-bottled hearty wine from well-established vines.

DELICATO VINEYARDS

12001 S. Highway 99, Manteca, California 95336

The Delicato Vineyards were established in 1924 by Gaspare Indelicato and his brother-in-law Sebastiano Luppino. With grape-growing experience gained in their native Sicily, they supplied wine grapes for the Eastern market. Today Indelicato's three sons operate an 8-million-gallon winery, in addition to selling bulk wine to other wineries. They produce generic and varietal table wines under the Delicato label, as well as sparkling wines, fruit and berry wines, ports and sherries.

SAMPLER SELECTION

Chenin Blanc. Light, fresh, fragrant, with an edge of sweetness.

Zinfandel. Produced and bottled from the company's own 67-acre vineyard. Redwood-aged. Good country wine.

EAST-SIDE WINERY

6100 East Highway 12, Lodi, California 95240

In 1934, a group of 130 local grape growers founded this cooperative winery, named for its location on the east side of town. The popular tasting room, made from a 50,000-gallon redwood storage tank, carries *Das Weinhaus* on the marquee, reflecting the German origins of most of the founders. Herman Ehlers was the winemaker for thirty-seven years, until his retirement in 1970. In addition to encouraging growers to plant the better varietals adapted to the region, including Ruby Cabernet, Ehlers produced a superb brandy that came forth anonymously from a famous Russian River winery which boasted of its merits as if it was their own. If you find Conti-Royale Brandy, one of the co-op's premium labels, pay tribute to its ten years of age and 80° proof softness with your finest crystal snifter.

Among the treasures of the 4 1/2-million-gallon winery, today run by Ernest Haas, is a mellow Angelica Antigua Mission 1773 produced from Mission grapes, aged in wood for eight to ten years. The Royal Host label for generic wines is well known in the Eastern market, but the premium wines are bottled under the Conti-Royale label. The Dry Sherry won a Grand Sweepstakes Award in 1972 at the Los Angeles County Fair, a distinction that is not granted easily or often.

SAMPLER SELECTION

Grey Riesling. A fresh and fruity edition of the Chauché Gris French varietal, matching more famed rival brands.

Petite Sirah. Under the Conti-Royale label, this sturdy red wine with Rhône Valley characteristics is dry and full-bodied.

A mountain of German-oak barrels dwarfs Eli Callaway and winemaker Steve O'Donnell

Ruby Cabernet. The hybrid vine was especially created for the growers in this area; they make some of its best wine.

Angelica Antigua. This "Mission 1773" example of the mellow, sweet wine from Padre Serra's grape makes one a believer.

FICKLIN VINEYARDS

30246 Avenue 7 1/2, Madera, California 93637

The late Walter Ficklin, Sr., came to Fresno as a grape grower in 1911. With the encouragement of viticulturists of UC–Davis he planted some acres of Portuguese port-wine varieties—Tinta Cão, Tinta Madeira, Souzão, and Touriga—as an experimental lot among his table grapes. With his sons David and

David Ficklin, whose Tinta Port ranks with the finest

Walter, Jr., he planned to make the first California port wine exclusively from Portuguese varieties. The grapes were hand-harvested in separate clusters, only the finest going to the crusher for open fermentation on the skins. With hand plungers the pomace was punched down to extract color, old brandy was added at just the precise moment indicated by the sugar readings, and the wine was aged in oak barrels for several years. Like the British blenders in Oporto, young David soon acquired, with passing harvests, a large inventory of aging wines. Every lot had its own number. He knew every cask, oval, and barrel as a parent knows his children, and like children, some day they would mature and be married.

In the early fifties, Walter Ficklin came to Los Angeles with the first Ficklin Tinta Port, with its label printed by the prestigious Grabhorn Press. A wine merchant in those days, I accepted the privilege of introducing it with great pleasure. Today, Ficklin Port is well known and is appreciated for its excellence. David's son Peter, now in his early twenties, is the third generation of the family to continue along the winemaker's path.

SAMPLER SELECTION

Ficklin Tinta Port. Every bottle could be poured the day you buy it, but further age brings greater bouquet. In the glass the wine is rich, ruby red, slightly bronzed on the edges.

FRANZIA BROTHERS

Highway 120, Ripon, California 95366

After arriving from Italy, in the 1890s, Giuseppe Franzia began his life in the New World as a truck farmer near Stockton. In 1906 he acquired the present Franzia Ranch to grow grapes for the Eastern market. With his five sons, Joseph, John, Frank, Louis, and Salvatore, in 1932 he established the winery known as Franzia Vineyards and Champagne Cellars, which in the ensuing decades was to become one of the largest in the state. The goal was sound, standard wines at popular prices.

A contract to supply bulk-process Franzia Cham-

CENTRAL VALLEY AND SOUTHERN CALIFORNIA WINE LABELS

pagne to Western Airlines for their highly advertised "Champagne Flights" zoomed the volume and propelled the image of Franzia into prominence. In April 1972 the company went public with one of the first stock offerings to come from a California winery. An offer from the Coca-Cola Bottling Co. of New York caused some rumblings in the family before the sale took place: three young Franzias split off to form the J F J Bronco Winery; two sons of Giuseppe remained with the new corporate organization. Under the new ownership the 4,000 acres of the Franzia Ranch are being planted to premium varietals with an eye on steeper competition ahead.

SAMPLER SELECTION

Chablis Blanc. In magnums and gallons, this is the "house wine" of many restaurants. Fair-quality, standard wine.

Robust Burgundy. Aiming for its "Hearty" competitor's business. Standard red wine with a slightly sweet edge.

E. & J. GALLO WINERY

600 Yosemite Boulevard, Modesto, California 95353

The Gallo brothers, who were brought up in their father's vineyard west of Modesto, made their

Julio Gallo and chief enologist Charles Crawford in Gallo's laboratory

first wines in 1933 in a small rented warehouse. Their present accomplishments represent hard work and intelligence. Ernest and Julio are today the owners of a winery with a 226-million-gallon fermenting and storage capacity, and annual sales in excess of $200 million. The warehouse for wine storage is big enough to swallow a whole freight train, including the caboose. There are batteries of insulated storage tanks, some holding a million gallons. Gallo makes its own bottles in an inferno where caldrons of molten glass feed an assembly line 24 hours a day, 365 days a year.

The newest incredible happening at Gallo is a man-made "cave" 20 feet high, with a total area of 100,000 square feet, all under 5 feet of earth. It will contain 650 4,000-gallon oak tanks made in Yugoslavia. The "cellar" will have total cooperage for 2.6 million gallons of oak-aged premium varietals.

Howard Williams, semiretired vice-president of Gallo, told me, "Until the late 1950s, the wine business was mostly port, sherry, and muscatel, with table wines a scant 25 percent. Table wines were delicate, hard to handle. What was needed was a proven package. Ernest Gallo alone taught the trade how to sell wine, through his distributors in one city after another." Today Gallo sells more than a third of the wine consumed in America.

The varietal wine program, launched in 1974, was the result of almost thirty years of planning. It involved scientific agriculture in experimental vineyards started in the 1940s, a continuous process of testing, planting over 500 varieties of grapes, reclaiming hundreds of acres and transforming them from wasteland to productive vineyard and orchard. The varietal program was initially delayed because the finer varieties such as Barbera, Ruby Cabernet, and Zinfandel were being blended into existing generic wines. Hearty Burgundy got better and better; today it even has some—not much, but some—Cabernet Sauvignon from the Napa Valley in addition to Petite Sirah, Ruby Cabernet, Carignane, Zinfandel, and Barbera. But a full program of varietals—Cabernet Sauvignon, Pinot Noir, Chardonnay, and Johan-

George Thoukis, Gallo enologist, tours the winery with enophile Burgess Meredith

nisberg Riesling—to be aged in Yugoslavian oak before bottling is a possibility before 1980.

Julio Gallo gives his energies to the vineyards, with the same concern that Ernest devotes to merchandising. Dr. Charles Crawford, chief enologist, oversees Gallo's winemaking in all classifications. Each category of wines is under the direct supervision as well of Dr. George Thoukis, enologist with Gallo for seventeen years. Every afternoon, Julio Gallo tastes wines in the laboratory with Dr. Crawford, Dr. Thoukis, and others. Ernest joins them when time permits.

There are more than forty-eight different Gallo wines, and each of them, along with the ports, sherries, varietals, and generics, is tasted in those laboratory sessions when day is done. Often competitors' products in masked bottles are arranged in a blind tasting for comparison.

Boone's Farm Apple Wine and Strawberry Hill, also apple-based, are among the best-selling wines in the United States. The newest of the carefully engineered products is E. & J. Brandy; smooth, "charcoal-filtered," and easy to sip, it is almost sure to be a success, according to marketing reports.

The translation of art into industry, without the loss of inspiration, is the genius of the whole Gallo

(overleaf) A. Perelli-Minetti & Sons (California Wine Association) at Delano, with a capacity of over 14,000,000 gallons of wine and brandy

organization. It is consistent with the brothers' drive for perfection, their desire to put something better and better into bottled wines, which has made the Gallo winery in Modesto the largest in the world and one of the greatest influences in the world of wine.

SAMPLER SELECTION

Gallo Champagne. The pride of the winery now bears the name Gallo. Extra dry, fruity, Charmat-process, modestly priced.

Sauvignon Blanc. The driest of the varietals in corked bottles. Clean, smooth, fragrant, and brilliantly finished.

Chablis Blanc. Popular house wine and bar wine, too good to omit from this listing. (Hearty Burgundy is a companion red wine.)

Livingston Cream Sherry. Can compare with the best of Bristol. Rich, mellow, one of America's greatest buys.

GIBSON WINE COMPANY

Grant Line Road at Highway 99, Elk Grove, California 95624

In 1943 wealthy stockbroker Robert Gibson acquired the Elk Grove Winery south of Sacramento, not far from his large cattle ranch in Roseville, where he also raised golden pheasants. The handsome game bird became the trademark for some of his wine labels. He chose to specialize in fruit and berry wines; apricot, raspberry, strawberry, each has its own true fragrance, and the colors are jewel-bright. A perfectionist, Gibson established new standards of excellence in the translation of pure berry nectars into wine.

Gibson died in 1960. The winery is owned today by the Sanger Wine Association of Tulare County, a group of 140 grape growers who also own cellars in Covington, Kentucky, where bulk shipments of their California wines are bottled for Eastern distribution.

The old winery, originally a gas-engine works, still produces the fine fruit and berry wines, plus a prize-winning honey mead. In 1970 an attractive tasting room was opened, in which the Sanger table wines are also presented.

SAMPLER SELECTION

Gibson's Old Fashioned Raspberry Wine. Would you believe fresh raspberries cost more than premium Chardonnay grapes?

Wassail Honey Wine. As classically beautiful as the legendary mead of Lancelot and Guinevere. Bright, golden, sweet.

GIUMARRA VINEYARD CORP.

P.O. Bin 1969, Bakersfield, California 93303

The founder of the winery, Giuseppe ("Joe") Giumarra, came to America from Sicily in 1906. At thirteen he began his new life in the New World with a pushcart, selling bananas in Toronto. Joe Giumarra in his seventies still moves merrily among the grape harvesters "manicuring" some of the most beautiful clusters of table grapes ever grown.

The Giumarra farms include 11,000 acres growing potatoes, apricots, plums, cotton, milo-maize (for chicken feed), table grapes, and wine grapes. The winery operation began in 1946, with younger brother John in charge, and expanded from dessert wines into a program of varietal table wines in 1974. In the first year the Zinfandel came home with a gold medal from the Los Angeles County Fair. Each successive Zinfandel vintage has been another prizewinner. On the wall of the tasting room are gold medals for the '73 Petite Sirah and '73 Cabernet Rouge. The Giumarra Barbera is Piedmontese in style, with a spicy, regional taste that supports the case for an appellation recognizing the individuality of this Central Valley wine region.

SAMPLER SELECTION

French Colombard. A very fruity vintage wine, flowery-fresh bouquet, interesting melon taste. Splendid white wine.

Chenin Blanc. Pleasing balance of fruit acidity with 2.2 percent residual sweetness for popular appeal.

Barbera. Full-bodied, with hints of *amarone* taste in the complex middle-body. Regional distinction.

Cabernet Rouge. Completely proving the merits of the hybrid Ruby Cabernet × Carignane. Soft, fragrant wine.

GUILD WINERIES AND DISTILLERIES

One Winemasters' Way, Lodi, California 95240

Guild is the nation's largest grower-owned cooperative producer of wine and brandy products. Its membership of nearly 1,000 grape growers owns seven wineries throughout the state, with central blending, bottling, and warehouse facilities in Lodi. In 1971, Guild acquired the Roma Winery in Fresno, with the famous Cresta Blanca label; it is operated today as a separate entity, its vineyards and winery in Mendocino, its marketing administration apart, in San Francisco, under its own president, Herbert Drake.

Under Robert M. Ivie's leadership, Guild has moved into a strong third position in the industry, after Gallo and United Vintners. As a result of Ivie's discriminating business sense, the marketing has been simplified and the list of wines cut down to known and demonstrated winners like Vino da Tavola and Famiglia Cribari.

Guild's prestige label, aside from Cresta Blanca, is Winemasters' Guild. The wine took more than half a dozen years to perfect, but now has a winning hands-across-the-sea tie to winemaking guilds of Europe. French, German, and Italian cooperatives have associated themselves with the California growers. All the middlemen have been passed over so that good basic titles of well-known European wines can be brought into this market at competitive pricing. In June 1977 I visited the co-op that sends Bordeaux wines from St. Émilion. They are pleased with the arrangement, and the wines are excellent.

SAMPLER SELECTION

French Colombard. Winemasters' Guild makes a stylish wine of this new popular "mid-varietal"—sweet-edged, soft.

Cabernet Sauvignon. Winemasters' Guild deepens this popular variety with some Mendocino grapes from its membership.

Zinfandel. Under the same label, this is a winner in price and dependable quality.

Burgundy (Famiglia Cribari). Either dry or mellow, it is a competitor of the Hearty one.

HARBOR WINERY

610 Harbor Boulevard, West Sacramento, California 95831

Charles H. Myers, who teaches English at Sacramento City College, is a self-taught winemaker. His romance with the grape began more than twenty years ago, and he has been encouraged by such experts as Sacramento's leading wine merchant, Darrell Corti, André Tchelistcheff, and grape grower Bernard Rhodes. He was among the first to discover the rich depths of Zinfandel grapes from the Deaver Vineyard of Amador County. The modest winery in West Sacramento today produces Zinfandels and Chardonnays from selected vineyards. Darrell Corti snags the lion's share of the wines for his store in Sacramento.

A rare specialty is an Amador County wine made from hundred-year-old Mission grapevines in harvest seasons when the cooler climate brings the grapes to perfect, sugar-laden ripeness. Following an old Roman winemaking method, additional grape concentrate is added to the fermenting wine, with champagne yeasts that raise the alcohol naturally until fermentation stops. Myers calls the wine Mission de Sol—Blanc de Noirs.

SAMPLER SELECTION

Chardonnay (Napa Valley). Fermented in 500-gallon stainless-steel tanks, aged in French oak. Silky, dry, regal.

Zinfandel (Amador County). Neither filtered nor fined; a dry vintage wine from the Deaver Vineyard. Big, noble wine.

Mission de Sol (Blanc de Noirs). From Mission grapes, a luscious, sweet, vintage wine, naturally almost 16 percent alcohol.

MONTEVIÑA

Route 2, Box 30A, Plymouth, California 95669

Once more the accent is on Zinfandel here in the Shenandoah Valley of Amador County. The young enterprise, established in 1973 by retired banker W. H.

Field, has son-in-law Cary Gott, trained at Fresno State, as winemaker. Monteviña has a whole group of Zinfandel wines, including Zinfandel Nuevo, exhibiting fragrance and complexity. But there's also Cabernet Sauvignon and Sauvignon Blanc and more in store from Monteviña's 165 acres of vines, which include Piedmont's Nebbiolo, certain to make a wine worth looking for.

SAMPLER SELECTION

White Zinfandel. You can have it Dry or Sweet and each is a conversation piece when poured.

Zinfandel Montino. A vintage wine, ruby-red, and deeply complex.

Monteviña Montenero. A Corti-inspired blending of Zinfandel and Barbera grapes. Big, fragrant, bold, complex.

Zinfandel Nuevo (Shenandoah Valley). Produced by the carbonic-maceration method, accenting berryness. Suggests Beaujolais.

Sauvignon Blanc (Amador County). A superb wine of extraordinary dry fruitiness; the complex flavors suggest pineapple.

PAPAGNI VINEYARDS

31754 Avenue 9, Madera, California 93637

Southeast of Madera, set among its own vines, is a bold new winery out to prove that really fine table wines can be produced here. In October 1976, Angelo Papagni and his wife journeyed to Milan to accept gold medals for three wines competing with their European counterparts at the Terzo Concorso Enologico Internazionale: their Madera Rosé, 1973 Madera Barbera, and Moscato d'Angelo. "For our family's first wines to win in Europe is the achievement of a lifetime," Angelo told me.

In 1912, Demetrio Papagni had arrived in the San Joaquin Valley from Puglia, the hot winemaking region in the heel of the Italian boot. From the beginning, Papagni Vineyards shipped tons of wine grapes to the Eastern seaboard (including Canada), mostly for home winemakers. In 1973, Angelo Papagni, the American-born son, decided to make

Angelo Papagni in his modern new winery at Madera

table wines with his own grapes, accepting the challenges of Region IV; he realized that the sandy loam soil, with some calcium but no lime, had potential. His studies in viticulture at Fresno State had readied him with understanding, plus some daring.

The jury is still out about his Chardonnay. There's no argument, however about the Italian delight Moscato d'Angelo, which undergoes the same slow, cool fermentation Louis M. Martini gives the celebrated Moscato Amabile. Another Papagni specialty is an oak-aged Alicante Bouschet, vintage and estate-bottled. That is daring: the most vulgar, misprized grape in the grape growers' ampelography treated with the concern given the noble Pinot and Cabernet! Papagni may not have received a gold medal for it yet—but here among wine buffs recognition has already arrived.

SAMPLER SELECTION

Moscato d'Angelo. As seductive as sweet, cold, fresh grapes juiced right into your mouth; 12 percent residual sugar.

Spumante d'Angelo. The same wine in a sparkling edition. Less exciting somehow, despite the honest bubbles.

Barbera (Madera). Vintage wine, aged in wood, with light body and style, complexity in nose and taste.

Alicante Bouschet (Madera). Vintage wine, oak-aged, with an aromatic spicy bouquet; haunting charms.

SAN ANTONIO WINERY

737 Lamar Street, Los Angeles, California 90031

Within sight of the Los Angeles City Hall, the San Antonio Winery is, according to its owners, "the last producing winery in the City of the Angels." It was saved to become Cultural Historical Monument Number 42, honoring Santo Cambianica, the founder, who began winemaking here in 1917 with grapes from nearby San Gabriel. The winery is named after the patron saint of Padua, in northern Italy, where Cambianica came from.

There are now eight "branch winery" retail stores in suburban southern California. San Antonio wines, made in downtown Los Angeles from grapes of several vinegrowing areas, are sampled and sold along with wine-related items—glasses, corkscrews, wine racks, bread, cheese, books.

SAMPLER SELECTION

French Colombard. A sweet-edged, fresh and fruity wine; popular price and popular appeal.

Velvet Chianti. In competition at the Los Angeles County Fair, this mellow blending has won top awards.

Almondoro. A Marsala-type wine, almond-flavored; excellent for zabaglione.

TOURING CALIFORNIA WINE TRAILS

"We could, in the United States, make as great
a variety of wines as are made in Europe, not
exactly of the same kinds, but doubtless as good."
                                              —Thomas Jefferson

During the last decade in California, Jefferson's prophecy has had a gratifying measure of fulfillment. Seven out of every ten bottles of wine consumed in the United States are produced in California, and their varieties are legion, their quality excellent. The widely publicized wine boom of the seventies gave a renewed luster to the name California, not only multiplying the number of wine buyers but inspiring in them a lively desire to visit the source of their enjoyment.

One hour's drive from San Francisco you can find yourself in Wine Country, U.S.A. Only ten years ago, a Pullman parlor car with a wine bar and a few lounge chairs sufficed to take care of pilgrims visiting the Charles Krug Winery in the Napa Valley, and August Sebastiani in Sonoma thought that an old railroad caboose with a pot-bellied wood-burning stove and a wine bar was an adequate reception room for those coming to visit his winery. Today, neither could accommodate the visitors who come even in one hour to the wineries along the vintage trails.

The allure of California wine country, and of the wine itself, depends in large part upon the nature lover in all of us. A vineyard is only a farm, and a winery a kind of factory; you can discount right now the free glass of wine in the tasting room as the big draw. This is a countryside "Disneyland," with seasonal festivals, to be sure, but I believe the appeal of the vineyards is to something more basic than merely the carnival spirit.

In the heart of each of us there is a response to the land. For some, it may be spiritual: the hills and valleys,

Thomas Jefferson wine exhibition, The Wine Museum of San Francisco

THE TAVERN: THOMAS JEFFERSON AND WINE IN EARLY AMERICA

forests and rivers, vineyards in growth cycles—all are evidence of God's hand. For history buffs, El Camino Real is a stirring experience rather than a concrete freeway between San Diego and Sonoma; it is the Mission trail of Padre Junípero Serra, and romantics see him still, strolling through the fields strewn with wildflowers. Some may be moved by the redwood groves, as serenely quiet as a cathedral, or by the bracing salt sea air of the coastal bays of Monterey and Carmel, or by craggy Mendocino. Others delight in the paradox of a bit of vineyard in downtown Los Angeles, a retreat beneath a grape arbor in the shadow of City Hall.

Eureka! ("I have found it!") is California's state motto. Wherever you find it—the memorable experience—however you find it, is up to you, but haste is the enemy of meaningful touring. A *New York Times* correspondent recently wrote a story for its Travel section on the "Highs and Lows of a California Wine Tour," in which he reported visiting seven wineries in nine hours! His account, while it is proof that this can be done, becomes a cautionary guide for anyone hoping to come away from such an experience with happy memories and increased wine wisdom.

There are certain ground rules that apply to all travelers to the wine country, whether they be casual visitors or dedicated and adventurous seekers of wine experience and knowledge:

- Weekdays are pleasanter than weekends, since you are less likely to encounter crowds.
- Don't schedule more than four winery visits in any one day.
- Lodgings for the night should be booked firmly in advance.
- Take notes. Memory is the winetaster's greatest asset, for taste is fugitive. A tasting diary complete with winery name, names of wines tasted, vintages, your ratings, and descriptions, prices, availability, and so on, will prove an invaluable comparison index.
- If you are serious about a specific winery or have professional ties to the wine world, write well in advance, giving the date and time of your

THE WINE MUSEUM

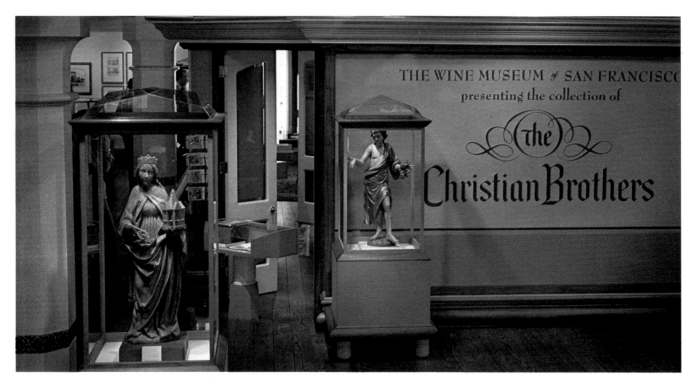

Entrance to The Wine Museum of San Francisco

arrival and requesting an appointment. Schedules are difficult to keep in wine country, and hosts are used to late-arriving guests who have been delightfully detained by a tasting at the previous stop; however, every effort should be made to extend the courtesy of promptness. California has laws prohibiting the serving of alcoholic beverages to persons under twenty-one years of age. Since wine is in this category, even watered wine at table is not permitted. Exceptions for your well-mannered offspring, however good a palate they may have developed at home, should not be requested.

What season of the year is best for wine touring? The logical answer is autumn, during the harvest, but that is when winemakers have the least time to spend in conversation. In winter, when the vines are dormant, the pace of work inside the winery permits more leisure. Walks through the bare, pruned vineyards are bracing; the air is clear for photographing great vistas. In spring, it is blossom time in the surrounding orchards, the first green appears in the vineyards, and

with June come the little jade beads that will develop into berries. Summer swells the berries, everything is lush and green, and tourists are everywhere. . . . In a word, the best time for you to come to the vineyard is when you have the most time to spend.

With these few points understood, geography becomes the next order of consideration. The divisions of California wine country are somewhat arbitrary. The wineries covered in the preceding pages are arranged alphabetically within four principal areas: the North Coast counties of Sonoma, Mendocino, and Napa; the Bay Area and Central Coast counties; the South Central Coast counties; and the Central Valley and Southern California counties. In this chapter the highlights of each area will be described, with suggestions of points of interest to see in addition to the vineyards.

WINE TOURS STARTING
FROM SAN FRANCISCO

In a light moment Robert Mondavi once described Oakville, the village town in the Napa Valley where his winery is located, as "the navel of Bacchus." In a more serious vein, San Francisco can certainly be called "the heart of California wineland," historically, culturally, and economically. Researchers can find the California Historical Society at 2090 Jackson Street. The winegrowers' own public relations and information bureau, the Wine Institute, at 165 Post Street, maintains files of information and photographs, with courteous staffers eager to assist wine pilgrims. The most beautiful repository of wine-related art and objects is The Wine Museum of San Francisco. An hour or so spent in this handsome Mission-inspired building overlooking Fisherman's Wharf will put the projected vineyard tour in full perspective. The collection of artifacts is organized around themes of the grape, the harvest, the vintner, wine in mythology, and the celebration of life and wine.

Almost forty years ago, Alfred and Hanna Fromm, with Alfred's brother, Norman, and partner, Franz W. Sichel, began assembling artistic expressions of man's joy in wine from all over the world. The collection grew to include drawings, watercolors, etchings, sculptures, paintings, porcelains, and drinking vessels from the major winegrowing countries. The Museum, administered with the cooperation of The Christian

Brothers, was inaugurated in January 1974. It is open daily except Mondays and holidays. Admission is free. The Museum also maintains a library of rare books on wine. The collection includes works in six languages, the earliest from 1587, as well as major contemporary volumes on wine. Wine students and writers may, upon application to the Museum, make use of these books. Write to The Wine Museum, 655 Beach Street, San Francisco, CA 94109.

A number of tours to the Napa and Sonoma areas are available. Gray Line Sight-Seeing offers nine-hour bus tours out of San Francisco every Monday, Wednesday, and Saturday, leaving at 9:00 A.M. These include stops at the Robert Mondavi Winery and at Sebastiani, with lunch included.

Should you be interested in a more personal or extended tour arranged specifically for you or your group, and going beyond the heavily traveled tourist routes, there are a number of possibilities. One specialist in private tours is Lou Gomberg, who has spent his life among the vintners, knows them all, and enjoys their friendship and profound respect. He might even, schedules and fee permitting, accompany you as guide. You can address him at Tours/Wine Tours, Ltd., 26 O'Farrell Street, San Francisco, CA 94108, or phone (415) 362–5071.

San Francisco from the highway overlook across the bay

Tourist attractions abound along the wine roads

Another well-qualified tour guide for the Napa Valley is John Thoreen, formerly director of wine programs at Sterling Vineyards. A teacher, writer, and enthusiastic wine connoisseur, he provides a service that is less conventional, more individual. Thoreen offers an intensively educational "Five-Day Tutorial in Napa Valley," with its base of operations at the new and comfortable Wine Country Inn. For further information and brochure, write to The Wine Tutor—John Thoreen, 1423 Foothill Boulevard, Calistoga, CA 94515, or phone (707) 942-5242.

You can, of course, do a little homework and go it alone at your own pace. Absolutely essential for planning your trip is the booklet "California's Wine Wonderland," available free from the Wine Institute in San Francisco. It lists all the wineries that are open to visitors in thirty-two of California's fifty-eight counties, giving addresses, telephone numbers, and visiting hours and also indicating which wineries are visitable by appointment only. It not only includes county maps but tells which wineries have picnic facilities and tastings. And it is indexed, which makes it a real treasure. Write to Wine Institute, 165 Post Street, San Francisco, CA 94108.

NORTH COAST COUNTIES

Forty years along the wine trail have taught me that flexibility can result in delightful experiences bearing out the words of the eighteenth-century poet John Gay: "From wine what sudden friendship springs!" The pleasures of the road, particularly in the wine country, often lie in a change of pace. Some days are long, some are short, and sometimes it rains. "Life is the thing that happens to you while you are making other plans." Impromptu and unanticipated happenings should be expected. The journey to Napa, Sonoma, and Mendocino might well include side trips to the tempting diversions of Fort Ross, Sea Ranch, Little River, Mendocino's rocky coast, and famed Benbow. Equally tempting excursions entice the wine tourist in Alameda, Santa Clara, Santa Cruz, and Monterey. The day-by-day schedule that follows is not meant to be an exact blueprint for "doing the wine country"; it is intended to serve as a basic outline for your own individual odyssey.

First Day. As you leave San Francisco in the morning, the toll-free, northbound traffic across the Golden Gate Bridge is lighter on your side of the road, while the southbound lanes are jammed with commuters from Marin County. A first temptation occurs just over the bridge, where there is an overlook for photographing San Francisco, seen on the other side of the bay in all its legendary beauty, its spires rising, sometimes into the mist. Just beyond San Rafael, on the right, over the crest of the hill, is the Marin County Court House, a Frank Lloyd Wright architectural masterpiece. Only a few miles ahead is a vista of San Quentin. Farther along you turn east and head for Sonoma, the logical first stop in any wine tour. Route 121 is well marked and leads directly to the central square of the historic town, where, on June 14, 1846, the first "Bear Flag" of the Republic of California was raised.

A slow drive around the old Plaza will adjust your time frame to the last century as you observe the old buildings, many restored to their nineteenth-century state. General Mariano Guadalupe Vallejo's soldiers might still inhabit the barracks in a balconied building in the style of architecture known as Monterey-California although it originated here. On a corner stands the Mission San Francisco Solano de Sonoma, and just one block west, at Number 2 Spain Street, is the Sonoma Cheese Factory. All the cheeses here are superb, the specialty being their own Sonoma Jack. But you can also buy—if you are inspired to grow your own—some Zinfandel and Sauvignon grapevines, already bench-grafted onto sturdy rootstock, packed with planting instructions. You can even buy a little two-bladed cork-puller to tuck into the glove compartment of your car.

Half a mile farther west on Spain Street is the house of General Vallejo—named after a nearby foothill with a flowing stream called "Crying Mountain" by the Indians—Lachryma Montis. This is now the proprietary name of a wine blend produced by Buena

Sonoma Plaza

Vista Winery, a big, bold red wine you may be tasting later in the afternoon on your visit to Count Agoston Haraszthy's winery a few miles northeast of the Plaza.

The Vallejo dwelling is a state historical monument, impeccably maintained. It is a thoroughly delightful Victorian gingerbread house, a house of seven marble fireplaces. Still furnished, it seems to have been left by the family only moments ago; the children's toys are still on the floor in the drawing room. In the carriage-house museum, you may see a repoussé silver berry spoon presented as a prize to the General as "Maker of Best Red Wine—1858," which no doubt pleased him, since there was a gentle rivalry in winemaking between the Vallejo and Haraszthy families.

You may linger an hour or so here, and then be on your way to Glen Ellen. This is Jack London country, and his 1,400-acre domain is now open to the public as the Jack London Historical State Park. Still standing is the gaunt stone skeleton of Wolf House,

destroyed by an arsonist the day before its completion. But Charmian London built another house, of the same native volcanic stone—the House of Happy Walls, which contains many fascinating memorabilia of the romantic novelist, including London's handwritten diary.

This might be the place for your first picnic lunch of wine, fruit, and cheese. "Fill your glass and let us look at the parchments of the dreamers of yesterday who dreamed their dreams on your own warm hills." From these hills you can look to the east and see the Mayacamas Mountains, which divide Napa from Sonoma, topped by the Monte Rosso Vineyard of Louis M. Martini, with vines in both counties.

This is also the neighborhood of the Grand Cru, Kenwood, and Hanzell wineries, all of which may be visited by appointment. If your schedule will not permit the Glen Ellen visits, then, after exploring Sonoma's Plaza, proceed a few blocks east of town to Sebastiani. A winery tour is offered here in which old winemaking methods are shown, demonstrating the striking contrast with the new stainless-steel and centrifuge technology. At the conclusion of the tour, participants are rewarded with a sampling of wines in the charming tasting room with its memorabilia of the founding family. One such winery tour is almost enough; certainly if you've seen one bottling line, you've seen them all. Nevertheless, at every winery, I go along to listen to the guide; one never knows when one will learn something new.

West of town, the Sebastiani family has a large varietal vineyard in Schellville, where a large new modern winemaking facility may be constructed. At present it is a vineyard, wild bird sanctuary, and tree-shaded picnic site for guests of the Sebastiani family or for group tours, by special arrangement.

There are two more wineries to see this first afternoon, Buena Vista and Hacienda Wine Cellars (which has its own private picnic area). Both wineries, once owned by Frank Bartholomew, show the artistic touch of the dedicated custodian of the Haraszthy legend. If time permitted, a whole day could be spent here. You might even acquire a private locker in Hacienda Wine

Cellars and store away a case or two of Clair de Lune Chardonnay for your next visit.

Dinner at Au Relais, 691 Broadway, on the main street leading to the Sonoma Plaza, concludes our first day. This *Holiday* magazine award restaurant belongs to Harold Marsden and his wife, who keep their little house by the side of the road as neat as new paint. There is a rose garden for outside dining, a popular bar, and a wine list that offers selections from wineries you might not have time to visit.

El Pueblo Motel, on the western edge of Sonoma, has the best overnight accommodations, with a swimming pool for cooling off after a hot summer day. You will need reservations at any time of year, but especially during the Vintage Festival in September. Write to El Pueblo Motel, 896 West Napa Street, Sonoma, CA 95476, or phone (707) 996-3651.

Second Day. You leave the Valley of the Moon and Jack London country for Sonoma's other principal wine region, the Russian River Valley. About a dozen wineries, clustered in the wooded hills and valleys, have formed their own promotional organization, the Russian River Wine Road. Their brochure has a map and capsule winery information, and can be obtained by writing to Russian River Wine Road, P.O. Box 127, Geyserville, CA 95441.

Route 12 out of Sonoma is a slow local road; it intersects Highway 101 near Santa Rosa, the home of

Dining in the patio of Au Relais in Sonoma

horticulturist Luther Burbank. His Memorial Gardens, maintained by the city of Santa Rosa, are open daily, admission free. Late March through early April is apple-blossom time in the valley. Grapevines are only beginning to put out bud-break leaves on gnarled stumps, but everywhere along the side roads bloom orchards of exquisite beauty. Here and there a chimneyed hop kiln pokes up above the trees, an architectural remnant from earlier times.

Follow Highway 101 north to Windsor, where the Guerneville off-ramp will take you along the Russian River as it winds to the coast and Fort Ross. But on the way, stop at fascinating Korbel Champagne Cellars, near Rio Nido. At Korbel you can witness the classic *méthode champenoise* bottle fermentation of sparkling wines and visit the handsome tasting room and souvenir shop. The second-morning stop might be at Sonoma Vineyards on the way back to Windsor. One of California's most handsome contemporary wineries, designed by a student of Frank Lloyd Wright, Sonoma presents concerts, operettas, and ballet performances in the summer months in an open green-lawned court between two of the building's wings.

If you continue north on Route 101 nearly to Geyserville, you can lunch at Souverain of Alexander Valley, another of the valley's leading architectural gems, inspired by the local hop kilns. In its open courtyard, summertime brings a series of theater concerts. Information can be obtained (and reservations made) by writing Souverain Cellars, P.O. Box 528, Geyserville, CA 95441. The restaurant is a delightful experience; open windows overlook vineyards with the Mayacamas Mountains as backdrop. The multi-million-dollar winery installation, now owned and controlled by a group of grape growers, has a tour that is well worth taking, even if you have already seen one winery. Little Trentadue is only paces away, and Simi and Dry Creek are among the nearby vineyards you should see if possible.

Overnight accommodations at Los Robles Lodge, one mile north of Santa Rosa, are comfortable and convenient. While the Lodge is large, having banquet and convention facilities, it also rejoices in the personal touch of owner Claus Neumann, whose executive chef is responsible for catering many of the local winery affairs. The dining room features a California/Continental cuisine, with a seafood buffet on Friday nights. Write to Los Robles Lodge, 925 Edwards Avenue, Santa Rosa, CA 95401, or phone (707) 545–6330.

Third Day. There are several options at this point. You may wish to drive north—visiting Geyser Peak and Pedroncelli en route—to the Ukiah region, where you will find Fetzer, Parducci, and Weibel. Or you could swing coastward and take time out at any one of three delightful havens for escapists. Heritage House at Little River, just below Mendocino, is a hundred-year-old white-frame hostelry with charming guest cottages whimsically named Scott's Opera House, The Barber Pole, Country Store, and Ice Cream Parlor. Write to Heritage House, Little River, CA 95456, or phone (707) 937–5885. Little River Inn, another white-frame structure, set among redwoods and facing the blue Pacific, is equally popular. The sea is often storm-tossed, always invigorating to view. Write to Little River Inn, Little River, CA 95456, or phone (707) 937–5942. At Sea Ranch Lodge, down the coast, one can find solitude that's both wild and peaceful. Write to Sea Ranch Lodge, Sea Ranch, CA 95456, or phone (707) 785–2371.

Returning from the coast toward Highway 101, Route 128 winds through Anderson Valley, where, by appointment, you might visit the little Husch winery and stop at Edmeades to have a taste of extraordinary wine made from Baldwin, Spitzenberg, and Golden Delicious apples. Fermented in French-oak puncheons, the apple wine is bottle-aged as tenderly and lovingly as Chardonnay, whose finesse it suggests.

If you do not have time for the coastal digression, then on this third day, after luncheon at Souverain, take Route 128 or the Alexander Valley Road southeast to Calistoga and the Napa Valley.

In August Calistoga celebrates Sam Brannan Days. Here you'll learn how this boomtown of the last century got its name. It was Sam Brannan, California's first millionaire, who first published the earth-shaking headline "Gold Discovered in California," which brought the forty-niners from all over the world. Indians had long cherished this area for its hot springs.

A guided tour at Charles Krug, St. Helena

(There's a geyser that spouts a column of steam 60 feet into the air as regularly as Old Faithful in Yellowstone.) Sam planned to create a great spa, complete with racetrack, to rival Saratoga Springs in New York. After one glass too many, in a promotional speech to potential investors, he announced: "This will be the greatest Calistoga spa in Sarifornia!" The name Calistoga endured, but his hotel did not. Evidence of the racetrack remains at the Calistoga Soaring Center, where fair weather and kindly breezes attract dozens of graceful and silent gliders that ride the windflow up into the blue.

There are still mud baths, mineral pools, and expert masseurs at Dr. Wilkinson's Hot Springs, open all year round and with comfortable accommodations. Write to Dr. Wilkinson's Hot Springs, 1507 Lincoln Ave., Calistoga, CA 94515, or phone (707) 942–4102. Pete's Delicatessen, on Lincoln Avenue in the center of town, is the most popular rendezvous, and a source of great sandwiches to take out for your next winery picnic.

Your next stop might well be Schramsberg, producer of California's outstanding champagnes, the

247

historic winery rapturously described by Robert Louis Stevenson in *Silverado Squatters*. Sterling Vineyards, the occasional setting for grand opera on its sky-high terrace, is a favorite rendezvous for tourists; its funicular offers the most unusual winery tour—self-conducted—in California.

You could spend a whole week and only begin to cover the wineries in the Napa Valley. Among my favorite stops are the two mentioned above, and, from north to south, Freemark Abbey (where lunch at the Abbey Restaurant is popular with winemakers because of the excellent food and service), Beringer, Louis M. Martini, Heitz, Beaulieu, Inglenook, Sutter Home, and, off the Silverado Trail, Joseph Phelps, Stag's Leap Wine Cellars, and The Christian Brothers at Mont La Salle. By appointment only, Mayacamas is an idyll for a leisurely visit.

The newest Napa Valley attraction for the winery visitor is Domaine Chandon in Yountville, the long-hoped-for offspring of Moët & Chandon of Épernay, France. The handsome new winery building was dedicated with full ceremony on April 23, 1977, and was launched with the smashing of two beribboned bottles of bubbly—Moët Brut Imperial and Domaine Chandon Napa Valley Brut. The winery is open every day but Tuesday and Wednesday and features, besides conducted tours, a handsome restaurant with open fire-

Outdoor opera at Sterling Vineyards

place and views of the landscaped grounds. The cuisine is French, naturally, supervised by a young disciple of Paul Bocuse. The restaurant, open for luncheon and dinner, seats only sixty. Reservations are advisable; phone (707) 944-2467.

Overnight lodging is deluxe at the Silverado Country Club, with its two 18-hole Robert Trent Jones golf courses, eight championship tennis courts, and four swimming pools for the inhabitants of the 180 condominiums. For reservations, write Silverado, 1600 Atlas Peak Road, Napa, CA 94558.

More intimate is the new Wine Country Inn, a handsome hideaway for wine pilgrims within walking distance of Freemark Abbey. This 14-room hostelry overlooking the vineyards was built by Ned Smith and his sons and decorated by his wife, Marge. There's no television, no radio, no telephone service, no room service, no pool, but there are rooms with fireplaces, beautiful views, privacy. Buffet-style Continental breakfast is included in the room rate. As its brochure says, the inn offers "a chance to unwind in country comfort." Reservations are absolutely essential. Write to The Wine Country Inn, 1152 Lodi Lane, St. Helena, CA 94574, or phone (707) 963-7077.

The Magnolia Hotel in Yountville is an unbelievable treat. Only four rooms! The two-story building, of locally quarried, hand-hewn granite blocks, was constructed in the last century, and was the home of Ray and Nancy Monte. They grew up in the valley, and were the creators of the adjacent shopping complex, Vintage 1870. The Magnolia is for lovers and honeymooners. The price of your room includes full breakfast and the best French toast you'll ever eat, served with homemade port-wine syrup. For the restaurant in the cellar a French chef prepares five-course dinners with rotating menus of some sixteen different entrées. One sitting and only forty-eight places make advance reservations essential. For reservations write to Magnolia Hotel, 6529 Yount Street, Yountville, CA 94599, or phone (707) 944-2056.

Next door to the Magnolia Hotel is The Court of the Two Sisters, for coffee and the best cookies, cakes,

A field of poppies, the State flower of California

Burgundy House in Yountville

pastries, and quiche imaginable, made by two elderly widows, Hilda and Leona. A few more steps will take you into Vintage 1870, a maze of shops built into an old winery building. Bring money. You'll find irresistible temptations in cookery equipment, wines, books, edibles, and potables galore. By all means plan to have lunch at the Chutney Kitchen, and don't miss the soup du jour.

Another overnight lodging possibility is just up the road at Burgundy House. It, like the Magnolia Hotel, is a nineteenth-century stone building. Mary Keenan, who operates an antique shop in the lobby, is mistress of this small inn. The decor is "greenhouse-funky" and you can buy the furniture in your room to take home, if you must have it. For reservations write to Mary Keenan, Burgundy House, 6711 Washington Street, Yountville, CA 94599, or phone (707) 944–8927.

Most of the tasting rooms in the wineries close at 5:00 P.M. You can make the Robert Mondavi Winery in Oakville your last stop on this third day, and after a tour and tasting, return to San Francisco (have coins ready for the toll over the Golden Gate Bridge) for dinner, possibly at the Blue Boar on Lombard Street. For the ultimate in spoiling yourself with comfort and service, Nob Hill offers the best hotels—the Stanford Court, the Fairmont, and the Huntington, to name a few.

BAY AREA AND CENTRAL COAST COUNTIES

First Day. Starting once again from San Francisco, weather or whim can dictate your direction—eastward across the bay to Alameda, stopping at Wente, Concannon, and Weibel, as a one-day excursion, or southward toward Monterey and Carmel, with way stops at Mirassou, just below San Jose, and the Paul Masson Vineyards in Saratoga. The Masson winery tour is one of the finest, with a dramatic historical film preceding it. Music at the Vineyards concerts on summer weekends, at the original winery founded by Paul Masson in the Santa Cruz Mountains, consist of chamber music and opera performances from San Francisco, with champagne intermissions on the terrace overlooking the Santa Clara Valley. For program schedules write to Paul Masson Music at the Vineyards, P.O. Box 97, Saratoga, CA 95070.

Route 17 out of Los Gatos offers the leisurely tourist a stop at the Henry Cowell Redwoods State Park near Felton, to see the great sequoias—1,737 acres of them—survivors of a former geologic age, now represented by only two species, the big tree and the redwood. Ring counts on the great trunks indicate some may have been seedlings centuries before the birth of Christ.

This Santa Cruz Mountain area has its own cluster of small wineries, to be visited by appointment only: David Bruce, Ridge Vineyards, Mount Eden. Near the coast is Bargetto, well worth an afternoon visit while you're en route to Monterey, and an added attraction is passing through the artichoke fields of Castroville.

The Monterey Peninsula is a vacation land that offers many options for overnight lodging. Three possibilities to be considered are: the Carmel Highlands Inn, Highway 1, Carmel, CA 93921, phone (408) 624–3801; La Playa Hotel, Eighth Avenue and Camino Real, Carmel, CA 93921, phone (408) 624–6476, and Quail Lodge, Carmel Valley Golf and Country Club, Carmel Valley, CA 93921, phone (408) 624–1581. Dining and sightseeing in Monterey and Carmel rate equal billing. This is Steinbeck country, and in a former sardine factory on Cannery Row can be found one of

Rainy-day tourists learn about a stainless-steel receiving hopper

the state's best restaurants, named, of course, The Sardine Factory. Sumptuous food, generously served, reflects the high standards of the owners Ted Balestreri and Bert Cutino. In season, the Monterey Bay prawns are a special delicacy, not to be missed.

Second Day. A stop in the morning at Carmel Mission will afford photographers ideal light on the eastward-facing chapel where Padre Junípero Serra is entombed. Continue down to Big Sur, just for the beauty of Highway 1, or head for Salinas and the wineries of the newly emerging Monterey County region. Just before leaving Monterey, visit the tiny Monterey Peninsula Winery, belonging to two dentists who have become winemakers, Roy Thomas and Dick Nuckton. It is an opportunity to pick up full-bodied Zinfandels and Cabernet Sauvignons seldom found in the retail market.

The first winery to visit at Gonzales, The Monterey Vineyard, originally built with a capacity of 100,000 to 150,000 cases, today handles only 20,000 to 25,000 cases of nine varietal wines from 600 acres of bearing vines.

By special arrangement, you can visit the Paul Masson Winery facilities at Soledad, a model of up-to-the-minute technology set among plots of flourishing

251

Vitis vinifera, growing on their own varietal rootstock.

For the truly dedicated winelover this day's climax, and possibly the chief reason for coming to Monterey County, would be a visit to Chalone Vineyard near the Pinnacles National Monument. The newly constructed winery, built by Dick Graff and his young brothers, is a sight to see. Arrangements for the visit must be made by mail, which will also bring instructions for finding the winery, tucked away in the wild, sun-drenched hills. Write to Chalone Vineyard, Stonewall Canyon Road, The Pinnacles, Soledad, CA 93960.

For some wine tourists, the next day will be devoted to the journey to Los Angeles. If time allows, travel via the dramatic coastal route of Highway 1, with a pause to visit San Simeon, or take Highway 101, east of Monterey, and stop at Salinas, where John Steinbeck's house is maintained by local charity groups as a small restaurant. The Steinbeck House, a one-story bungalow in the heart of Salinas, is just as the author described it in *East of Eden*. The landscape southward along Highway 101, crisscrossing the Salinas River, is the setting of *Red Pony* and *Of Mice and Men*.

Paso Robles is a good halfway stop, with a chance

Winter tourists can watch bare vines being pruned

to visit the Hoffman Mountain Ranch winery. There is a tasting room on the highway which is open to the public, just in case you failed to write ahead for an appointment to visit the winery.

Near Santa Barbara, in the Santa Ynez Valley, is The Firestone Vineyard and Winery, not far from the delightful Danish village of Solvang. If there is time, both are worth seeing.

A WINE TOUR STARTING FROM LOS ANGELES

At one time, the first true vinifera vineyard in California was thriving in Los Angeles where the Union Station now stands. Today, if you want to visit a winery right in downtown Los Angeles, you can enjoy a picnic lunch with sample wines in the outdoor grape arbor at the San Antonio Winery, 737 Lamar Street (about 1 1/2 miles northeast of City Hall, via Main Street). The experience offers all the rural charm of a vineyard miles from the city's din. An hour's drive from the center of Los Angeles takes you to Guasti, where, at 9900 Road you can visit the headquarters of Brookside in the historic old winery whose museum documents the most important winemaking in southern California. This is one of the most venerable and largest wine companies in the Cucamonga district.

Although it cannot compare with the pilgrimages in northern California, a two-day excursion from Los Angeles to the Central Valley counties can, nevertheless, be memorable.

There are one-day trips to Temecula, just above San Diego, by appointment to visit the Callaway Vineyard & Winery, taking dinner that night at El Adobe de Capistrano near old Mission San Juan Capistrano.

First Day. Leave Los Angeles via the Hollywood Freeway, taking Route 5 toward Bakersfield, over the famed Grapevine to Route 99, then along the Edison Highway to the Giumarra vineyard and winery. In late August there is an opportunity to watch the luscious table grapes being packed by hand for the world market. Just a few miles toward the Tehachapi Mountains is the Bear Mountain Winery. Here visitors

The great bells at Mission San Juan Capistrano date from 1813

Dinner at The Imperial Dynasty in Hanford is fit for a Chinese emperor

has two or three motels and hotels to choose from, and host Richard Wing will gladly make reservations.

Second Day. Richard Wing and The Imperial Dynasty were saved for the last and crowning experience of wine touring in California. On the drive back to Los Angeles, if it is between mid-March and May, the road will take you past field after field of orange poppies, the California state flower, mingled with blue and white lupine—hundreds and thousands of acres of wildflowers in bloom on the alluvial benchlands of the great Tehachapi Mountains. Man does not live by wine alone.

The California wine trail is today a noble route, well worth getting to know better. There are unquestioned delights and adventures generously offered everywhere, waiting to be found.

are welcome, and they have a chance to taste an almost 100 percent Green Hungarian wine that, in itself, is reason for optimism about the quality of wine production in this warm region. But more than the winery visits, the event that will make this journey memorable is a Chinese banquet in Hanford, 200 miles north of Los Angeles. Planeloads of gourmets have flown all the way from New York just to dine at The Imperial Dynasty, 2 China Alley, Hanford, phone (209) 582–0087. The size of your party is immaterial. Richard Wing, upon consultation, will prepare foods for you that you will someday tell your grandchildren about. For example a tiny breast of squab in a corona of Bing cherries, resting on a slice of honeydew melon, garnished with plump green grapes and slivered almonds, the whole glistening with a ginger sauce. The wine list rivals that of Manhattan's "21" Club in depth and breadth. Richard Wing is not only a great chef but a philosopher and an enophile; after dessert he may engage you in a winetasting dialogue, or, with the treasures of the Imperial Dynasty's cellars to draw on, you can have your own summit tasting, pitting a rare Stag's Leap or Chalone wine against whatever comparable French wine you might choose. The little town

Richard Wing, owner-chef of The Imperial Dynasty

A knight in armor stands guard over Château Montelena's prize vineyards

BIBLIOGRAPHY

Building a wine library at home is a continuing pleasure. The key word is "continuing," for the fascinating subject of wine has been reflecting man's preoccupation with the nectar of the grape for more than six thousand years. For both writer and reader it is a study that never palls. And of course there continue to be new vineyards and new wineries, and even new vine species. The first vintage tour is invariably a prelude to any number of successive pilgrimages to wine countries ...everywhere. One book leads to another, and through this continuing pleasure the novice becomes the seasoned connoisseur.

The following list is not an exhaustive compendium, nor even a significant fraction of the titles in my own library. Rather it is a selection of reliable texts which may, by expanding awareness, add to the pleasures of living with wine.

Adams, Leon D. *The Wines of America.* Boston: Houghton Mifflin Company, 1973.

Amerine, Maynard A., and Singleton, V. S. *Wine—An Introduction for Americans.* Berkeley and Los Angeles: University of California Press, 1965.

Bespaloff, Alexis. *A Guide to Inexpensive Wines.* New York: Simon & Schuster, 1973.

Broadbent, J. M. *Wine Tasting.* London: Wine & Spirit Publications, Ltd., 1971.

Chroman, Nathan. *The Treasury of American Wines.* New York: Crown Publishers, Inc., 1973.

Church, Ruth Ellen. *Entertaining with Wine.* Chicago: Rand McNally & Company, 1976.

Fadiman, Clifton, and Aaron, Sam. *The Joys of Wine.* New York: Harry N. Abrams, Inc., 1975.

————. *Wine Buyers Guide.* New York: Harry N. Abrams, Inc., 1977.

Gillette, Paul. *Enjoying Wine.* New York: The New American Library, A Signet Book, 1976.

Haraszthy, A. *Grape Culture, Wines, and Wine-Making.* New York: Harper & Brothers, 1862.

Johnson, Hugh. *The World Atlas of Wine.* New York: Simon & Schuster, 1971.

Leedom, William S. *The Vintage Wine Book.* New York: Random House, Vintage Books, 1975.

Lichine, Alexis. *Alexis Lichine's New Encyclopedia of Wines & Spirits.* New York: Alfred A. Knopf, 1974.

Melville, John. *Guide to California Wines.* New and revised fourth edition by Jefferson Morgan. San Carlos: Nourse Publishing Company, 1972.

Morgan, Jefferson. *Adventures in the Wine Country.* San Francisco: Chronicle Books, 1971.

Ramey, Bern C. *The Great Wine Grapes and the Wines They Make.* Burlingame, California: Great Wine Grapes, Inc., 1977.

Robards, Terry. *The New York Times Book of Wine.* New York: Quadrangle/The New York Times Book Co., 1976.

Roberge, Earl. *Napa Wine Country.* Portland, Oregon: Graphic Arts Center Publishing Co., 1975.

Schoonmaker, Frank. *Frank Schoonmaker's Encyclopedia of Wine.* New York: Hastings House, 1967.

Stevenson, Robert Louis. "The Silverado Squatters," in *The Travels and Essays of Robert Louis Stevenson.* New York: Charles Scribner's Sons, 1918.

Thollander, Earl. *Back Roads of California.* Menlo Park, California: Lane Magazine & Book Company, 1971.

Thompson, Bob, and Johnson, Hugh. *The California Wine Book.* New York: William Morrow and Company, Inc., 1976.

Yeadon, Anne and David. *Wine Tasting in California.* Los Angeles–San Francisco: Camaro Publishing Co., 1973.

SUPPLEMENTARY MATERIAL

Sunset Pictorial—*California Wine.* Menlo Park, California: Lane Magazine & Book Company, 1973.

California Wineries Series: Vol. I, *Napa Valley;* Vol. II, *Sonoma & Mendocino;* Vol. III, *Central Coast;* Vol. IV, *South Coast & Inland Valleys* (Summer '78). St. Helena, California: Vintage Image, 1975/1978.

California Wine Tour Series: Vol. I, *Napa Valley;* Vol. II, *Sonoma & Mendocino;* Vol. III, *Central Coast;* Vol. IV, *South Coast & Inland Valleys* (Summer '78). St. Helena, California: Vintage Image, 1977/1978.

Map: *The Wineries of the Napa Valley* 12 x 17". Price 25¢, from Napa Valley County Development Council, P.O. Box 876, Napa, CA 94558.

ACKNOWLEDGMENTS

In the genesis of the present volume two good friends were involved, and I thank them first and foremost. It was William T. Shirer, an enthusiast of California wine, who made the suggestion that led me to write my first wine book, *California's Best Wines,* in 1948. And it was Alfred A. Knopf who suggested, after reading that manuscript, that I should write such a book in the autumn of my life. Now, thirty years later, having reached three-score and five, after forty working years spent among the vineyards of my home state, I have followed his sage advice.

The book itself is a tribute to my friends in the vineyards. However, there are a few other special acknowledgments that I should like to add.

All winelovers should be grateful for the existence of the research center in San Francisco called the Wine Institute. Its president emeritus, Harry Serlis, has my enduring gratitude not only for his friendship but for his open-minded dealing with problems and suggestions, his gracious and prompt solutions to dilemmas. Today's president, John de Luca, brings an equally supportive presence that augurs well for the continued growth of the Institute in this new day with its difficult problems. Wine writers in particular are often confronted with questions that tax their resources. The Wine Institute's Harvey Posert is not only always available; he anticipates our needs and generously shares material that would enrich our writings.

To those two good elder statesmen of the California wine industry, Otto Meyer, the retired president of Paul Masson Vineyards, and Alfred Fromm, the still-active head of Fromm & Sichel, applause and gratitude. To Jim Lucas of Fromm & Sichel, my thanks for keeping me informed of industry statistics.

Over the years it has been my privilege to watch Julio and Ernest Gallo as they single-mindedly pursued the goals of wine quality that they share with likeminded consumers. Only a track record of honest reporting without condescension could have won a journalist like myself access to these two very private people, and I am grateful that their doors have been and still are open to me.

And there are my colleagues on the *Los Angeles Times:* Carolyn Murray, editor of *Home* magazine, and restaurant editor Lois Dwan of *Calendar,* with whom I share enthusiasm for our wine-and-food assignments for the Sunday editions.

My gratitude to the staff of Lawry's California Center, where I teach a weekly wine class: Richard and Ralph Frank, Lorraine Petitfils, Vicki Vance, and winekeeper Luba White, who have grown, along with my students, in wine consciousness.

I am grateful to Maynard Amerine for looking over this text and making valuable suggestions—and for writing the foreword to it. To my copy editor, Ruth Eisenstein, a very special thanks for her talent and skill in turning some rough phrasing into silky syntax for which I shall get credit but always know it was her good eye and mind that brought it about.

From the beginning, I have enjoyed a happy working relation with my chief editor, Darlene Geis, who has helped to shape the book, encouraged me when the task seemed endless, and patiently sifted through hundreds of my pictures with me to be sure the best of them were used. In the long process I believe this New Yorker has wholly succumbed to my chauvinistic championing of California wines. And so my book, just in the editing, has already won one convert.

The friendships that have "sprung from wine," to use John Gay's words, have been too many to list fully. But among the friends in wine to whom I owe particular thanks are Florence and Sam Aaron, Burgess Meredith, Drs. Jean and Wallace Tourtellotte, Jean Leon, Price Hicks, Hernando Courtright and Peter Korzilius of the Beverly-Wilshire Hotel, James Nassikas of the Stanford Court and Richard Swig of the Fairmont Hotel in San Francisco, Patricia Delaney, Ralph Graves, and Cal Whipple of Time, Incorporated, Doris and Joe Walsh, Alvin Malnik, Carolyn and Leonce Picot, Dr. William and Marcia Bond, Nancy and Carroll O'Connor, Cleo and Lester Gruber, Ella, Adelaide, and Dick Brennan, Paul Kovi and Tom Margittai, Augustin V. Paege, Patrick Teraill, Alexis Lichine, Curtis Harrington, Gerald Asher, Alexander McNally, Tony Valone, and Glenn Ford—and this is an abbreviated list.

My two closest friends in wine, after decades of working closely together, are André Tchelistcheff, to whom this book is dedicated, and James Andrew Willett, whose inspiration, support, and assistance made the completion of the work possible.

ROBERT LAWRENCE BALZER

Santa Ana, California
March 17, 1978

258

INDEX

(Monterey County), 16–17; Le Blanc de
Blancs, 54, 197; Pinot Chardonnay
(California), 38, 197; Sauvignon Blanc, 197;
tasting room of, *196
Werner, Karl, 221
West Sacramento, Calif., 232
West's White Prolific, 45
Wetmore, Charles, 62, 64, 97, 168, 176
Wetzel, Harry H., Jr., 90; Harry H., III
("Hank"), 90
Wheeler, Dan, 185–86
Whitehouse, David, 163
White Pinot (wine), 42, 52
Wild Horse Valley, 159
Wildwood Vineyards, 96
Williams, Howard, 226
Willmes press(es), *43, 118
Wilson, Winston, 134
Windsor, Calif., 119, 246
Wine: aging methods, 43, *56, 60, 71, *88,
*157, 221; containers, *185; determinants
of its quality, 16, 87–88; enhancement of
food, 146, 150; storing of, 186; storing of,
in glass-lined tanks, *47
Wine Advisory Board, 37
Wine country, California, touring of, 235–54;
Bay Area and Central Coast counties,
251–52; ground rules for travelers, 236,
241; Los Angeles, starting from, 252–54;
North Coast counties, 244–50; San
Francisco, starting from, 241–52
Wine Country Inn, 244, 248
Wine history, California, major periods (in
chronological order): Mission (1769–1834),
80; Pioneer (1835–61), 81; Founders'
(1861–1919), 81–82; Post-Repeal
(1932–45), *18, 81; Prestige (1946–65),
81; Corporate Investment (1965–74), 82,
85; Financial Adjustment and Post-Boom
Crisis (1974–76), 85–86, 208
Wine Institute, 242, 244; Health and Social
Welfare Committee, 107
Wine labels: Bay Area and Central Coast,
*179; Central Valley and Southern
California, *225; Mendocino and Sonoma,
*109; Napa, *145; South Central Coast,
*209; varietal, *63; wrap-around, 191
Winemasters' Guild, 232
Wine Museum of San Francisco, *238, *241,
242; Thomas Jefferson wine exhibition at,
*236, *237
Winepresses: basket, *60, *171; cylindrical,
*58; Willmes, *43, 118
Wine Review, 189
Winery Lake Vineyard, 123, 127, 163, 189
Wines & Vines, 189
"Wines by Wheeler," 185
Wines of America, The (Adams), 74
Winespell, 16, 20
Wine Stomp, 210

Wine Tutor, 244
Wing, Richard, 254, *254
Winiarski, Barbara, 159; Warren, *159
Winkler, A. J., 36, 45, 62, 200
Wisconsin, 90
Wolf House, 245
Wood, Laurie, 140
Wood, role in aging of wine, 106. See also
Cooperage
Woodside, Calif., 197
Woodside Vineyards, 197–98; Cabernet
Sauvignon, 198; Chardonnay, 198; Pinot
Noir, 198
Woodward, William P., 205
Wright, Frank Lloyd, 244; student of, 120,
246

Y

Yettem, Calif., 220
York, Andrew, 210; Wilfred, 210
York Mountain Winery, 210
Young, Robert, Vineyard, 177
Young's Market Company, 92
Yountville, Calif., 127, 137, 163, 248, 250
Yverdon Vineyards, 164; Cabernet Sauvignon
(Napa Valley), 164; Johannisberg Riesling
(Napa Valley), 164

Z

ZD Wines, 123; Chardonnay (Sonoma), 123;
Gewürztraminer (Winery Lake Vineyard),
123; Pinot Noir (Napa), 123; Zinfandel
(Amador), 123
Zellerbach, James D., 86, 105–6
Zepponi, Gino, 123
Zepponi Vineyard, 123
Zind-Humbrecht cellars, Alsace, 24
Zinfandel Rosé(s), California, 76
Zinfandels, California, 74, *75, 76, 128, 191

PHOTOGRAPH CREDITS